WORD JOURNEYS

Solving Problems in the Teaching of Literacy

Cathy Collins Block, *Series Editor*

Engaging Young Readers:
Promoting Achievement and Motivation
Edited by Linda Baker, Mariam Jean Dreher, and John T. Guthrie

Word Journeys:
Assessment-Guided Phonics, Spelling, and Vocabulary Instruction
Kathy Ganske

WORD JOURNEYS

Assessment-Guided
Phonics, Spelling,
and Vocabulary Instruction

◆

KATHY GANSKE

◆

THE GUILFORD PRESS
New York   London

© 2000 The Guilford Press
A Division of Guilford Publications, Inc.
72 Spring Street, New York, NY 10012
www.guilford.com

Printed in the United States of America

This book is printed on acid-free paper.

Last digit is print number: 9 8 7 6 5 4 3 2 1

Library of Congress Cataloging-in-Publication Data

Ganske, Kathy.
    Word journeys : assessment-guided phonics, spelling, and vocabulary
instruction / Kathy Ganske.
        p. cm. — (Solving problems in the teaching of literacy)
    Includes bibliographical references and index.
        ISBN 1-57230-559-2 (pbk.)
        1. Vocabulary—Study and teaching.   2. English language—Orthography
and spelling—Study and teaching.   3. Reading—Phonetic method.
    I. Title.   II. Series.
LB1574.5 G25 2000
372.63'2—dc21   00-035374

Chapter opening photographs by Jeanie Eye.

The author acknowledges with appreciation the work of Chris Jennison, Senior
Editor; Anna Brackett, Senior Production Editor; and the rest of The Guilford
Press staff for making this book a reality.

*To all those with a curiosity about words
and most specially to Philip, who has shared
in so many of my own word journeys.*

About the Author

Kathy Ganske, PhD, is an assistant professor in the Department of Reading at Rowan University, Glassboro, New Jersey, where she teaches graduate and undergraduate courses in literacy and supervises the reading clinic. Before receiving her doctorate from the University of Virginia, she was a long-time classroom teacher in primary through upper elementary grades and taught in many regions of the country. Kathy is a popular consultant and leader of inservice workshops.

◆
Preface

I have written *Word Journeys: Assessment-Guided Phonics, Spelling, and Vocabulary Instruction* so that teachers and students can experience the advantages of exploring words through a student-centered approach that is interactive and inquiry-based. The book is grounded in developmental spelling research (Henderson, 1990; Templeton & Bear, 1992) and is intended as a practical guide to help you understand what your students already know about words and to assist you in planning appropriate and engaging instruction. It is divided into two sections.

Part I—Understanding Children's Word Knowledge. Few spelling errors are random. Rather, they are demonstrations of the writer's level of understanding of how the English spelling system works. As children progress through a stage of spelling development, they tend to "use but confuse" (Invernizzi, Abouzeid, & Gill, 1994) features typical of that stage. Unless teachers are informed, they are likely to view the misspellings that result as mere errors and not as indications of what to teach, and when. Part I is intended to open the window on children's word knowledge so that teachers and others can begin to view the information afforded by children's spellings with informed eyes and thoughtful minds. Chapter 1 describes the stages of spelling development and provides a look at readers and writers at each stage through student snapshots. Chapter 2 explains how to assess children's knowledge of words with the Developmental Spelling Analysis (DSA), a dictated word inventory.

Part II—Fostering Children's Word Knowledge. Once you have a clear understanding of your students' orthographic knowledge, you can tailor instruction to match students' needs. This portion of *Word Journeys* addresses instructional issues. Chapter 3 discusses how to use DSA results to get started with word study. It describes considerations for selecting words, explains how to guide students through a word sort, and provides ideas for word study activities, including those that relate to word play. Most of the suggestions in this chapter are general and apply to students at any stage of spelling development.

Chapters 4 through 7 have a different format from the previous three chapters. Each focuses on a particular stage of spelling development—letter name, within word pattern, syllable juncture, and derivational constancy—and is organized around the orthographic features that are relevant to that stage. Features are introduced one at a time and include a description of specific instructional strategies, a reference to the appendix page location of appropriate supplemental words, and a chart that outlines a possible sequence for teaching the feature. Although you can determine starting points for instruction from your inventory results, when using categorization activities like word sorting you may be unsure of what to contrast with a given feature under study and uncertain of when to move on to a new feature. The sequence of contrasts presented in the charts will provide direction in these areas. Keep in mind that *each series of sorts is just one of many that could be used.* The orderings illustrate what word study might look like across the various stages. This big picture will enable you to engage your students in word study with greater confidence and ease by providing a foundation on which to build your expertise. The framework should be used with flexibility—for some features, it may be desirable to use all of the sorts; for others, only some or none at all. This will depend on the needs of students. In time, you may wish to develop sorting sequences of your own.

Chapter 8 addresses questions that teachers commonly ask about word study. It is followed by supplemental word lists and an appendix of forms used for implementing assessment-guided word study. So that you can be an active learner, I have also included two hands-on activities (an error sort and sample inventories to score).

This book could not have been written without the many researchers, teachers, students, parents, and friends whose work or comments gave me cause to wonder about words and to reflect on students' word learning. I hope it will similarly inspire you.

Contents

Introduction

It has been more than 25 years since linguist Charles Read (1971) first excited the educational community with his observations of preschool children's spelling inventions. In his investigations, Read repeatedly noted a logic behind the young children's spellings. They systematically matched the names of alphabetic letters they knew to the speech sounds they were trying to write, relying heavily (although tacitly) on points of articulation—in other words, on where the sounds were formed in the mouth. This strategy resulted in consistent letter omissions and substitutions—less prominent sounds were easily overlooked (LAD for *land*), and letter names that produced similar sounds were interchanged (GAM for *jam*). Read's now classic study ignited the interest of other researchers. Children's spelling errors, their inventions made in the absence of a complete knowledge of the spelling system, were seen as a means for understanding their word knowledge, which was thought to underlie both spelling and word recognition.

The work of Edmund Henderson and his students and colleagues at the University of Virginia confirmed and extended Read's findings (Beers, 1980; Beers & Henderson, 1977; Henderson, Estes, & Stonecash, 1972; Gentry, 1980). Their research suggested a stagelike progression of spelling development through which children advance from a reliance on sound to more pattern-based strategies as their experience with print and the English spelling system broaden. Further spelling studies, especially those targeting older students (Bear, Truex, & Barone, 1989; Schlagal, 1989; Templeton, 1983), led to refinements in the theory and elucidated the role of meaning in learning to spell.

Eventually, Henderson (1990) outlined a model of developmental spelling that encompassed the preschool years through adulthood. He divided the spectrum into five periods, or stages, each with a name describing students' spelling behavior at that particular time—preliterate, letter name, within word pattern, syllable juncture, and derivational constancy. The stage that best characterizes a child's spelling is known as the child's *stage of development*. This differs from child to child, even within the same class, because children progress at different rates through the stages. As they advance, they learn to negotiate increasingly more abstract spelling relationships, beginning with individual letter–sound associations and moving on to the greater complexities of pattern and meaning connections.

Over the years, examinations of children's spellings have also provided strong support for the relatedness of reading and writing (Ehri, 1980, 1997; Gill, 1989; Invernizzi, 1992; Juel, Griffith, & Gough, 1986; Zutell & Rasinski, 1989). Results have suggested that the two subjects should be taught in a more integrated fashion and that activities that engage children in looking carefully at words will benefit their ability to read words as well as to write them. *Orthographic knowledge*, or knowledge of the spelling system, is of central importance to both—when writing words, students are trying to map letters to sounds, and when reading they are attempting to match sounds to letters (Adams, 1990).

Still other studies have examined the spelling errors of students with dyslexia and learning disabilities in order to gain a better understanding of their learning difficulties and, in turn, to discover the most beneficial instructional practices for them. Worthy and Invernizzi (1990) found that the spelling errors of students with learning disabilities were similar to those of normally achieving students when the students were matched by developmental spelling level rather than by age or grade level. This and other studies have highlighted the need for developmentally appropriate instruction for these students (Moats, 1983; Sawyer, Lipa-Wade, Kim, Ritenour, & Knight, 1997).

Increased understanding of children's orthographic knowledge has led to new possibilities for the teaching of spelling that give greater consideration to the developmental differences typically found among students within a classroom (Bear & Templeton, 1998; Bloodgood, 1991; Cramer, 1998; Cunningham, 1995; Gentry & Gillet, 1993; Wilde, 1990; Zutell, 1998). These possibilities, coupled with the growing interest in integrating the language arts, have prompted many teachers to abandon traditional approaches in favor of alternative methods, such as the use of theme-based words, words from children's writing, high-frequency word lists, and word study (Henderson, 1990). The central focus of this book is *word study*, a learner-centered, hands-on approach that has evolved over the years as a result of developmental spelling studies and direct classroom application.

Although English has a highly complex spelling system, it is far more regular than it appears on the surface. One reason it appears to be irregular is that the pronunciation of particular letters and letter combinations often vary. For example, notice the sound of the underlined letter in each of the following words—*game, fudge, rough, resign* and *pillow, pilot, combination, special*. At first glance, teaching children to read and spell words with such letter–sound variations may seem like a nearly impossible task. Indeed, if word learning is approached in a word-by-word manner, it may be. However, more is involved in learning words than just memory. Rather than being based on a simple one-letter equals one-sound organization, our spelling system reflects the interplay of sound, pattern, and meaning relationships. As Henderson reflected: "Those who set out to remember every letter of every word will never make it. Those who try to spell by sound alone will be defeated. Those who learn how to 'walk through' words with sensible expectations, noting sound, pattern, and meaning relationships, will know what to remember, and they will learn to spell English" (1990, p. 70). In word study, students are taught to explore the sound, pattern, and meaning relationships among words through various compare and contrast strategies known as *word sorts*. By examining words encountered in their reading and used in their writing, children discover consistencies that enable them to generalize their understandings to other words and, thereby, learn to read and spell more efficiently.

Helping children learn to "walk through words" requires informed teachers who know where each student is along the continuum of spelling knowledge and who use this information to plan instruction that is appropriate for diverse needs. Unfortunately, the process of determining the word knowledge of a class of 25 to 30 students can be time-consuming and confusing. Word knowledge within a classroom typically spans several grades and several different stages of spelling development. Recognizing spelling errors is easy, but knowing how to interpret them for meaningful instruction is difficult without a firm understanding of the way word knowledge develops. This may explain why many teachers' instructional decisions related to spelling are still based on grade level, rather than being developmentally appropriate. One goal of this book is make it possible for all teachers to view their students through a developmental lens in a manner that is considerate of the many time demands placed on them.

There are several ways to learn about children's orthographic knowledge. Students' reading and writing are two important means that should be used on an ongoing basis. However, they should not be the only methods for determining what to teach and when to teach it. Students often understand more than they can apply, or at least apply consistently, in their reading and writing. Also, in the case of writing, the types of errors may be limited by the topic or the writer's confidence.

Research has shown that the understanding students have about words can be revealed with a simple dictated spelling inventory (Perfetti, 1992; Templeton & Bear, 1992). A dictated word list enables teachers to quickly assess students' levels of spelling development. The *Developmental Spelling Analysis* (DSA; Ganske, 1999), described in Chapter 2, makes it easy for teachers to identify each child's stage of development and to distinguish the orthographic features that students are currently negotiating from those they either already know or have no idea about. Such information enables teachers to design instructional experiences that build systematically on what students know.

Although having many opportunities to read and write is essential for spelling development, for most students it is not sufficient. A more guided approach is needed (Invernizzi, Abouzeid, & Gill, 1994; Templeton & Morris, 1999), one that helps students know what to look for and how to recognize what they are seeing as they explore words. Even students who seem to have a natural knack for spelling benefit from and are stimulated by developmentally appropriate activities that are within their "zone of proximal development" (Vygotsky, 1978). Students learn about words in supportive contexts where the concepts are neither too easy nor too hard. This allows them to use their prior knowledge and to connect new understandings to old—in other words, to expand their knowledge of how words work in the security of what they already know (see Figure I-1). This scenario by no means requires a humdrum exploration of words; quite the contrary.

During my last 10 years as a classroom teacher, I used word study as a natural bridge between reading and writing. Reading and writing provided the purpose and the vehicle for learning about words, and word study served as the means for strengthening and advancing students' understanding of words so they could read and write more fluently. Besides enhancing children's phonics, spelling, and vocabulary knowledge, word study (and word play) promoted discussion, language appreciation, critical thinking, curiosity, and a greater interest in reading and writing. And to top it off—we all had fun in the process!

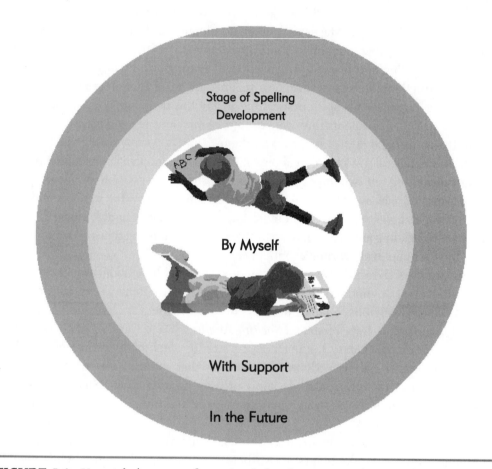

FIGURE I-1. Vygotsky's zone of proximal development. When students are given instructional support within their zone of proximal development—namely, at their stage of spelling development—they are able to draw upon what they already know to expand their knowledge of words. With increased understanding and continued support, aspects of orthography that were formerly too difficult ("In the Future") become negotiable.

PART I

◆◆◆

Understanding Children's Word Knowledge

CHAPTER 1

◆

A Developmental Perspective

Matching words to sentences.

Completing an upper-level blind written sort with words like legendary, teachery, *and* category.

Chapter at a Glance

◆

This chapter provides an overview of the five stages of spelling development outlined by Henderson (1990)—preliterate, letter name, within word pattern, syllable juncture, and derivational constancy. Because the term *emergent* is now widely used to describe the period of children's literacy development before the letter name stage, for purposes of clarity I have used it in place of *preliterate* in the pages that follow. In order to highlight the literacy development of students at each stage, I have included student snapshots that show their reading, writing in context, and dictated inventory spellings. Discussion of the last four stages also includes a descriptive listing of the specific orthographic features targeted by the Developmental Spelling Analysis (DSA). These features, as well as others, are described in detail in the instructional sections of Part II.

STAGE I: EMERGENT SPELLING

◆

This first stage of spelling development includes the writing attempts of children who are not yet reading. It is a period of emergent literacy and a time during which children's understandings about writing vary considerably. Some may pretend-write with scribbles or random marks, while others reveal greater understanding through their more linear and wave-like writing. As children see others writing, start to notice print around them, and begin to write letters themselves (often those of their name), their pretend-writing takes on a more conventional appearance. Words are rendered with strings of letters and letter-like symbols. Although this writing has the look of real writing, there is no relationship between the letters used and the sounds represented (see Figure 1-1). This type of writing is sometimes called *prephonetic*.

In order to begin to understand the *alphabetic principle*, the concept that letters stand for speech sounds, children must not only have some knowledge of the alphabet but must also be phonemically aware. *Phonemic awareness* is an awareness of the sounds (*phonemes*) that make up spoken words. Phonemes roughly correspond to letters, but the connection is not one to one. For example, the word *mat* has three phonemes—/m/-/ă/-/t/, and *spend* has five—/s/-/p/-/ĕ/-/n/-/d/, but *chick* and *shade* each have just three—

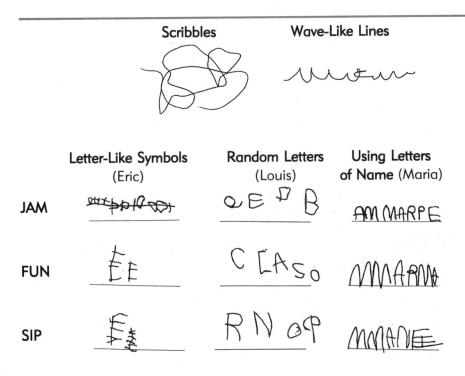

A Kindergartner's Journal Writing and Drawing

FIGURE 1-1. Snapshots of emergent spellers: Prephonetic writing.

/ch/-/ĭ/-/k/ and /sh/-/ā/-/d/. Many simple, enjoyable activities have been devised to help children develop phonemic awareness (see, for example, Adams, Foorman, Lundberg, & Beeler, 1998; Blevins, 1997; Ericson & Juliebo, 1998; Yopp & Yopp, 1997). Reading aloud to children and engaging them in rhyming and alliteration games and other types of sound play are activities that can easily be used by teachers and parents (Fitzpatrick, 1998; Yopp, 1992, 1995).

As children acquire the alphabetic principle, they learn to use their letter-sound knowledge to match spoken words with words in print and develop a *concept of word* (Morris, 1981). Teachers often foster this understanding by pointing to words as they read aloud big books, dictated experience stories, and nursery rhymes, such as those in Bruce Lansky's *The New Adventures of Mother Goose*. Repeated readings enable children to memorize the text and provide models of fingerpoint reading. By observing how the children later "read" and track the same text, teachers can discover much about their print knowledge. For example, consider the rhyme "Jack be nimble; Jack be quick. . . ." Children who have not acquired the alphabetic principle may show directionality with a sweep of their finger as they recite but will not be able to accurately point to individual words. By contrast, children who associate letters with sounds will use this understanding to guide their finger, knowing that if they're saying "be," their finger needs to point to a group of letters that starts with *b*, not with *J* or *n*. Even as children begin to develop a concept of word, words like *nimble* cause confusion, because syllables tend to be mistaken for words, and with each new syllable they move their finger along. Greater print experience helps children realize that, even though it makes sense to point to "nimble" when saying /n/-/ĭ/-/m/, it does not make sense to point to "Jack" when saying /b/-/l/, and they learn to self-correct the mismatches.

Along with their increased knowledge of print come advances in children's writing. Attention to sound is apparent. At first, only the most prominent sound in a word may be perceived and recorded, and this may or may not be the initial one; K for *come* and D for *dog*, but T for *cut*. As children become more conscious of word boundaries in their tracking of text, their spelling reflects this. Both the initial and final consonant sounds are recorded (RN for *run* and LT for *elephant*). Writing at this time often lacks spacing between words; at first glance it may even appear to be a random string of letters (see Figure 1-2). However, because these spellers do include part of the words' sounds, closer scrutiny usually discloses an interpretable message. Not surprisingly, this type of writing is called *semiphonetic* writing.

STAGE II: LETTER NAME SPELLING

◆

Students who are in the letter name stage have only recently achieved a concept of word and begun to read. Because the beginning reader's sight vocabulary and orthographic knowledge are limited, reading and writing are slow processes, punctuated by many pauses. Reading out loud buys time for the novice reader to figure out unknown words, and picture clues and predictable text lend much-needed support. Predictable text has repetition, rhyme, rhythm, an obvious sequence (often cumulative), or a combination of these patterns that enable young readers to anticipate words. Among children's many favorites are *Time for Bed* by M. Fox, *Is Your Mama a Llama?* by D. Guarino, *Polar Bear, Polar Bear, What Do You Hear?* by B. Martin, Jr., and *Jump Frog, Jump* by R. Kalan. *Choral reading* and *echo reading* also support beginning readers. During choral reading,

No Word Boundaries

DeResse's story—completed independently on the computer—reveals his knowledge of the alphabet and his rudimentary ability to use the alphabet to communicate through writing "... <u>now</u> <u>i</u> <u>know</u> <u>my</u> <u>abc</u>'s <u>next</u> <u>time</u> (<u>y</u>)won't yo<u>u</u> <u>sing</u> (<u>y</u>)with <u>me</u>."

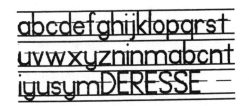

Captioned Picture with No Word Boundaries
"My sister played with me."

Late Emergent/Early Letter Name Spellings

LM	FN	SB
JAM	FUN	SIP

FIGURE 1-2. Snapshots of emergent spellers: Semiphonetic writing.

the teacher and students read out loud together; in echo reading, the teacher reads a line and then the students read the same line.

Writing, too, is labor-intensive at this stage. Words are formed deliberately and with determination in a sound-by-sound fashion. To ease the task of writing, teachers sometimes have students write part of a story and dictate the rest, or encourage "buddy-writing" with a friend or an older student. They also give students opportunities to create personal versions of favorite patterned books and read alouds, like *Brown Bear, Brown Bear, What Do You See?* by B. Martin, Jr., and *The Very Hungry Caterpillar*, by E. Carle. Supplied with a copy of portions of the text, students complete the sentences with their own innovations—as "Little bird, little bird, *what do you see? I see a* worm *looking at me.*" In classrooms where beginning readers and writers predominate, students who demonstrate more advanced understandings are often sought out by their peers for assistance during reading and writing workshops.

Letter name spellers (Read, 1975) rely on the *names* of letters to spell words. Approaching each word one sound at a time, they seek out the letter name that most closely matches the sound they are trying to reproduce. Some sounds have a more direct match than others. Consider, for example, the word *bake*. The "buh"—*b*, "aye"—*a*, and "kuh"—*k* are much more straightforward for these young spellers than are the sounds in *drip*. In the latter word, there is no direct letter name for either the "jr" sound of the *dr* or for the short *i* vowel sound. When this happens, children choose the letter name with the closest "feel" (place of articulation) to the sound they are trying to represent. This approach frequently leads to an unconventional spelling, as in the case of *drip*. Here, either *j* or *g* may be used for the beginning element, since both letter names result in a "juh" sound—"jay" and "gee." The letter name *h* is even a possibility, because "aich" also comes close to the desired sound. The short vowel in *drip* presents another problem. Because there is no letter named "ih," the letter name chosen by the child is the one that feels most like the short *i* sound. In this instance, the closest match is not the correct letter *i*, which causes the jaw to drop when pronounced and is formed farther back in the mouth, but the letter *e*.

An experiment with a partner or a mirror will illustrate how this letter-naming strategy works. While making the short *i* sound, notice the outside shape of your mouth as well as the inside feel. Then compare this feel and look to each of the vowel letter names— *a, e, i, o,* and *u*. Almost no change occurs when you shift from the short *i* sound to naming the letter *e*, which is why letter name spellers commonly substitute *e* for *i* in short vowel words. Although spellings like JEP, GEP, HEP (or even JP, GP, or HP at the beginning of this stage) for *drip* are certainly nonstandard, they are well-reasoned attempts by novice writers seeking to make sense out of our English spelling system. Because children at this stage represent most of the sounds in their words, and because the names of alphabetic letters serve as their guide, letter name spellings are also known as *phonetic* or *alphabetic* spellings.

Letter name features include the following:

• *Initial and final consonants* are usually the first features with which the letter name speller becomes competent. However, a few consonant confusions often persist during this stage (KAT = *cat*, CAD = *sad,* and YAT = *wet*).

• *Initial consonant blends and digraphs* are made up of two consonants. In a consonant blend, the sound of each consonant is maintained (*bl* and *st*), while the two consonants in a digraph produce a single, simple sound (*ch* and *sh*). A good mnemonic for keeping blends and digraphs straight is to remember: the word <u>*bl*</u>*en*<u>*d*</u> starts and ends with a blend, and the word *digra*<u>*ph*</u> ends with a digraph. Letter name spellers' representations of initial consonant blends and digraphs are often incomplete (GAB = *grab* and TAT = *that*).

• *Short vowels* are written with many substitutions. These are predictable and tend to appear as follows: B<u>A</u>K = *b<u>a</u>ck* (no change), P<u>A</u>T = *p<u>e</u>t*, F<u>E</u>T = *f<u>i</u>t*, G<u>I</u>T = *g<u>o</u>t*, and M<u>O</u>D = *m<u>u</u>d*.

• *Affricate* refers to the speech sound heard when the beginning of *job* or *chop* is pronounced. Several letters and combinations of letters besides *j* and *ch* also produce this sound in English—for example, the *g* in *gym* and the letters *t* and *d* before *r* (*drop* and *trot*). The names of some letters—*g, j,* and even *h*—also make these sounds. Because writers at this stage depend on the sounds of letter names and how they are formed in the mouth to spell words, they often substitute one letter or letter combination for another when an affricate sound is involved (JROM = *drum*, GOB = *job*, HRE = *tree*, and CHRAP = *trap*). The choice of substitution varies and reflects what the child knows. For example, a child named Charlie is likely to rely on *ch*.

• *Final consonant blends and digraphs*, like their initial counterparts, are often incomplete (DIS = *dish*). Frequently, the incompleteness stems from an omitted *m* or *n* preceding the final consonant (BOP = *bump* or LAD = *land*). The nasal quality of /m/ and /n/ causes these sounds to be overshadowed by the consonant that follows, making it easy for the sound-conscious letter name speller to overlook them. Inclusion of the *preconsonantal nasal* is an accomplishment that typically marks the end of the letter name stage.

Although they do not warrant instructional attention at this stage, two additional characteristics of the letter name speller should be highlighted—their omission of silent, long vowel markers (BOT = *boat* and SHAD = *shade*) and of vowels in unstressed syllables (PAPR = *paper* and TMATO = *tomato*). The absence of these letters is not surprising given the letter name speller's reliance on sound. The student snapshot in Figure 1-3 is an in-depth look at a letter name speller.

STAGE III: WITHIN WORD PATTERN SPELLING

◆

Students in the within word pattern stage have developed sight word vocabularies that enable them to read without the support of patterned or familiar text. Word recognition is further aided by a growing knowledge of the orthographic system. Rather than relying on letter-by-letter and sound-by-sound processing, learners at this stage are able to chunk parts of words and process them in a more automatic fashion. The resulting increased fluency is evidenced in children's phrase-by-phrase reading, which replaces their former word-by-word approach, and in their greater expression. As reading becomes faster, out-loud reading changes to silent reading. For both reading and writing, greater efficiency means that students have more attention available for constructing meaning. Books comprised of chapters become accessible and capture students' interests. These are simple at first and include stories like A. Lobel's *Frog and Toad Together*, and C. Rylant's *Henry and Mudge*. In time, longer chapter books with more complex plots supplant these. School and family situations are popular topics, as are mysteries. Among children's favorite are Patricia Reilly Giff's adventures of the kids at Polk Street School, Anne Cameron's stories about Julian, Louis Sachar's misadventures of Marvin Redpost, Jon Sczieska's Time Warp Trio, and Johanna Hurwitz's humorous

Thomas entered second grade as a beginning reader. Although his sight vocabulary was limited to just a few words, he was able to fingerpoint to memorized text and self-correct mistakes. He was eager to learn, full of energy, and put his all into reading and writing. Although partner reading was always an option during DEAR (drop everything and read) time, one day Thomas chose to sit near me and "reread" a patterned story that he and several other children had choral and echo read that morning. He knew they would be working with the story again the next day, and obviously wanted to be on top of the situation. I could hear him flipping pages and whisper-reading the text over and over. Finally, he turned to me and proudly announced, "I'm getting to be such a good reader I don't even have to look at the words!" As amusing as this story is, it strikes a keynote regarding literacy learning. Although beginning readers need the support of familiar text, as teachers we must be sure we help them progress beyond a dependence on context and picture clues for word reading so that they truly do increase their sight vocabularies and their understanding of letter–sound associations. This can be done by moving from story, to sentence strips, to individual words.

The spellings below, from the letter name feature list given in September, reveal Thomas's strong understanding of initial and final consonants—only *b/p, c/k,* and *w/y* were confused. His more limited knowledge of short vowels, affricates, blends, and digraphs is also evident. Thomas correctly spelled *map, bet, rub, grab, slid,* and *fast*.

got	GAT		went	YATH
win	YNH		cap	KAP
fed	FAD		hop	HAP
rub	ROP		fit	FAT
ship	SEPH		jet	JAT
plan	PAND		drum	JUM
that	TATH		much	MUH
bump	BUP		chop	TAP
with	YET		trip	RAT
dish	BCH			

By the middle of January, Thomas's word knowledge had progressed considerably. He relied less on picture clues and memory for the story, and more on his growing sight vocabulary and knowledge of letters and sounds. Cumulative stories held a special interest. Although longer and more challenging, they still provided support through repetition and rhyme. Thomas and a friend were delighted when they discovered Bill Grossman's wonderful variation of the "I know an old lady who swallowed a fly" tale—*My Little Sister Ate One Hare*—and decided

(cont.)

FIGURE 1–3. Snapshot of a letter name speller: Thomas.

to present it to the class. With serious determination (and many giggles), they practiced reading the story, which tells of a little girl who gobbles down everything from one hare to nine lizards "and their gizzards" but can't handle the ten peas on her dinner plate. Needless to say, the reading rated a 10 with all but the squeamish.

On the January DSA reassessment, Thomas spelled 19 of the letter name words correctly. Problems persisted with digraphs and affricates (SIP for *ship*, THOP for *chop*, MUTH for *much*, JRUM for *drum*); with consonant *w* (YITH for *with*); and with short *e* (WINT for *went*). Although Thomas's instructional needs were clearly still at the letter name stage, a few of his spellings on the within word pattern list showed that he was beginning to discover that all words are not spelled sound by sound—CUOT for *cute*, MIET for *might*, CYIET for *quite*, and POEINTE for *point*.

Weekend news writing (Fraser & Skolnick, 1994) became an anticipated part of our Monday morning routine soon after it was tried. It gave the children another occasion for meaningful writing (and purposeful reading and sharing) and afforded me time to work with small groups of children on word study. Thomas's weekend news from the time of his January inventory assessment illustrates his confusion with the digraph *th* and short *e*, his ability to spell some of his sight words correctly (*have* and *good*), and his use of classroom environmental print (*Saturday* and *weekend news*). Long vowel markers are absent here.

Weekend News
On saturday
me and sistr wi
sla rodeg tin I
wint to have
sum hot koko.
it was good hot
koko tin I had
to go hom tin
I had to goto

beb I had a Fun
Weekend.

FIGURE 1–3. (*cont.*)

tales of Aldo. Children also find books from Joanna Coles' *Magic School Bus* series engaging. The amazing adventures of wacky Ms. Frizzle and her class and the factual information presented in the books attract students.

Advances in word knowledge affect students' writing, too, making it easier and more fluent. A noticeable result of this is longer pieces. Children at this stage consider their audience more and, unlike beginning writers who often assume that readers and listeners know more than they actually do, take care to include plenty of details. *And, then,* and *next* can get quite a workout as writers strive to tell the *whole* story.

Their greater experience with print leads children at this stage to a heightened awareness of how words work and, consequently, to more conventional spelling. The once-logical letter name spellings of BAK for *bake* and RAN for *rain* are not confirmed by the within word pattern speller's ever-increasing sight vocabulary—such spellings just don't "look right." Short vowel substitutions gradually disappear at this stage, and long vowel markers appear. Pattern mastery, especially the marking of long vowels, is at the heart of this stage of development. The many ways of representing long vowel sounds in English can make this a confusing process and cause within word pattern spellers to ponder "Which pattern, and when?" For example, although the *a–consonant–e* pattern is correct in *wave*, it is not correct in *train, play, eight, they,* and *great*. Furthermore, finding that a pattern works one time with a particular pronunciation is no guarantee that it will work with another—for example, *I liked the <u>tale</u> about the gingerbread man,* but *My dog's <u>tail</u> is very long.* In their efforts to come to terms with these difficulties, children often overgeneralize and misapply their understandings (MAIK = *make* or HIDE = *hid*).

Within word pattern features include the following:

• *Vowel–consonant–e* patterns are frequent. Despite early confusions (BAIK = *bake*), these patterns are usually the first to be used with confidence by within word pattern spellers.

• *R-controlled vowel patterns,* those in which *r* follows a vowel or a team of vowels, are often substituted for each other (HERT = *hurt,* FEER = *fear*). Reversed letter order is also common (GRIL = *girl,* BRID = *bird*).

• *Other common long vowels* include vowel teams like *ai, ay, ee, ea, oa,* and *ui,* as well as *igh, i–consonant–consonant* (*find* and *wild*), and *o–consonant–consonant* (*cold* and *post*). Using but confusing is apparent in spellings like BOET for *boat* and POAK for *poke,* or TITE for *tight* and SPIGHT for *spite.*

• *Complex consonant units* (Venezky, 1970) include the following types: (1) three-consonant clusters (*scr, tch*), (2) two-consonant units that result in the sound of a single letter (*ck, kn*), and (3) consonant and vowel units (*dge, qu*). Errors such as SKRAP and SCAP for *scrap,* QWEEN for *queen,* BRIGDE for *bridge,* and BICKE for *bike* are common.

• *Abstract vowels* are vowel patterns that are neither long nor short. Most of the patterns consist of two vowels that form a *diphthong,* a speech sound that begins with one vowel and glides into the next as in the following words: *p<u>ou</u>t, c<u>ow</u>, f<u>ew</u>, b<u>oi</u>l, t<u>oy</u>.* Other patterns include the vowel teams of *oo* (*foot* and *boot*) and *au* and *aw* (*caught* and *paw*). Spelling difficulties often result from confusion of the patterns, like COWCH for *couch* and POYNT for *point*.

In addition to increasing their knowledge of patterns, within word pattern spellers need opportunities to explore meaning connections. A study of *homophones* (words that sound alike but are spelled differently) is not only fun for students but can clear up many writing confusions. Another meaning connection that students benefit from is the understanding that in English, actions that happened in the past are usually recorded with *ed*, regardless of how the ending is pronounced. Students' overreliance on sound when writing words of this type results in such spellings as BATID/*batted*, RIPT/*ripped*, and PEND/*penned*. The fact that *ed* endings sometimes require the dropping of a final *e* or the doubling of a final consonant is *not* an instructional issue until the next stage.

Despite the pattern complexities at this stage, as students read and examine words and exercise their understandings in their writing, they gradually sort out the correct use of patterns in single-syllable words. Their developing knowledge of pattern, sound, and meaning relationships, coupled with a steady acquisition of sight vocabulary, continues to strengthen their fluency in reading and writing. Although many students move into the within word pattern stage during second grade (see Figure 1-4), others who have difficulty with reading and writing may not reach it until much later (see Figure 1-5).

STAGE IV: SYLLABLE JUNCTURE SPELLING

◆

By the time they reach the syllable juncture stage (often in the intermediate grades), most students have become proficient readers and process print with considerable efficiency. Reading and writing to learn assume a greater emphasis as students explore new genres and expand their purposes. Content areas, like social studies and science, present students with increasingly difficult informational text, exposing them to more sophisticated vocabulary and to more complex spelling patterns. Content studies often pique students' interests in historical fiction and biographies for recreational reading. Favorite authors also drive student choice in reading material. In fact, it is not uncommon to find students at the syllable juncture stage scouring the library for just one more book by a well-liked author, like Judy Blume, Betsy Byars, Matt Christopher, Lois Lowry, Roald Dahl, Lloyd Alexander, Beverly Cleary, or J. K. Rowling.

Much of students' writing at this stage is done in response to what they are learning. They write to persuade, explain, describe, summarize, and question, using such forms as letters, essays, and various types of response logs to convey their ideas. Their writing voice becomes more distinctive, more personal, than earlier. The use of *dialogue journals* (Atwell, 1998) can be especially enjoyable at this time because the letters about books exchanged between teacher and student or pairs of students are often truly conversational.

Jason began second grade as a late letter name speller who was making the transition from beginning reading to more independent reading. He spelled 19 words correctly on the DSA given in September. His spellings indicated short *i* and short *e* confusions. Jason used short *i* correctly in just one word—WIN. In all but one of the other words (TRP for *trip*), he consistently substituted *e* (SHEP, WETH, SLED, FET, DESH). A few of his spellings at the within word pattern stage reveal a beginning awareness of long vowel marking—GAPE for *grape*, FERE for *fear*, STEPE for *steep*. Jason's sight vocabulary was growing, and it wasn't long after the year started that he was reading easy chapter books, such as those from the *Frog and Toad* and *I Can Read* series, with peer or teacher support. Although he occasionally whisper-read, more and more of his reading was done silently.

By January, Jason was ready to deal with patterns within words. On the spelling reassessment, he demonstrated a firm grasp of the vowel–consonant–*e* pattern and showed experimentation with other vowel patterns—GLAIR for *glare*, HERT for *hurt*, FEER for *fear*, FROUN for *frown*, STUED for *stood*, and PONTE for *point*. Jason spelled 14 words correctly on the within word pattern feature list.

His progress from relying on sound when spelling words to considering patterns is apparent in a comparison of his September spelling of *bridge* (BREJ) with that in January (BIREG).

As Jason's word knowledge increased, writing became easier and more fluent, as evidenced by his weekend news at the time of the spelling reassessment. It took up four and a half journal pages! His spellings are indicative of a growing understanding of English spelling. Typical of children at this stage and age, his account provides a "play by play" description of what happened.

Pittsbrag!

On friday rode an airplane to my dad's house alone. Onese we got home we blu up my Super Bowle in flateubul chair. My dad blu up most of it. After that we wated [watched] Sliders. Than I went to bed. The nexst morning I woke up erly. At 3:00 we went to a Penguin game. Penguins vs New York Raneger. New York wun 7 to 4. Than we went home and my dad made dunkin hines brounys. It tuck him 15 min. I ate one. I said "Yum!"!!! The nexst day we wached the Super bowle. Green Bay Patkers 35 to 21. I had a fun Weekend!

FIGURE 1-4. Snapshot of a within word pattern speller: Jason.

Sara also reached the within word pattern stage, but as a fifth grader. Although her DSA assessment revealed strong understandings of features at the letter name stage (all 25 words were correct), her demonstrated knowledge of sound–pattern relationships on the within word pattern list was considerably weaker (just 10 words were correct). Like Jason, Sara had no difficulty in spelling words with vowel–consonant–e, and as learners often do, she overgeneralized her grasp of this feature to other words (MITE for *might*, FRANE for *frown*, and STUDE for *stood*). Her experimentation with other patterns was limited to two words (STEAP for *steep* and GLAER for *glare*).

Finding a satisfying book was not an easy task for Sara—"too difficult" and "not interesting" choices left her sitting and gazing, rather than engaged. However, when she found or was introduced to a book she liked and felt comfortable with, it was difficult to draw her attention away. *Fruit Flies, Fish, and Fortune Cookies* by Anne Le Mieux was one such book. After reading for some time one day, Sara wrote the following entry in her dialogue journal:

> *Dear Mrs. G,*
>
> *I am reading <u>Fruit Flies, Fish, and Fortune Cookies</u>. It is a very good book. What happed was that Mary Ellen bracks her mom's mirow and her friend said that she would have bad luck for 7 years. So she said that she does not belive in that stuff.*
>
> *So the next day she finds out that her best friend is moveing to pares for 2 years so that is the frist thing. She thinks she will not tell her mom that she brock her mirow but she tells her that but her mom is not made that was one good thing. But when she was on her way to walk home she got sprayed by a skunk.*
>
> *I thank that this book is very good for me. I like when she thinks abot bad luck and then it comes. I think that you will like thime to.*
>
>

Your friend
and all ways will be,
Sara

>

Sara's ability to spell numerous sight words is apparent from her writing—WOULD, SAID, HAVE, GOOD, FRIEND. Although she used patterns correctly in many single-syllable words (for example, *out*, *home*, *spray*, *luck*), she misused them in others (such as , MADE for *mad*, BROCK for *broke*, BRACKS for *breaks*, FRIST for *first*). The understandings she develops at the within word pattern stage will serve as the basis for later learning at the syllable juncture stage when she will deal with issues like those in MOVEING and MIROW.

FIGURE 1-5. Snapshot of a within word pattern speller: Sara.

Spellers at this stage use most vowel patterns in single-syllable words correctly. Polysyllabic words and the issues accompanying them become the instructional focus. Students must learn to apply their pattern knowledge within syllables and across syllable boundaries. A primary question is whether to double the final consonant of a syllable in order to maintain the vowel sound—*hopping* and *dotted*, not HOPING and DOTED, and *butter* and *motel*, not BUTER and MOTTEL.

Syllable stress also needs to be taken into account at this stage. In polysyllabic words, syllables differ in the amount of stress, or accent, placed on them when they are pronounced. When syllables are stressed, the vowel sound is obvious. This simplifies the process of selecting the right pattern. However, unstressed syllables do not clearly identify the vowel and therefore are a source of numerous spelling errors. Compare, the second syllable in *contain*, which is stressed, to the second syllable in *villain*, which is not. Both have the same pattern, yet the second example is far more troublesome to spell (and read) than the first. Students' difficulties stem from the schwa sound that occurs in unstressed syllables. This sound, designated by the symbol (ə) and pronounced "uh," creates confusion for the syllable juncture speller because it can be represented by any of the five vowels (*again, agent, pencil, complete, focus*) as well as by various combinations of them. The student snapshots in Figures 1-6 and 1-7 illustrate the characteristics of learners at this stage.

Syllable juncture features include the following:

* *Doubling and e-drop with ed and ing endings* requires a firm understanding of how patterns work. For example, in order to correctly spell *baking*, a learner must first know that *bake* is spelled BAKE and not BACK or even BAIK. Then attention must be given to preserving the vowel's sound by dropping the final *e*, by doubling the final consonant, or by simply adding the ending (for example, *taping, tapping, tacking*).

* *Other doubling at the syllable juncture* also depends on pattern knowledge. In syllables that end with a long vowel sound, the quality of the vowel is maintained by not doubling the consonant (*silent*, not SILLENT). In contrast, a syllable that ends in a consonant and contains a short vowel retains its vowel sound through consonant doubling (*matter*, not MATER, and *cabbage*, not CABAGE). The latter syllable principle holds true for many words. However, because English includes numerous words borrowed from other languages that have undergone pronunciation changes, this rule has many exceptions (*rabbit*, but *habit*).

* *Long vowel patterns in the stressed syllable* present opportunities for the syllable juncture speller to apply pattern knowledge learned at the within word stage to words of more than one syllable—*complaint*, not COMPLANTE. Perhaps the strong relationship between this feature and those mastered at the previous stage accounts for the fact that it is often the first syllable juncture feature to be used with confidence.

* *R-controlled vowels in the stressed syllable* provide further opportunities for students to apply and extend their within word pattern knowledge (DISTERB = *disturb*).

* *Vowel patterns in the unstressed syllable* have a schwa sound (*trample* and *solar*) that lead to spelling confusions (TRAMPUL and SOLER). An examination of similar words (*sample, dimple, simple, temple*) can be of considerable help, as can meaning (*polar, similar, popular, regular* are all adjectives).

In second grade, Abigail demonstrated a sophisticated command of language. She was very verbal and took pleasure in both reading and writing. Her reading tastes varied from Laura Ingalls Wilder's *Little House* series to Mary James' *Shoebag*, the story of a cockroach who changes into a human. Abigail read with fluency, expression, and in-depth understanding, often adding an insightful remark to a book discussion. Writing was a favorite pastime that received much of her attention throughout the year. Free moments usually found her several pages deep in a new story, collaborating on a play, or playing with words for a poem, like the first line of this poem about rain: "Drip drop tiddle top, I woke up in the morning. . . ."

Abigail was already a syllable juncture speller in September. Her spelling assessment revealed a strong knowledge of patterns in single-syllable words and showed that she was negotiating spelling issues in longer words. Although she correctly spelled *trotted*, she had trouble with the doubling in *clapped* (CLAPED) and *swimming* (SWIMING). Other doubling confusions were also evident. She spelled *tennis* right but missed *pilot* (PILLITE) and *minnow* (MINO). Vowel patterns also caused her difficulty—*complaint* (COMPLANT), *disturb* (DISTERBE), and *trample* (TRAMPUL). Nonetheless, Abigail accurately spelled 12 of the 25 words.

By January, Abigail had sorted out many of the doubling and pattern questions and when reassessed spelled 20 of the words correctly. *R*-controlled vowel patterns and vowel patterns in unstressed syllables were still troublesome (SOLUTE for *salute* and BERDEN for *burden*). Abigail's weekend news at this time illustrates her proficiency in writing and spelling. She made only three spelling errors in her recounting of the sleepover—FIANALLY, SLEDED, and SATERDAY. Interestingly, the last is a word that appeared on the classroom calendar. Unlike Thomas, Abigail may have felt confident enough about her spelling to write the word without checking.

Robyn's Sleepover

We ran upstairs. And went to Jessica (Robyn's sister's) room, to play computer. After that we fixed a fort, in her room. Then we had macaroni and cheese, and hot dogs. Then we ran upstairs, and got ready for bed. It was 9:00. We told ghost stories. With the light off. Nothing scared us until "Ahhhhh" Robyn's mom came in the room. We turned on the light. And played with her stuffed animals. Then 1 hour later, we found out that Robyn had some M&M's in her room. We each had 9 M&M's. Then we went to bed.

The next morning at 7:30, Robyn and I went downstairs and made oatmeal. (It turned into watery-oatmeal-mush) I had a poptart instead. Then we went outside. I made a snowman, Robyn made a snowman. Caline, Robyn's dog took my mitten. We chased and chased after her. Fianally, we got it. After that we sleded down the hill. Then we had hot cocoa. I had to go home then. I had fun.

FIGURE 1-6. Snapshot of a syllable juncture speller: Abigail.

Like many of her peers in fifth grade, Gina was dealing with syllable juncture issues in her spelling. Her performance on the spelling assessment at the beginning of the year was strong at the within word pattern stage—the only word she missed was *bridge* (BRIGDE). Gina spelled 12 of the syllable juncture words correctly. Her strength was with vowel patterns in the stressed syllable. She missed just two *r*-controlled patterns (FERNESS for *furnace* and BIRDEN for *burden*) and only one long vowel pattern (COMPLANT for *complaint*). As the rest of her spellings reveal, her understanding of the other features at this stage was just developing. Her need to sort out spelling issues in polysyllabic words is also apparent in her journal entry below.

E-drop and doubling		Other doubling		Unstressed syllable	
SWIMMING		TENNIS		TRAMPLE	
MAKING		PILET	*pilot*	MAYOR	
TROTED	*trotted*	SOBBER	*sober*	POLER	*polar*
CLAPED	*clapped*	BAGIGE	*baggage*	FOUNTEN	*fountain*
PILEING	*piling*	MINOW	*minnow*	SULLUTE	*salute*

Gina was a fluent reader and enjoyed different genres—*The Great Gilly Hopkins*; *Black Star, Bright Dawn*; *Tuck Everlasting*. She knew what she liked in a book and readily and clearly expressed her ideas and reactions to her reading in her journal letters, as in the following entry:

Dear Mrs. Ganske,

I was reading a book called <u>Starring Sally J. Freedman as Herself</u>. I droped it on page 34. There wasn't enouf action, exitement, and laughs. It didn't have enouf to it. It was just about her. I dragged myself to read it. It was sort of like standding and waiting for the ball to come when you play soccer with the boys, but it never comes.

But there is a good side. I started a book that I think I am relly going to like. It's called <u>A Little Princess</u> by Frances Hodgson Burnett. It makes me wonder and be ciours. It looks so very intresting. I can't tell you much cauce I've only read 3 pages. So far I know the main charcter in this story is a rich girl named Sarah Crewe. I also know that Sarah is being sent away to "The Place" in Indianna from England. Judgeing by the back cover I think it's the boarding school their talking about. They make it sound like theire up on a hill on a dirty road in a carrige with fields sorounding them looking down on a cloud of mist and in the distane they see "The Place". More next Wedsenday.

Gina

FIGURE 1-7. Snapshot of a syllable juncture speller: Gina.

Common prefixes and suffixes, also known as *affixes*, are other issues faced by the syllable juncture speller. Students need to learn that prefixes and suffixes are separate meaning units and therefore remain unchanged when added to a base word (*misspelled*, not MISPELLED, and *really*, not REALY). A knowledge of prefixes and suffixes also helps in decoding and understanding unfamiliar words.

STAGE V: DERIVATIONAL CONSTANCY SPELLING

◆

This is the last stage of spelling development and one that continues through adulthood. Most of the words students encounter in their reading and many they use in their writing are of relatively low frequency and primarily of Greek and Latin origin. Although some students reach the derivational constancy stage by fourth grade, the majority are likely to be in seventh or eighth grade before they attain it (Ganske, 1999). Occasionally, students exhibit word knowledge characteristic of this period early in their school years; in fact, a kindergarten teacher shared the spellings of one such "expert" with me! However, just because they demonstrate a sophisticated understanding of words does not mean these young learners are ready for word study with derivational constancy features. They typically lack the necessary reading and writing connections. The text they choose to read reflects characters, happenings, and vocabulary that are more closely aligned with their age-related interests than with their word power. Similarly, although these young experts can spell low-frequency words when called upon to do so, they do not use them in their writing. By contrast, more mature derivational constancy spellers are confronting the orthographic features described below in their reading and are attempting to use them in their writing. They, like the fifth grader highlighted in Figure 1-8, are ready to address these issues through word study.

Unlike words studied at earlier stages, many of the words at this stage are related and derive from the same *root*. Roots, like prefixes and suffixes, carry meaning. Because they cannot be made any smaller without losing the meaning, they are known as *morphemes*. Some roots (often called *root words*) are intact words, as in *rereading*. However, most of the Greek and Latin roots that form the backdrop for word study at this stage are not— *transfer, audible, dictate*). Learning to preserve the meaning units of derivationally related words is the key issue confronting spellers at this stage. For example, in each of the following pairs of words, notice the consistency of the spelling–meaning connection, despite the pronunciation changes that are evident in the underlined letters: *condemn/condemnation, discuss/discussion, music/musician, compose/composition*. An awareness of this relationship can greatly facilitate spelling knowledge and enhance vocabulary acquisition.

Derivational constancy features include the following:

• *Silent and sounded consonants* occur in word pairs such as *hasten* and *haste*. Although the latter word is seldom misspelled at this stage, the former frequently is (HASEN). Being mindful of the meaning connection between these two words can help insure that students include the silent *t*.

Lance started fifth grade as a solid syllable juncture speller. By midyear, he had progressed to the derivational constancy stage, spelling 14 of these words and all but one word on the syllable juncture list correctly. Lance's spellings show that he was beginning to make connections between spellings and meanings but had much refining to do—as his invention for *inedible* reveals.

Silent/sounded		Consonant alternations		Vowel alternations	
DESIGN		EXPRESSION		DISPOSITION	
PROHIBITION		CONSUMPTION		INSPIRATION	
SOLEMN		DISRUPTION		STABILITY	
HEISON	*hasten*	PURSSUATION	*persuasion*	PROCLAMATION	
MUCSLE	*muscle*	POLITITION	*politician*	DEFINATE	*definite*

Latin-derived suffixes		Assimilated prefixes	
SUBMISSIVE		ACCUMULATE	
ETERNITY		SURPRESS	*suppress*
ASSURANCE		COLIDE	*collide*
INEATABLE	*inedible*	ERRESPONSIBLE	*irresponsible*
PERSISTANT	*persistent*	IMMOBAL	*immobile*

Lance was an excellent reader and read widely from the classroom and school libraries, as well as from outside sources. He particularly enjoyed action and adventure. This interest led him to nonfiction books like Jean Fritz's *Stonewall*, but also to the fantasy works of James Howe. During the course of the year, Lance devoured all of the Howe books he could find. The following entry from his dialogue journal in January shows his taste in reading material and illustrates his proficiency as a speller and writer.

Dear Mrs. Ganske,
    I am reading <u>Howliday Inn</u> by James Howe.
    What's happening in this story is while Chester and Harold are out looking for clues concerning Louise's dissapearence, they spy on Max and Georgette (also a dog). While discussing what they had heard Max, Lyle, Taxi (dog), and Georgette surround them and start saying accusations like "you don't really think Louise was murdered". The next day Harold awakes to find Chester missing. Jill and Harrison (the caretakers) say they don't see how Chester could have been poisened!
    My thoughts are the following. I like this book because of its non-stop action and suspense. For example I thought "oh my gosh" when Chester dissapeared. I like the characters because Harold thinks logic and Chester is a crazy thinker. I predict that Chester is not dead because of my background knowledge, I know that Chester is a main character and usually main character's don't die. I like how James Howe forms his characters. I think the combination of a logical thinker and an illogical thinker is great. I can't wait to find out what happens next.

                                         Sincerely,
                                         Lance

FIGURE 1-8. Snapshot of a derivational constancy speller: Lance.

• *Consonant changes* (or alternations) involve a predictable change in a consonant's sound or its sound and spelling. In the examples that follow, notice the changes that occur in the underlined portions of the words. Then note the types of misspellings that may result when students are not aware that words related in meaning are often related in spelling as well. Even when spelling changes occur, as in the last two examples, these tend to be predictable when considered by families of words (*consume/ consumption, resume/resumption*, and *conclude/conclusion, include/inclusion, allude/ allusion*).

confess → confession (sound)	CONFESION
presume → presumption (spelling/sound)	PRESUMTION
exclude → exclusion (spelling/sound)	EXCLUTION

• *Vowel changes* (or alternations) most often involve a change in the vowel's sound. Vowel sounds may shift from long to short, long to schwa, short to schwa, and schwa to short in the related form. The most common and probably most often misspelled words of this type are those that alter to a schwa sound. Changes from long to short give the speller the advantage of being able to use sound as a cue (*volcano → volcanic*); those altering to a schwa do not.

Again, the underlined letters of each of the following examples point out the change. Notice how much more obvious the vowel sound is in the first word than in the second. By thinking of a related word in which the vowel sound is clear, students make the task of spelling words like *composition* and *democratic* much easier.

compose → composition (long to schwa)	COMPESITION
democracy → democratic (short to schwa)	DEMICRATIC

Vowel alternations occasionally require a spelling change as well. However, as with consonant alternations, these are usually predictable if considered by families (*explain/ explanation, proclaim/proclamation*, and *exclaim/exclamation*.

• *Latin-derived suffixes* often have sound-alike counterparts, and this leads to confusion.

invisible, not INVISABLE, and *respectable,* not RESPECTIBLE
conference, not CONFERANCE, and *abundant,* not ABUNDENT

• *Assimilated prefixes* (also known as *absorbed prefixes*) are characterized by double consonants. However, unlike syllable juncture doubling, this doubling results from the fact that over time the final consonants of some prefixes have been absorbed or assimilated into the accompanying base word or root (*in + literate = illiterate, sub + press = suppress*, and *in + merse = immerse*). Most spelling errors related to this feature are due to a lack of doubling (ILITERATE, SUPRESS, and IMERSE).

Greek and Latin roots provide further areas for study at the derivational constancy stage. By realizing that spelling can signal a common root, students are able to make meaning connections among related words and thereby expand their vocabularies. For example, knowing that the root *rupt* means "to break" provides a clue to the meaning of other words with this same word part—*abrupt, bankrupt, eruption, interrupt*.

Through increasing experiences with reading and writing and through guided explorations of words, mature writers and readers discover how the sound, pattern, and meaning principles of English spelling interact. As the discussions in this chapter have shown, the process of acquiring such knowledge is a developmental one (see Figure 1-9). To aid students' progress, teachers need to know what orthographic understandings students already have. The Developmental Spelling Analysis described in Chapter 2 reveals this information.

Before moving on to the next chapter, you may want to check your understanding of stage-related features. Sort the word cards with student misspellings that are included in Appendix 2 into the appropriate categories. Begin by placing the five stage name cards as column headers. Then place each error card under the stage that characterizes the spelling. To see if you're correct, return to the feature descriptions earlier in this chapter. The spellings have been selected from examples that were discussed. An answer key appears as Figure 8-2 at the end of Chapter 8.

	Emergent		Letter name	Within word pattern	Syllable juncture	Derivational constancy
	Prephonetic	Semiphonetic				
Ages:	1 to 7		4 to 9	6 to 12	8 to 12	10+
Grades:	pre-K to mid-1		1 to 2	2 to 4	3 to 8	5 to 8+
	B∃IGT	N	PAN	PAN	PAN	PAN
	132TB	CM	SAM	STEM	STEM	STEM
	ERL88I	K	BIK	BIEK	BIKE	BIKE
	ABGE	HT	CRT	CHRAT	CHART	CHART
	∃A23	DD	DITD	DOTID	DOTED	DOTTED
	IABTT	Z	JREZL	DRIZUL	DRIZZEL	DRIZZLE
	BBEGBA	K	CRETSIZ	CRITUSIZE	CRITASIZE	CRITISIZE
	8BGRE	M	MGRT	MUJORTEA	MEJORATY	MEJORITY

Note: Grade-level ranges indicate grades at which a third or more students are likely to be at that stage of development (Ganske, 1999). **Emergent Stage:** This is a stage of *emergent* understandings. Children progress from prephonetic writing with no letter–sound association (B∃IGT for *pan*) to semiphonetic, "part sound," spelling (N for *pan* or CM for *stem*). **Letter Name Stage:** Students spell by sound, often matching the *names of alphabetic letters* to the sounds they wish to write (JREZL for *drizzle*). They learn to associate letters with their appropriate sounds (*drip*, not JREP). **Within Word Pattern Stage:** Students learn to use *patterns* to spell single-syllable words (*bike*, not BIEK and *chart*, not CHRAT). **Syllable Juncture Stage:** Because words of more than one syllable are the focus at this stage, students are confronted with new spelling issues that result from the *juncture* or *joining of syllables*, such as consonant doubling, dropping the final e before *ing*, and syllable stress (*dotted*, not DOTED). **Derivational Constancy Stage:** Students learn that related words—those with the same *derivation*, or origin—often share the same spelling pattern; the spelling pattern tends to remain *constant* despite changes in pronunciation (*critic/criticize* and *major/majority*).

FIGURE 1–9. Examples of students' spelling inventions by stage.

CHAPTER 2

◆

Assessing Word Knowledge
The Developmental Spelling Analysis

Independent reading during DEAR time.

Chapter at a Glance

Learning about the Screening Inventory
    Dictation
    Scoring
Learning about the Feature Inventories
    Dictation and Scoring
    Analyzing Feature Performance
    Recording Results
    Instructional Implications
    Feature Inventories A and B

◆

In order to tailor instruction appropriately for children, it is important for teachers to learn about their students' orthographic understandings. As previously discussed, ongoing monitoring of students' writing is one part of the information-gathering process (see Laminack & Wood, 1996, for a discussion of evaluating spelling in context); periodic assessment with a dictated word inventory, such as the Developmental Spelling Analysis (DSA), is another.

I devised the DSA with teachers in mind. Teachers typically have classes of 20 to 30 students and many curricular demands to meet. The often difficult and time-consuming process of analyzing and interpreting children's spellings for instructional purposes needs to be quick and easy. The DSA enables teachers to readily and confidently identify children's stages of spelling development, highlight specific strengths and weaknesses in featural knowledge so instruction can be timely and appropriate, and monitor progress over time. The DSA includes a Screening Inventory and two different, but parallel, Feature Inventories. The Screening Inventory identifies the developmental spelling stage of students. The Feature Inventories provide more specific information and are used to determine the particular instructional needs of students. Both components may be used with individuals, small groups, or an entire class. This chapter describes how the inventories are used. A summary of the key steps appears at the end of the chapter for future reference.

THE SCREENING INVENTORY

◆

The main purpose of the Screening Inventory (Figure 2-1) is to determine a child's stage of development so that the appropriate portion of the Feature Inventory can be dictated. The screening device consists of 20 words that become progressively more difficult. The words are grouped into sets of five, with each set focusing on a different stage of word knowledge, beginning with letter name. Although the Screening Inventory has been found to accurately identify a child's stage of development over 90% of the time (Ganske, 1999), it is not intended for repeated use with the same students. Once a child's stage of spelling development is initially established and the Feature Inventory is used, the Screening Inventory is no longer necessary.

Dictation

Consider the following guidelines before starting:

1. Be familiar with the inventory.
2. Minimize distractions, and encourage a relaxed atmosphere. I let students know that I will not be grading their papers but will instead use the information to understand how to help them learn more about words.

Directions: I am going to say some words that I want you to spell for me. Some of the words will be easy to spell, and some will be more difficult. When you don't know how to spell a word, just do the best you can. Each time, I will say the word, then use it in a sentence, and then I will say the word again.

1.	hen	The <u>hen</u> sat on her eggs.
2.	wish	The boy made a <u>wish</u> and blew out the candles.
3.	trap	A spider web is a <u>trap</u> for flies.
4.	jump	A kangaroo can <u>jump</u> high.
5.	brave	A <u>brave</u> dog scared the robbers.

*   *   *

6.	smile	A <u>smile</u> shows that you're happy.
7.	grain	One kind of <u>grain</u> is called wheat.
8.	crawl	The baby can <u>crawl</u> but not walk.
9.	clerk	The <u>clerk</u> sold some shoes to me.
10.	clutch	The <u>clutch</u> in the car needed fixing.

*   *   *

11.	palace	The king and queen live in a <u>palace</u>.
12.	observe	I like to <u>observe</u> birds at the feeder.
13.	shuffle	Please <u>shuffle</u> the cards before you deal.
14.	exciting	The adventure-story I'm reading is very <u>exciting</u>.
15.	treason	The man was found guilty of <u>treason</u>.

*   *   *

16.	column	His picture was in the first <u>column</u> of the newspaper.
17.	variety	A grocery store has a wide <u>variety</u> of foods.
18.	extension	The workers need an <u>extension</u> ladder to reach the roof.
19.	competition	There was much <u>competition</u> between the two businesses.
20.	illiterate	An <u>illiterate</u> person is one who cannot read.

Stop when a child has spelled 0 or 1 word correctly out of any set of 5.

FIGURE 2-1. The DSA Screening Inventory.

3. Instruct students to print their responses on the reproducible answer sheet found in Appendix 2 so that scoring will be easier. Sharpened pencils also help.
4. Speak clearly and distinctly when reading the items, but avoid over-emphasizing parts of the target word.
5. Dictate the number of the item, say the word, read the sentence, and then repeat the word before moving on to the next item. (Primary grade teachers may omit the sentence if the children find it distracting.)
6. Allow sufficient time for students to respond, but move along quickly.
7. Encourage reluctant spellers to write what they can.

Begin by dictating the first set of five words. Continue dictating succeeding sets as long as students are able to spell at least two of the words within the set. *As soon as someone spells only one or none of the words correctly, that child may stop.* In a small-group or individual setting, it is easy to monitor who should stop when. However, when a whole class is being assessed, use one of the following alternative approaches. Dictate the entire list to all students, watching for anyone who may be frustrated by words beyond the stopping point, so that you can quietly tell them they may stop if they wish. In classrooms where children's efforts at representing "big words" are routinely encouraged and respected, even the very young are usually willing to try. The dictation may also be spread out over more than one day, enabling you to review the results and determine which students need to stop. Regardless of which alternative you choose, be sure to observe the above criterion for stopping when scoring the papers.

Scoring

Score the Screening Inventory by awarding one point for each correctly spelled word. *If a child completed any sets of words beyond the stopping point, these words receive scores of zero, regardless of their spelling accuracy.* Record the number of correctly spelled items at the top of each child's paper. To identify the likely stage of development, locate the child's score on the chart in Figure 2-2.

As the chart reveals, a few scores suggest two possible stages instead of one. Students in transition from one stage to another tend to achieve scores at the upper end of one set or at the lower end of the following set—namely, scores of 5 or 6, 10 or 11, 15 or 16. These individuals often vary in their actual stage of development. For example, some students with scores of 10 or 11 are within word pattern spellers, while others are at the syllable juncture stage of development. Because of this variation, both stages are listed as possibilities. Performance on the Feature Inventory is used to determine which stage is more appropriate.

Students with scores of 1 or 0 on the Screening Inventory also tend to vary in their stage of development. Those with scores of 1 may or may not be at the letter name stage. Sometimes children achieve this score due to familiarity with a specific word on the list, and yet on the whole, they may not exhibit spelling knowledge characteristic of this stage. By contrast, a child who is unable to spell any of the first five words correctly may nonetheless exhibit considerable knowledge of individual spelling features. A close look at the

Inventory score	Predicted stage(s)
20	DC
19	DC
18	DC
17	DC
16	SJ/DC
15	SJ/DC
14	SJ
13	SJ
12	SJ
11	WW/SJ
10	WW/SJ
9	WW
8	WW
7	WW
6	LN/WW
5	LN/WW
4	LN
3	LN
2	LN
1	LN*
0	LN*

*Children who achieve scores of 1 or 0 may or may not be letter name stage spellers.

FIGURE 2-2. The Screening Inventory prediction chart: Identifying students' stage(s) of development from the Screening Inventory.

spellings of these children can determine the value of progressing with the Feature Inventory. In general, if the spellings indicate attention to initial and final sounds, and especially if a vowel has been included, dictation of the letter name portion of the Feature Inventory is recommended.

After you have identified a child's likely stage(s) of development on the chart, note the result on the answer sheet by circling the appropriate letter at the top: *L* for letter name, *W* for within word pattern, *S* for syllable juncture, or *D* for derivational constancy. When this process is complete, information can be gathered from the Feature Inventory. The Screening Inventory snapshots of Chris and Tracy in Figure 2-3 illustrate how this process works.

THE FEATURE INVENTORIES

◆

Two different Feature Inventories, Forms A and B, were developed for the DSA so that children would not become overly familiar with certain words as a result of repeated use. Each inventory has separate lists for the letter name, within word pattern, syllable juncture, and derivational constancy stages of word knowledge. The individual lists contain 25 words that focus on five different spelling features. Although the words are different for the two inventories, the orthographic features are the same.

The Feature Inventories are designed for flexible use and enable teachers to choose between a brief assessment option and a more comprehensive one. The procedures for the two are similar. The primary differences are that the brief approach provides teachers with less information and takes less time to administer than the more comprehensive approach.

With the brief option, information is gathered about a child's stage of development only. This provides useful instructional information and entails minimal dictation of words. Students with LN predicted as their stage complete the letter name list; those with WW complete the within word pattern list; those with LN and WW complete both; and so on. This option enables teachers to determine which features are areas of strength, which seem to be relatively weak, and how well the child can accurately spell words at this stage, thereby making it easy to plan appropriate instruction.

The comprehensive option provides the same instructional information as the brief approach. However, because it is more extensive, it enables teachers to assess the full range of a child's word knowledge, not just stage of development performance. While this makes the process somewhat more time-consuming, it insures that students begin responding to words that are relatively easy to spell, thereby building their confidence. The information that results from this approach leads to a *total inventory score*, which is useful for following children's progress from year to year as well as for comparing the progress of students.

One method is not better than another. The choice is a matter of the teacher's purpose, which may differ over the course of a school year. Most teachers prefer to gather comprehensive data once or twice a year to document overall progress, but rely on stage

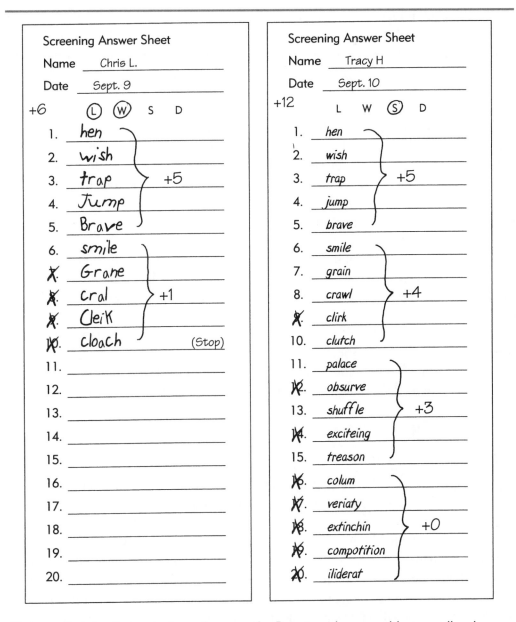

Chris spelled the first set of words correctly. But since he was able to spell only one of the second set, he did not attempt any more words. His score is 6. According to the chart in Figure 2–2, Chris is either a letter name or a within word pattern speller. Because both stages are possibilities, the *L* and the *W* are circled at the top of Chris's answer sheet.

Tracy completed all 20 words. She spelled 9 of the first 10 words accurately, plus *palace*, *shuffle*, and *treason* in the third set, before missing the entire last set. Tracy's score of 12 corresponds to the syllable juncture stage on the prediction chart, so *S* has been circled at the top of her paper.

FIGURE 2-3. Screening Inventory snapshots: Chris and Tracy.

of development information from the brief option at other times to keep them abreast of instructional needs. By supplementing the assessment results with regular observations of children's writing, teachers will be well prepared to make sound instructional decisions.

Whether to use Feature Inventory A or B at a given time is also a matter of choice. However, if an entire school or school division is using the DSA, it is best to come to agreement about when to use which form. This adds consistency to the process. Many schools base the decision on how the assessment is being used—one form for the brief option and the other for the comprehensive. Others specify that a certain form be used for a given reporting period—for example, Form A for the first and fourth quarters, and Form B all other times. At any rate, *dictating one inventory form more than twice to a child during a year is strongly discouraged*. It should not be necessary and could reduce the measure's reliability.

A detailed description of the comprehensive assessment option is presented below. Because the same general directions apply to the brief approach, it is not explained separately. The main procedural difference is that dictation for the brief option is done at the child's indicated stage(s) of development only, unless resulting performance on this list is stronger or weaker than expected. Such instances are few, but when the predicted stage proves not to be the actual stage of development, the previous or following list will also have to be dictated. An additional difference associated with the brief option is fewer scores to record, including no total inventory score.

Dictation and Scoring

Starting the Dictation

Make a list of which students will start at which stage. When determining these starting points, be sure to drop back one stage from that indicated by the Screening Inventory. For students with two suggested stages, go back one from the earliest stage predicted. For example, students who have within word pattern as their likely stage will begin with the letter name list. Those with predicted stages of within word pattern and syllable juncture will begin with the letter name list also. Because you cannot drop back a stage for predicted letter name spellers, they too will begin with the letter name list. Although dropping back is beneficial to most students, it is especially advantageous for children who have just moved into a new stage, because starting at their stage of development is likely to mean responses with many errors.

Once the list is compiled, begin dictation with the earliest stage needed. In most cases, this will be the letter name list. Oral directions are included at the beginning of each Feature Inventory form. The same general guidelines that were described for dictating the Screening Inventory should be kept in mind.

Scoring

Score all answer sheets for the first dictated list before dictating the next. The Feature Inventories are scored qualitatively so that children's knowledge of specific orthographic features can be determined as well as their ability to correctly spell entire words. The following point system is used:

2 = entire word is correctly spelled
1 = targeted feature is correct; entire word is not
0 = targeted feature is incorrect

Answer cards facilitate the scoring process. The cards have the targeted feature underlined and can be aligned with a student's answer sheet (see Figure 2-4). By placing the student's paper next to the corresponding answer card, it is easy to determine the amount of credit to award each word. The appropriate 2, 1, or 0 value is recorded beside each item. Letter reversals, such as *b* for *d*, are not considered errors.

ANSWER SHEET: FORM A

Stage ___LN___

1	1.	*jat*
O	2.	*chip*
O	3.	*Bat*
2	4.	*got*
2	5.	*Cap*
1	6.	*drom*
O	7.	*Bop*
1	8.	*Moch*
2	9.	*wiTh*
2	10.	*Map*
2	11.	*hop*
2	12.	*Plan*
O	13.	*Tat*
2	14.	*Slid*
O	15.	*mad*

DSA Form A: Letter Name Answer Card

1.	<u>j</u> et	D	16.	<u>gr</u> ab	B
2.	<u>sh</u> ip	B	17.	<u>ch</u> op	D
3.	b <u>e</u> t	C	18.	fa st	E
4.	<u>g</u> ot	A	19.	di <u>sh</u>	E
5.	c <u>a</u> p	C	20.	we <u>nt</u>	E
6.	<u>dr</u> um	D	21.	wi <u>n</u>	A
7.	bu <u>mp</u>	E	22.	<u>f</u> ed	A
8.	mu <u>ch</u>	D	23.	<u>tr</u> ip	D
9.	wi <u>th</u>	E	24.	<u>r</u> ub	A
10.	ma <u>p</u>	A	25.	f <u>i</u> t	C
11.	h <u>o</u> p	C			
12.	<u>pl</u> an	B			
13.	<u>th</u> at	B			
14.	<u>sl</u> id	B			
15.	m <u>u</u> d	C			

FIGURE 2–4. An answer card scoring example.

Determining Stage Scores

Once the items are scored, *tally* the number of *correctly spelled* words (those with a score of 2), and note the result at the top of the paper. Keep in mind that tally means to count, not add. The tallied result is the overall score for that stage. *Stage scores cannot exceed 25*, since there are only 25 words.

Dropping back a stage means that the first list should be one where most students exhibit strong understandings. In most cases, the stage scores on a student's initial list will fall in the range of 22 to 25. Those who are novice spellers at the letter name stage of development obviously are not starting out at a stage earlier than their predicted stage of development, and therefore they are not likely to perform as well. If a student does not achieve a score demonstrating confidence (22 to 25) on the first list and if that list was not the letter name list, it will be necessary at some point to drop back yet one more stage for this student.

Dictating the Next Feature List

The second feature list may be dictated the same day or on a subsequent day. Students responding to the words should include (1) those with the following stage as their predicted stage (the new "drop-back" group) and (2) all students who achieved stage scores of 12 or greater on the list just completed. Students with stage scores in the range of 0 to 11 do not need to proceed further. After the dictation, score the responses as described above.

Continuing the Process

Repeat the above steps until all students have a set of stage scores that demonstrate the full range of their word knowledge. In general, this means scores that extend from a level of confidence (22–25) down to relative weakness (0–11). However, novice spellers may not be able to achieve a score of 22 or greater, and advanced spellers may never attain scores as weak as 11.

Stage scores between 12 and 21 are indicative of a child's stage of development. Such scores reflect spelling features that are within the learner's zone of proximal development. In other words, the child shows some understanding of the features presented but not a complete grasp of them. It is here that instruction should be directed. By contrast, scores above 21 reveal few errors and little need for instructional support. Those below 12 suggest much confusion on the part of the speller and too many new issues to negotiate.

Occasionally, a score in the 0 to 11 range is used as the basis for determining a student's stage of development. This occurs when a child demonstrates confidence at one stage but falls short of reaching the stage of development range on the next. These children are in transition and are most often moving from the letter name stage to within word pattern. Spellers of this type are referred to as *early* (such as early within word pattern spellers). Figure 2-5 presents a summary of how to interpret stage scores.

Stage score (correctly spelled words)	Observations
22–25	**Secure Understandings** The speller is competent and confident at this stage and demonstrates firmly developed understandings.
12–21	**Stage of Development** The student is confronted with new spelling issues that challenge existing understandings about how the orthographic system works. As the student revises and refines previous notions in light of new information, features are likely to be used correctly at times but confused at others.
Below 12 (but with strong scores, 22–25, on the previous stage)	**Early Stage of Development (WW, SJ, DC)** Although there is much at this stage that the speller hasn't yet figured out about the spelling system, the student has a solid base of understandings from which to progress.
Below 12*	**Too Much Is Unknown** Without a firm understanding at the previous stage, scores below 12 reflect an overload of new issues. The logic behind the child's spelling is likely to deteriorate; even random spelling may occur.

*Note. Because there is no prior list at the letter name stage, spellers with feature knowledge that indicates letter–sound association, such as B or BT for *bet*, may be considered *early letter name* spellers.

FIGURE 2-5. Interpreting stage scores on the Feature Inventory.

Analyzing Feature Performance

After the dictation and scoring are finished, each child's feature performance needs to be analyzed. For most students, this means determining spelling strengths and weaknesses on one list—their stage of development list. Occasionally a student may have two stage scores that fall within the 12 to 21 range; if so, analyze both. In most cases, these are students who are in transition from one stage to another. Teachers also sometimes analyze two different lists for early spellers—the stage of development list and the previous one.

To learn how well students performed on a specific feature, tally the words that have this feature correctly represented. First, you will need to locate the five words that address the feature. This is easily done by referring to either the feature letters listed at the end of each line on the answer cards, or by using the words by feature chart found at the end of each Feature Inventory (see Figure 2-6). Once you have identified the five words,

DSA Form A: Syllable Juncture Answer Card

1. f <u>ur</u> nace   N
2. ma <u>king</u>**   K
3. s <u>ob</u> er*   L
4. compl <u>ai</u> nt   M
5. p <u>il</u> ot   L
6. t <u>er</u> mite   N
7. pol <u>ar</u>   O
8. pi <u>ling</u>**   K
9. cla <u>pped</u>**   K
10. esc <u>a</u> p <u>e</u>   M
11. dist <u>ur</u> b   N
12. tramp <u>le</u>   O
13. c <u>ir</u> cus   N
14. surv <u>i</u> v <u>e</u>   M
15. swi <u>mming</u>**   K

16. b <u>ur</u> den   N
17. ba <u>gg</u> age*   L
18. fount <u>ai</u> n   O
19. expl <u>o</u> d <u>e</u>   M
20. may <u>or</u>   O
21. s <u>a</u> lute   O
22. mi <u>nn</u> ow*   L
23. tro <u>tted</u>**   K
24. te <u>nn</u> is*   L
25. comp <u>e</u> t <u>e</u>   M

*A vowel must follow the underlined letters. One must also *precede* the underlined letters in words 17, 22, 24.
**A *single* vowel must precede the underlined letters.

Words by Feature, Form A

LN Stage

A	B	C	D	E
4	2	3	1	7
10	12	5	6	9
21	13	11	8	18
22	14	15	17	19
24	16	25	23	20

WW Stage

F	G	H	I	J
4	6	3	1	2
11	9	8	5	10
17	15	14	7	13
19	21	20	12	18
23	24	25	16	22

SJ Stage

K	L	M	N	O
2	3	4	1	7
8	5	10	6	12
9	17	14	11	18
15	22	19	13	20
23	24	25	16	21

DC Stage

P	Q	R	S	T
5	1	10	4	3
8	2	21	7	6
13	9	23	11	12
18	17	24	15	14
19	20	25	16	22

FIGURE 2-6. Ways of identifying features.

count those with a score of 1 or 2. Record the results at the bottom of the answer sheet. Carry out the process for all five features. Scores will range from 0 to 5. It is usually easiest to complete the analysis for all students at one stage before moving on to another. Labels for the identifying feature letters are listed on the class record found in Appendix 2. For example, at the letter name stage, A represents *initial and final single consonants*, B stands for *initial consonant blends and digraphs*, C is used for *short vowels*, and so on. Figures 2-7 and 2-8 trace the Feature Inventory assessments of Chris, an early within word pattern speller, and Tracy, a syllable juncture speller (see Figure 2-3 for the screening results for Chris and Tracy). To practice scoring and tallying feature performance, see the student samples included in Appendix 2. Answers are included in Figure 8-2 at the end of Chapter 8.

Chris's Screening Inventory score of 6 suggested two possible stages of spelling development—letter name and within word pattern.

The tally of Chris's correct spellings on the letter name feature list reveals a stage score of 22, indicating that this stage is one of confidence for Chris. Not only did he miss just 3 of the words, but as the absence of any 0 scores shows, Chris accurately represented the feature in all 25 words. Two of Chris's misspellings, CAPE for *cap* and PLANE for *plan*, resulted from the addition of an e-marker. This type of overgeneralization of the silent *e* is common among children who are within word pattern spellers and strongly suggests that the within word pattern stage is Chris's actual stage of spelling development.

On the within word pattern list, Chris achieved a stage score of just 10, making this the last feature list he completed. Although Chris's score falls below the expected 12–21 stage of development range, within word pattern is nonetheless the stage at which Chris is ready for instruction. Because of his strong score on the letter name feature list and his relatively weak stage score on this list, Chris is considered an early within word pattern speller. Contrary to his

Stage ___LN___   Name ___Chris L.___

Date ___Sept. 14___

+22

2	1. Jet	2	16. Grab
2	2. ship	2	17. Chop
2	3. Bet	2	18. fast
2	4. Got	2	19. Dish
1	5. Cape	2	20. went
2	6. Drum	2	21. win
2	7. Bump	2	22. fed
2	8. much	2	23. trip
2	9. With	1	24. rob
2	10. Map	2	25. fit
2	11. hop		
1	12. Plane		
2	13. that		
2	14. Slid		
2	15. mud		

FIGURE 2-7. Feature Inventory snapshot of an early within word pattern speller: Chris.

performance on the letter name list, his achievement on the within word pattern list is characterized by many words with incorrect features. Clearly, Chris still has much to learn about the use of patterns in English spelling.

Feature analysis results for Chris's stage of development are noted at the bottom of his within word pattern answer sheet. As his strong performance on feature F shows, Chris is using a final e to mark long vowels. He spelled this feature correctly in all five of the targeted words (CUTE, SMOCE, GRAPE, DRIVE, and RIPE). However, Chris also used the final e to mark the long vowels in *steep*/STEPE, *might*/MITE, and *least*/LESTE. These spellings and his 0 score for this feature (H) indicate that Chris has not yet learned other common ways to mark the long vowel. His knowledge of *r-controlled vowel patterns*, feature G, is considerably stronger. As his correct spellings for *girl*, *short*, *fear*, and *hurt* demonstrate, Chris is beginning to use this feature with *consistency*. Although experimentation with *complex consonant units* and *abstract vowels* is apparent (*flock*/FLOCK, *stood*/STOUD, and *point*/POEINT), Chris's understanding of these features (I and J) is minimal.

Stage	WW	Name	Chris L.
		Date	Sept. 15

+10

0	1. pach	0	16. qwite	
2	2. couch	2	17. grape	
0	3. stepe	0	18. yone	
2	4. cute	2	19. Drive	
0	5. bridj	0	20. Kost	
0	6. glair	2	21. hurt	
0	7. skrap	0	22. poeint	
0	8. mite	2	23. ripe	
2	9. girl	2	24. fear	
0	10. frowne	0	25. pant	
1	11. smoce			
2	12. flock			
0	13. stoud		F G H I J	
0	14. leste		5 4 0 1 1	
2	15. short			

FIGURE 2-7. (*cont.*)

Tracy's Screening Inventory score of 13 predicted the syllable juncture stage of spelling development. However, before dictating this list of the Feature Inventory, Tracy's teacher dropped back to the within word pattern stage. These words were expected to be relatively easy for Tracy, and indeed they were. She spelled 22 of them correctly. Strong feature performance is also noted at this stage. The only word with a 0 score is *glare*, which Tracy recorded as GLAIR.

Tracy's word knowledge at the syllable juncture stage is less secure. Her performance, typical of stage of development spelling, is characterized by the use and misuse of various spelling features. She correctly spelled 14 of the words but misrepresented the targeted feature in numerous other words. Tracy's spellings reveal that she is beginning to sort out the spelling issues at this stage. Appropriate activities that support her experimentation will make this process easier.

Because Tracy's stage score was in the 12 or greater range on the syllable juncture list, she also responded to words at the derivational constancy stage. However, her stage score on this list is minimal. The issues confronting her were just too many and too complicated.

The results of the feature analysis completed at Tracy's stage of development are shown at the bottom of her syllable juncture answer sheet. In order to

Stage	WW		Name	Tracy H.		Stage	DC		Name	Tracy H.
	+22		Date	Sept. 14			+2		Date	Sept. 17
2 1. patch		1 16. quiet				0 1. elecrition		0 16. hostillady		
2 2. couch		2 17. grape				0 2. imprestion		2 17. eruption		
2 3. steep		2 18. yawn				0 3. inmachure		0 18. veicile		
2 4. cute		2 19. drive				1 4. permisive		0 19. condem		
2 5. bridge		2 20. coast				2 5. hymn		0 20. pervistion		
0 6. glair		2 21. hurt				0 6. comend		0 21. admeration		
2 7. scrap		2 22. point				0 7. grevinse		0 22. eresestabile		
2 8. might		2 23. ripe				0 8. moisen		1 23. composistion		
2 9. girl		2 24. fear				0 9. asumtion		1 24. majoraty		
1 10. frowne		2 25. paint				0 10. exspination		0 25. confadent		
2 11. smoke						0 11. dependend				
2 12. flock						0 12. acomadate				
2 13. stood						0 13. resighn				
2 14. least						0 14. safice				
2 15. short						0 15. encridibile		*(cont.)*		

FIGURE 2-8. Feature Inventory snapshot of a syllable juncture speller: Tracy.

determine the number of words with a correct feature, Tracy's teacher notes the identifying letter after each word with a correct feature and then simply counts the number of times a particular letter is recorded.

Two areas of strength are apparent in Tracy's use of the polysyllabic words that are the basis of syllable juncture spelling—her use of *long vowels* and *r-controlled patterns* (features M and N, respectively). Tracy accurately employed each of these features in four of the five words. COMPIETE and FERNACE are the two exceptions. The other three features indicate weaker understandings. Tracy shows a beginning awareness of the e-drop and doubling principles (feature K). She recorded *making* and *trotted* correctly but failed to apply the principles in *piling, swimming,* and *clapped.* Her understanding of *other syllable juncture doubling* (feature L) is also developing, as is her knowledge of *unstressed syllable patterns* (feature O).

Appropriate instruction in the features at the syllable juncture stage will enable Tracy to progress in her orthographic knowledge so that she will soon be able to handle the difficult challenges associated with spelling words at the next stage—derivational constancy.

FIGURE 2–8. (*cont.*)

Recording Results

The Class Record

Sometimes it is helpful to view the results of an entire class at a glance. By highlighting everyone's strengths and weaknesses, you can identify children with common needs and group them for explicit instruction. The chart shown in Figure 2-9 and included in Appendix 2 serves this purpose. It provides space for recording students' names, the number of words spelled correctly at each stage (stage score), performance on particular features, and a total inventory score. Steps for recording results from the comprehensive assessment option follow. Recording procedures for the brief option are basically the same; there are just fewer stage scores to record and no total inventory score.

1. *Arranging the papers.* Spend a few minutes organizing the student papers. The investment is well worth it. It will speed up the recording process and result in a clearer and easier-to-interpret class profile. Begin by compiling each student's answer sheets into a set. Putting the stage of development list on the top is helpful. Next, organize the sets according to the students' stage of development. Papers belonging to the letter name spellers will be in one stack, those of the within word pattern spellers in another, and so forth. Finally, order each of the stacks from strongest stage of development score to the weakest.

2. *Entering the names.* Start with any derivational constancy spellers, and enter their names down the left side of the class record. Continue in like manner with students at the other stages of development, ending with the letter name spellers.

3. *Recording the stage scores.* Transfer each student's stage scores to the appropriate columns of the chart. Some of the student's stage score space will be blank at this time.

4. *Recording the feature results.* Next, record the feature scores for each child's stage of development. Students in transition to a new stage and early spellers may have two sets of feature scores. Figure 2-10 shows part of a class record completed to this point.

5. *Determining a total inventory score.* Stage scores are needed for all four stages in order to ascertain the total inventory score. After scores from the assessment have been recorded, the blank stage scores may be extrapolated from the recorded information. To obtain the additional scores: (a) assume a stage score of 25 for all stages preceding one with an achieved score of 20 or greater, and (b) assume a stage score of 0 for all stages following one with an achieved score of 11 or less. Once the new scores are recorded, add up the four stage scores to arrive at the total inventory score (see Figure 2-11). Total inventory scores will range from 0 to 100. As noted earlier, this score enables you to compare a student's progress across time as well as to compare the progress of different students. However, a total inventory score is not necessary for planning appropriate instruction.

The Student Profile

The student profile, included in Appendix 2, may be used as a long-term record of individual student performance. It can easily be placed in a student's portfolio. As revealed by the completed form in Figure 2-12, the profile highlights word knowledge at three

**DSA
Class Record**

		A	Initial & Final Consonants	
		B	Initial Consonant Blends & Digraphs	**LN STAGE**
		C	Short Vowels	
		D	Affricate	
		E	Final Consonant Blends & Digraphs	
			STAGE SCORE	
		F	Long Vowels (VCe)	
		G	R-Controlled Vowels	**WW STAGE**
		H	Other Common Long Vowels	
		I	Complex Consonants	
		J	Abstract Vowels	
			STAGE SCORE	
		K	Doubling & e-Drop with ed & ing	
		L	Other Syllable Juncture Doubling	**SJ STAGE**
		M	Long Vowel Patterns (Stressed Syllable)	
		N	R-Controlled Vowels (Stressed Syllable)	
		O	Unstressed Syllable Vowel Patterns	
			STAGE SCORE	
		P	Silent & Sounded Consonants	
		Q	Consonant Changes	**DC STAGE**
		R	Vowel Changes	
		S	Latin-Derived Suffixes	
		T	Assimilated Prefixes	
			STAGE SCORE	
			TOTAL INVENTORY SCORE	

FIGURE 2–9. Part of a blank class record.

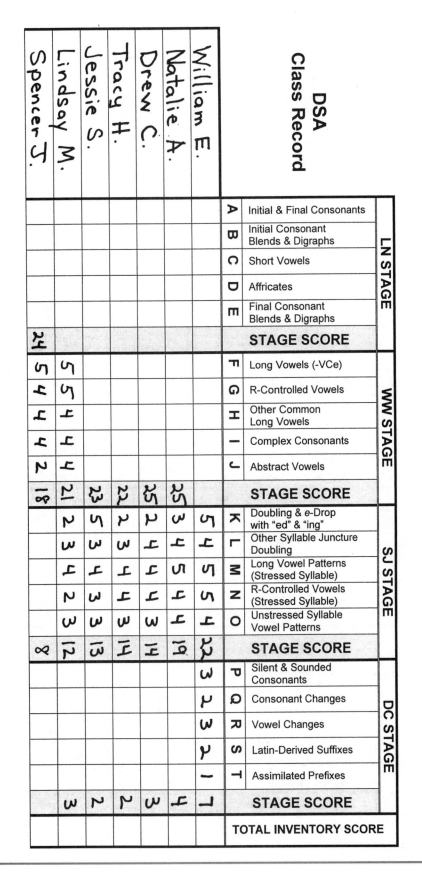

Stage	Code	Feature	William E.	Natalie A.	Drew C.	Tracy H.	Jessie S.	Lindsay M.	Spencer J.
LN STAGE	A	Initial & Final Consonants							
LN STAGE	B	Initial Consonant Blends & Digraphs							
LN STAGE	C	Short Vowels							
LN STAGE	D	Affricates							
LN STAGE	E	Final Consonant Blends & Digraphs							
LN STAGE		**STAGE SCORE**							24
WW STAGE	F	Long Vowels (-VCe)						5	5
WW STAGE	G	R-Controlled Vowels						5	4
WW STAGE	H	Other Common Long Vowels						4	4
WW STAGE	I	Complex Consonants						4	4
WW STAGE	J	Abstract Vowels						4	2
WW STAGE		**STAGE SCORE**		25	25	22	23	21	18
SJ STAGE	K	Doubling & e-Drop with "ed" & "ing"	5	5	3	2	2	5	2
SJ STAGE	L	Other Syllable Juncture Doubling	4	4	4	3	3	3	3
SJ STAGE	M	Long Vowel Patterns (Stressed Syllable)	5	5	5	4	4	4	4
SJ STAGE	N	R-Controlled Vowels (Stressed Syllable)	5	5	4	4	4	3	2
SJ STAGE	O	Unstressed Syllable Vowel Patterns	4	4	3	3	3	3	3
SJ STAGE		**STAGE SCORE**	22	19	14	14	13	12	8
DC STAGE	P	Silent & Sounded Consonants	3						
DC STAGE	Q	Consonant Changes	2						
DC STAGE	R	Vowel Changes	3						
DC STAGE	S	Latin-Derived Suffixes	2						
DC STAGE	T	Assimilated Prefixes	1						
DC STAGE		**STAGE SCORE**	1	4	3	2	2	3	
		TOTAL INVENTORY SCORE							

FIGURE 2-10. Part of a class record showing recorded scores for stages that were assessed and analyzed.

45

DSA Class Record

Dana L.	Taylor W.	Nathan T.	Miranda S.	Susan P.	Elizabeth M.	Hannah D.	Steven W.	Spencer J.	Lindsay M.	Jessie S.	Tracy H.	Drew C.	Natalie A.	William E.	Code	Category	Stage
5	5	5													A	Initial & Final Consonants	LN STAGE
4	4	5													B	Initial Consonant Blends & Digraphs	
3	4	3													C	Short Vowels	
3	3	4													D	Affricates	
3	3	3													E	Final Consonant Blends & Digraphs	
16	16	18	25	23	24	23	25	24	25	25	25	25	25	25		STAGE SCORE	
			5	5	4	4	5	5	5						F	Long Vowels (-VCe)	WW STAGE
			2	4	4	4	3	4	5						G	R-Controlled Vowels	
			4	3	2	3	3	4	4						H	Other Common Long Vowels	
			2	2	3	2	4	4	4						I	Complex Consonants	
			2	3	1	2	3	2	4						J	Abstract Vowels	
6	7	9	12	12	13	14	18	18	21	23	22	25	25	25		STAGE SCORE	
									2	5	2	2	3	5	K	Doubling & e-Drop with "ed" & "ing"	SJ STAGE
									3	3	3	4	4	4	L	Other Syllable Juncture Doubling	
									4	4	4	4	5	5	M	Long Vowel Patterns (Stressed Syllable)	
									2	3	4	4	4	5	N	R-Controlled Vowels (Stressed Syllable)	
									3	3	3	3	4	4	O	Unstressed Syllable Vowel Patterns	
0	0	0	2	3	2	6	5	8	12	13	14	14	19	22		STAGE SCORE	
														3	P	Silent & Sounded Consonants	DC STAGE
														2	Q	Consonant Changes	
														3	R	Vowel Changes	
														2	S	Latin-Derived Suffixes	
														1	T	Assimilated Prefixes	
0	0	0	0	0	0	0	0	0	3	2	2	3	4	7		STAGE SCORE	
22	23	27	39	38	39	43	48	50	61	63	63	67	73	79		TOTAL INVENTORY SCORE	

FIGURE 2–11. A completed class record.

DSA Student Profile

Name: Tracy H. School: Wordstone Elementary

Grade	2		3		4						
Teacher	Brown		Gardner		Johnson						
Date	9/98	5/99	9/99	5/00	9/00						
Form	A	A	A	A	A						
Total Inventory Knowledge											
Total Inventory Score	32		44		63						
Stage Knowledge											
Derivational Constancy	0		0		2						
Syllable Juncture	0		4	11	14						
Within Word Pattern	8	15	17	23	22						
Letter Name	24		23		25						
Feature Knowledge											
T—Assimilated Prefixes											
S—Latin-Derived Suffixes											
R—Vowel Changes											
Q—Consonant Changes											
P—Silent & Sounded Consonants											
O—Unstressed Syllable Vowel Patterns				2	3						
N—R-Controlled Vowels (Stressed Syllable)				3	4						
M—Long Vowels (Stressed Syllable)				4	4						
L—Other Syllable Juncture Doubling				2	3						
K—Doubling & e-Drop with "ed" & "ing"				1	2						
J—Abstract Vowels	0	2	3	4							
I—Complex Consonants	1	3	3	4							
H—Other Long Vowels	2	3	3	5							
G—R-Controlled Vowels	2	4	5	5							
F—Long Vowels (-VCe)	5	5	5	5							
E—Final Consonant Blends & Digraphs	5										
D—Affricates	5										
C—Short Vowels	4										
B—Initial Consonant Blends & Digraphs	5										
A—Initial & Final Consonants	5										

FIGURE 2-12. A completed student profile.

different levels—the feature, the stage, and the total inventory. A student's progress in acquiring an understanding of the 20 features that comprise the inventories is noted in the *Feature Knowledge* area. This information is especially helpful for documenting the progress of novice spellers, who often make considerable gains in their knowledge of specific orthographic features but are unable to spell many, if any, entire words correctly. The *stage knowledge* portion of the chart reflects a child's ability to correctly spell words at each of the four stages. The *total inventory knowledge* section provides a quick indicator of progress by highlighting changes in a child's overall spelling knowledge from year to year. Space is available for recording name, school, grade, teacher, dates of testing, and form used.

The directions for completing the class record apply to filling out the student profile. In fact, teachers who use the class record typically just transfer the data to the individual student records. There are, however, two key differences in the forms. The class record displays information on many students but for just one assessment, while the student profile summarizes the performance of just one student but across many different testings.

As shown in Figure 2-12, Tracy's progress has been followed since second grade. Form A has been used exclusively for the beginning and end of the year assessments entered on the chart. The results from Form B, which is reserved for any additional midyear evaluations teachers may wish to do, have not been recorded. Teachers at Tracy's school use the comprehensive option each September in order to gather information on students' word knowledge at their stage of development and to derive an overall score. At other times, they use the brief option. This is why fewer scores are recorded for the end of the year. This type of plan works well; as the example illustrates, progress is clearly visible, and yet assessment time is minimized.

Instructional Implications

Organizing Groups

Because most students in a given classroom vary in their word knowledge, instruction should accommodate different needs. When it is limited to a whole-class format, many students are not engaged in activities at their stage of development. Small-group instruction provides an alternative, enabling students to explore the spelling features they are beginning to use, but are using inconsistently—those within their zone of proximity. The process of determining who needs what in order to organize small groups is made easy with the class record. Because assessment is carried out several times during the year, the groupings that result are not static, but change as students change in their knowledge of how words work. When forming groups, take into consideration the students' stages of development, the strength of their stage of development scores, and their knowledge of specific features. Three groups used with flexibility are manageable and usually sufficient for meeting the needs of a classroom. Often, the groups correspond roughly to particular stages or to features, if everyone is at the same stage.

When stage is used as the basis for grouping, students are still likely to differ somewhat in their knowledge of particular features. This is normally not a problem. Review is helpful, even for those with a firmer grasp of the features. However, the needs of an early speller may be quite different from those of a more advanced speller at the same stage. Sometimes it is best to group early spellers with the strongest of the previous stage. Teachers occasionally express concern about whether the groups they have set up are the "right ones." There is little to worry about when you keep in mind that group reorganization can occur at any time and that it needs to if a student is either overly or insufficiently challenged.

Starting Instruction

When planning appropriate activities for a group or an individual, start with an area of strength. *Resist the temptation to target instruction at the weakest features first.* Spelling is a developmental process with new understandings unfolding from previous ones. For instructional strategies to be beneficial, they must move forward from the child's secure knowledge base. Beginning with what is known allows children to feel confident and in control of their own learning. New issues are confronted as hurdles, not as barriers.

When working with a group, start with a feature that is a strength for everyone. Feature scores of 4 and 5 are indicative of this. The selected feature is usually from the students' current stage of development, but can be from the previous stage. Once students are familiar with the instructional routine and the various types of activities they'll be doing, somewhat weaker scores can become the focus.

After a feature has been chosen, compare-and-contrast activities, like word sorts (Morris, 1982; Barnes, 1989), which are described in Chapter 3, may be used to help students gain tacit as well as explicit understandings about words. Through sorting activities, students categorize words by sound, pattern, and meaning. They learn to identify the general characteristics of a particular feature—what it *is* and what it *is not*—and to apply their understandings to other words. As children progress in their knowledge of spelling features, they are still likely to remain at a given stage of spelling development for a year and a half or more. Once their feature knowledge becomes solid, it generally takes time before the spelling of entire words (which have several features that must be dealt with at once) becomes secure. Students need time to work with a given feature, to assimilate their new understandings, and to review old issues.

A Classroom Example

To see how small instructional groups are determined with the class record and how instruction is started, let's go through the process with the class depicted in Figure 2-11. Although William's stage scores on the syllable juncture (22) and derivational constancy (7) lists indicate that he is at the latter stage of development, his achievement is that of an early speller. This, coupled with the fact that he is the only student in his class at this stage, makes it likely that his needs will best be met, at least initially, by interaction with the syllable juncture spellers. Natalie, Drew, Tracy, and Jessie are solid syllable juncture spellers, with stage scores ranging from 19 to 13. They will benefit from planned activities at this stage.

Lindsay exhibits scores within *two* stages of development. She is nearly secure in her knowledge at the within word pattern stage (feature scores of 4 and 5 and a stage score of 21). Her ability to correctly spell words at the syllable juncture stage (12), as well as her feature performance, is similar to that of Jessie, Tracy, and Drew. Lindsay is an eager and hard-working student, and this, too, needs to be taken into account when deciding how to best meet her needs. She will most likely function well in the syllable juncture group.

Spencer, Steven, Hanna, Elizabeth, Susan, and Miranda all demonstrate strong understandings at the letter name stage. As their stage scores on the within word pattern list, which range from 18 to 12, attest, they are ready to clarify and extend their knowledge of pattern-related issues.

Nathan, Taylor, and Dana, the last three students listed on the class record, show considerably less spelling competence than their classmates. Their knowledge of features is just becoming secure at the letter name stage; they will benefit most from instruction focused on features at this stage.

When initially establishing groups, don't overlook clues from the total inventory score column, if these scores are available. A large break between adjacent scores—such as that between Lindsay's total (61) and Spencer's (50), or between Miranda's (39) and Nathan's (27)—signals considerable differences in word knowledge. The needs of these students are not likely to be met by the same instructional strategies.

The initial instructional groups for the classroom example are as follows:

LN	WW	SJ
Nathan	Spencer	William
Taylor	Steven	Natalie
Dana	Hanna	Drew
	Elizabeth	Tracy
	Susan	Jessie
	Miranda	Lindsay

As their feature scores of 4 and 5 suggest, students in the syllable juncture group exhibit a strength in their use of *long vowel patterns in the stressed syllable*—feature M. This is a good starting point for instruction. Polysyllabic words may be used for the instruction, or, if desired, instruction may begin with a very brief review of long vowel patterns in single-syllable words, a within word pattern issue. In either case, categories similar to the following are likely to be compared and contrasted:

Single-syllable words	Polysyllabic words
flap space stain gray	chapter bracelet failure crayon

A good place to begin instruction with the within word pattern group is feature F— long vowels spelled with *vowel–consonant–e*. Here again, all students achieved scores of 4 and 5. Words with a silent-*e* marker may be contrasted with short vowel words (such as *bake, line, joke, plane* and *slam, grin, flop, plan*). *R-controlled patterns* or *other long vowel patterns* are likely features for follow-up. Because the students' understanding of feature J—*abstract vowels*—is relatively weak, this feature would not receive attention until later.

For Nathan, Taylor, and Dana instruction should begin with a brief review of *initial and final consonants* (feature A) or *initial blends and digraphs* (feature B). Both features are strengths for all three children. Word families that incorporate blends and digraphs may be a good follow-up to turn the focus to short vowels. In time, the word family categories may be collapsed into contrasting short vowel categories. For example:

Word family sort 1				Word family sort 2				Short vowel sort 3	
an	*ap*	*at*	→	*in*	*ip*	*it*	→	short *a*	short *i*
can	clap	bat		skin	lip	bit		bat	bit
fan	map	cat		pin	skip	hit		can	spin
man	slap	hat		spin	rip	sit		flat	hit
plan	tap	flat		win	snip	spit		clap	lip
								fan	pin
								hat	skip

Before moving on to a more in-depth look at instructional considerations in Part II, here is a summary of the assessment steps discussed in this chapter. Word lists and answer cards for Forms A and B of the Feature Inventory follow the summary.

THE ASSESSMENT

◆

Steps in Brief

Step 1: Dictating the Screening Inventory

1. Dictate the list in sets of five.
2. Continue the dictation as long as students get two or more words correct within a given set of five.
3. Stop the dictation when students score only 1 or 0 correct in a set of five.
4. Determine the number of correctly spelled words, and record this number at the top of the students' papers.
5. Refer to the Screening Inventory prediction chart.
6. Circle the predicted stage(s) for each student.

Step 2: Dictating the Feature Inventory, Comprehensive Option, for Forms A and B

1. Drop back one stage from that predicted by the Screening Inventory. (For students with two predicted stages, go back one stage from the earliest stage predicted.)
2. Dictate the feature list for that stage, and score the items with a 2, 1, or 0.

3. Record the number of correctly spelled words (those with a 2) at the top of the student's paper. This is the stage score; it will not exceed 25.

4. If a student's stage score is 12 or more, continue dictating words from the next feature list. Proceed until a stage score of 11 or below is achieved. Then stop the dictation.

5. If the stage score for the *first* dictated feature list does not establish a confidence level (22 or greater), drop back to the previous list. Figure 2-13 shows likely scenarios for dictating the lists.

Step 3: Completing the Feature Analysis

1. Analyze feature performance on a child's stage of development list. This list has
   a. A stage score of 12–21 or
   b. A stage score of 0–11 if only the letter name list was dictated or if mastery (22–25) was demonstrated on the previous list.

2. Tally the number of words with a *correct feature* (include items with scores of 1 or 2 in the count). Carry out the process for each of the five features. Note the tally results at the bottom of the student's paper. Individual feature scores will range from 0 to 5.

Step 4: Recording Results on the Class Record

1. Enter the stage scores from the top of each student's papers on the class record. (No stage score will exceed 25.)

2. To obtain stage scores for lists that were not dictated, do the following:
   a. For any stage score of 20 or greater, assume and enter 25 for all previous lists.
   b. For any stage score of 11 or less, assume and enter 0 for all more advanced lists.

3. Add up all four of an individual's stage scores to get the total inventory score.

4. Record the feature analysis results in the appropriate spaces.

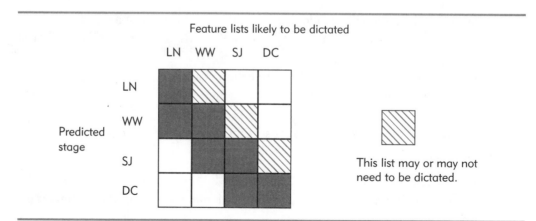

FIGURE 2-13. Likely scenarios for feature list dictation.

DSA Feature Inventory, Form A

Directions: I am going to say some words that I want you to spell for me. Some of the words will be easy to spell and some will be more difficult. When you don't know how to spell a word, just do the best you can. Each time, I will say the word, then use it in a sentence, and then I will say the word again.

DSA Form A: Letter Name Feature List

1.	jet	The jet made a safe landing.
2.	ship	The ship sailed across the water.
3.	bet	I bet you will finish the book today.
4.	got	The boy got a new dog.
5.	cap	The new baseball cap was red.
6.	drum	We could hear the drum beat.
7.	bump	The bump on his head hurt.
8.	much	The boy didn't have much homework.
9.	with	My brother will come with us.
10.	map	The woman looked at a map of the city.
11.	hop	A rabbit can hop.
12.	plan	The class will plan a party.
13.	that	What is making that noise?
14.	slid	The player slid into second base.
15.	mud	There was mud on the floor.
16.	grab	She had to grab her hat in the wind.
17.	chop	Please chop the carrots into pieces.
18.	fast	The girl is a fast runner.
19.	dish	The dish fell and broke.
20.	went	The car went past our house.
21.	win	Let's try to win the game.
22.	fed	The farmer fed the cow hay.
23.	trip	The family took a trip to the beach.
24.	rub	I will rub the penny to make it shine.
25.	fit	The dress did not fit the girl.

DSA Form A: Within Word Pattern Feature List

1. patch   The pirate had a <u>patch</u> over his eye.

2. couch   His grandmother sat on the <u>couch</u> reading.

3. steep   The hill was very <u>steep</u>.

4. cute   Everyone thought the baby was <u>cute</u>.

5. bridge   The <u>bridge</u> had to be fixed.

6. glare   The <u>glare</u> of the sun made it hard to see.

7. scrap   A <u>scrap</u> of paper was found on the floor.

8. might   It <u>might</u> rain tomorrow.

9. girl   The <u>girl</u> opened the envelope.

10. frown   You could tell by her <u>frown</u> that the woman was upset.

11. smoke   <u>Smoke</u> came out of the chimney.

12. flock   A <u>flock</u> of geese flew overhead.

13. stood   The boy <u>stood</u> on his tiptoes to reach the box.

14. least   The opposite of *most* is <u>*least*</u>.

15. short   The girl has <u>short</u> hair.

16. quite   It is <u>quite</u> sunny outside today.

17. grape   The <u>grape</u> juice tasted good.

18. yawn   When you're tired, you sometimes <u>yawn</u>.

19. drive   They will <u>drive</u> to the grocery store.

20. coast   It's fun to <u>coast</u> downhill on a bicycle.

21. hurt   The old man fell and <u>hurt</u> his back.

22. point   The teacher asked the child to <u>point</u> to the letter *b*.

23. ripe   A banana is <u>ripe</u> when it is yellow.

24. fear   He has a <u>fear</u> of the dark.

25. paint   The men were going to <u>paint</u> the house.

DSA Form A: Syllable Juncture Feature List

1. furnace   The <u>furnace</u> was broken, so it was cold in the house.

2. making   The children were <u>making</u> paper airplanes.

3. sober   The family became very <u>sober</u> when they heard the news.

4. complaint   A <u>complaint</u> was made about the restaurant's food.

5. pilot   The <u>pilot</u> made a safe landing on the runway.

6. termite   A <u>termite</u> is a harmful insect.

7. polar   The <u>polar</u> bear lives in cold regions.

8. piling   They were <u>piling</u> the books into stacks.

9. clapped   Everyone <u>clapped</u> at the end of the play.

10. escape   The criminal tried to <u>escape</u> from the police.

11. disturb   The sign said: Do Not <u>Disturb</u>.

12. trample   Horses will <u>trample</u> the flowers if they walk on them.

13. circus   We saw a clown at the <u>circus</u>.

14. survive   We need water in order to <u>survive</u>.

15. swimming   Many people enjoy <u>swimming</u> in a pool.

16. burden   The man carried his <u>burden</u> up the steps.

17. baggage   The men loaded the <u>baggage</u> onto the plane.

18. fountain   You can drink water at a <u>fountain</u>.

19. explode   We could see the firecrackers <u>explode</u> into beautiful colors.

20. mayor   The townspeople elected a new <u>mayor</u>.

21. salute   The soldiers will <u>salute</u> the flag when it passes.

22. minnow   We saw a <u>minnow</u> in the pool of water.

23. trotted   The pony <u>trotted</u> up the hill.

24. tennis   The <u>tennis</u> ball bounced out of the court.

25. compete   The athletes will <u>compete</u> on Saturday.

DSA Form A: Derivational Constancy Feature List

1. electrician — The <u>electrician</u> came to fix the light.

2. impression — Their <u>impression</u> of the movie was favorable.

3. immature — Thumb-sucking is an <u>immature</u> behavior.

4. permissive — The <u>permissive</u> parents allowed their children to run around the theater.

5. hymn — The congregation sang a <u>hymn</u> during the church service.

6. commend — The captain came to <u>commend</u> the officer for his work

7. grievance — The worker filed a <u>grievance</u> against the company.

8. moisten — <u>Moisten</u> the envelope flap to make it stick.

9. assumption — Because of the dark sky, her <u>assumption</u> was that it would rain.

10. explanation — Give an <u>explanation</u> for what happened in the experiment.

11. dependent — A baby is <u>dependent</u> upon others.

12. accommodate — The hotel will <u>accommodate</u> 200 people.

13. resign — His boss is going to <u>resign</u> from his job.

14. suffice — Four bottles of ginger ale will <u>suffice</u> for the punch.

15. incredible — The story of the 100-pound tomato was <u>incredible</u>.

16. hostility — There was <u>hostility</u> between the Indians and the settlers.

17. eruption — The volcanic <u>eruption</u> occurred at 6:30 A.M.

18. vehicle — An automobile is a <u>vehicle</u>.

19. condemn — They will <u>condemn</u> the bridge, since it is unsafe.

20. provision — The man's will contained a <u>provision</u> for his grandchildren.

21. admiration — The mother looked at her baby with <u>admiration</u>.

22. irresistible — The cookies were <u>irresistible</u> to the little boy.

23. composition — The <u>composition</u> was five pages long.

24. majority — The <u>majority</u> of the people voted in the election.

25. confident — He was <u>confident</u> he could solve the riddle.

DSA Form A: Letter Name Answer Card

1. <u>j</u> et   D

2. <u>sh</u> ip   B

3. b <u>e</u> t   C

4. <u>g</u> ot   A

5. c <u>a</u> p   C

6. <u>dr</u> um   D

7. bu <u>mp</u>   E

8. mu <u>ch</u>   D

9. wi <u>th</u>   E

10. ma <u>p</u>   A

11. h <u>o</u> p   C

12. <u>pl</u> an   B

13. <u>th</u> at   B

14. <u>sl</u> id   B

15. m <u>u</u> d   C

16. <u>gr</u> ab   B

17. <u>ch</u> op   D

18. fa <u>st</u>   E

19. di <u>sh</u>   E

20. we <u>nt</u>   E

21. wi <u>n</u>   A

22. <u>f</u> ed   A

23. <u>tr</u> ip   D

24. <u>r</u> ub   A

25. f <u>i</u> t   C

DSA Form A: Within Word Pattern Answer Card

1. pa <u>tch</u>   I
2. c <u>ou</u> ch   J
3. st <u>ee</u> p   H
4. c <u>u</u> t <u>e</u> F
5. bri <u>dge</u>   I
6. gl <u>are</u>   G
7. <u>scr</u> ap   I
8. m <u>igh</u> t   H
9. g <u>ir</u> l   G
10. fr <u>ow</u> n   J
11. sm <u>o</u> k <u>e</u>   F
12. flo <u>ck</u>   I
13. st <u>oo</u> d   J
14. l <u>ea</u> st   H
15. sh <u>or</u> t   G

16. <u>qu</u> ite   I
17. gr <u>a</u> p <u>e</u>   F
18. y <u>aw</u> n   J
19. dr <u>i</u> v <u>e</u>   F
20. c <u>oa</u> st   H
21. h <u>ur</u> t   G
22. p <u>oi</u> nt   J
23. r <u>i</u> p <u>e</u>   F
24. f <u>ear</u>   G
25. p <u>ai</u> nt   H

DSA Form A: Syllable Juncture Answer Card

1. f <u>ur</u> nace   N
2. ma <u>king</u>**   K
3. s <u>ob</u> er*   L
4. compl <u>ai</u> nt   M
5. p <u>il</u> ot*   L
6. t <u>er</u> mite   N
7. pol <u>ar</u>   O
8. pi <u>ling</u>**   K
9. cla <u>pped</u>**   K
10. esc <u>a</u> p <u>e</u>   M
11. dist <u>ur</u> b   N
12. tramp <u>le</u>   O
13. c <u>ir</u> cus   N
14. surv <u>i</u> v <u>e</u>   M
15. swi <u>mming</u>**   K

16. b <u>ur</u> den   N
17. ba <u>gg</u> age*   L
18. fount <u>ai</u> n   O
19. expl <u>o</u> d <u>e</u>   M
20. may <u>or</u>   O
21. s <u>a</u> lute   O
22. mi <u>nn</u> ow*   L
23. tro <u>tted</u>**   K
24. te <u>nn</u> is*   L
25. comp <u>e</u> t <u>e</u>   M

*A vowel must follow the underlined letters. One must also *precede* the underlined letters in words 17, 22, 24.

**A *single* vowel must precede the underlined letters.

DSA Form A: Derivational Constancy Answer Card

1. electri <u>c</u> ian**   Q
2. impre <u>ss</u> ion**   Q
3. <u>imm</u> ature   T
4. permiss <u>ive</u>   S
5. hy <u>mn</u>   P
6. <u>comm</u> end   T
7. griev <u>ance</u>   S
8. moi <u>st</u> en   P
9. assum <u>pt</u> ion**   Q
10. ex <u>plan</u> ation   R
11. depend <u>ent</u>   S
12. <u>acc</u> ommodate   T
13. resi <u>gn</u>   P
14. <u>suff</u> ice   T
15. incred <u>ible</u>   S

16. hostil <u>ity</u>   S
17. erup <u>t</u> ion**   Q
18. ve <u>h</u> icle*   P
19. conde <u>mn</u>   P
20. provi <u>s</u> ion**   Q
21. ad <u>mir</u> ation   R
22. <u>irr</u> esistible   T
23. com <u>pos</u> ition   R
24. <u>ma</u> jority   R
25. con <u>fid</u> ent   R

*A vowel must *precede* and follow the underlined letter.
**A correct vowel (or consonant) must precede and follow the underlined letter(s).

Words by Feature, Form A

LN Stage

A	B	C	D	E
4	2	3	1	7
10	12	5	6	9
21	13	11	8	18
22	14	15	17	19
24	16	25	23	20

WW Stage

F	G	H	I	J
4	6	3	1	2
11	9	8	5	10
17	15	14	7	13
19	21	20	12	18
23	24	25	16	22

SJ Stage

K	L	M	N	O
2	3	4	1	7
8	5	10	6	12
9	17	14	11	18
15	22	19	13	20
23	24	25	16	21

DC Stage

P	Q	R	S	T
5	1	10	4	3
8	2	21	7	6
13	9	23	11	12
18	17	24	15	14
19	20	25	16	22

DSA Feature Inventory, Form B

Directions: I am going to say some words that I want you to spell for me. Some of the words will be easy to spell and some will be more difficult. When you don't know how to spell a word, just do the best you can. Each time, I will say the word, then use it in a sentence, and then I will say the word again.

DSA Form B: Letter Name Feature List

1. path   We walked on the <u>path</u>.
2. camp   The family will <u>camp</u> at the park.
3. lap   They ran one <u>lap</u> around the track.
4. drop   She tried not to <u>drop</u> the vase.
5. top   A <u>top</u> can spin round and round.
6. rip   Try not to <u>rip</u> the paper.
7. cut   Scissors can <u>cut</u> paper.
8. shop   The toy <u>shop</u> was closed.
9. chin   Your <u>chin</u> is below your mouth.
10. van   Dad drives us to school in his <u>van</u>.
11. wet   The grass is <u>wet</u> after a rain.
12. nest   There were three eggs in the <u>nest</u>.
13. glad   I am <u>glad</u> the work is done.
14. hot   Summertime can be very <u>hot</u>.
15. dig   Dogs like to <u>dig</u> holes.
16. rich   The <u>rich</u> man lived in a castle.
17. tub   The <u>tub</u> has water in it.
18. hunt   The Indians used to <u>hunt</u> buffalo.
19. this   What is <u>this</u> thing?
20. yes   The teacher answered "<u>Yes,</u>" to my question.
21. spot   The girl has a <u>spot</u> on her new dress.
22. trot   Horses sometimes <u>trot</u>.
23. fish   There are many <u>fish</u> in the ocean.
24. crib   The baby was sleeping in a <u>crib</u>.
25. job   He drives 10 miles to his <u>job</u>.

DSA Form B: Within Word Pattern Feature List

1. broke   The glass <u>broke</u> when it fell.

2. burn   Be careful, so you don't <u>burn</u> your finger.

3. pine   The <u>pine</u> tree was very tall.

4. spoil   Put the meat in the refrigerator, so it won't <u>spoil</u>.

5. scare   Some people <u>scare</u> easily.

6. queen   The <u>queen</u> waved good-bye from the castle door.

7. cube   Each side of a <u>cube</u> is shaped like a square.

8. scrub   Cinderella had to <u>scrub</u> the floor.

9. slide   It's fun to go down the <u>slide</u>.

10. storm   The <u>storm</u> blew down a tree.

11. train   The <u>train</u> arrived on time.

12. brick   That <u>brick</u> building is a school.

13. growl   We heard the dog <u>growl</u> at the stranger.

14. peach   The <u>peach</u> was very juicy.

15. dawn   It begins to get light at <u>dawn</u>.

16. tight   His jacket was too <u>tight</u>.

17. catch   The little boy tried to <u>catch</u> the ball.

18. mound   The baseball pitcher stepped onto the <u>mound</u>.

19. sheet   The <u>sheet</u> of paper was covered with lines.

20. shook   She <u>shook</u> the grass off her coat.

21. roast   You can <u>roast</u> marshmallows over a fire.

22. dirt   There was a lot of <u>dirt</u> on the floor.

23. ridge   Their house is on top of the <u>ridge</u>.

24. frame   The picture has a wooden <u>frame</u>.

25. clear   The water is very <u>clear</u>.

DSA Form B: Syllable Juncture Feature List

1. cabbage   The <u>cabbage</u> was cut up for the salad.

2. concern   They showed their <u>concern</u> by offering to help.

3. taping   "Why are you <u>taping</u> that shut?" she asked.

4. advice   It is good <u>advice</u> to rest when you're sick.

5. sturdy   The bench is well-made and <u>sturdy</u>.

6. thirty   There were <u>thirty</u> people at the party.

7. mountain   The skiers raced down the <u>mountain</u>.

8. tailor   A <u>tailor</u> makes clothing for people.

9. spotted   A Dalmatian is a <u>spotted</u> dog.

10. refrain   Please <u>refrain</u> from kicking the table.

11. solar   They heat their house with <u>solar</u> energy.

12. shallow   The <u>shallow</u> water was frozen.

13. skipping   She keeps <u>skipping</u> the last line.

14. contain   What does the box <u>contain</u>?

15. dimple   You could see her <u>dimple</u> when she smiled.

16. purchase   The family decided to <u>purchase</u> a new car.

17. parade   The band marched in the <u>parade</u>.

18. grabbed   The football player <u>grabbed</u> the ball and ran.

19. extreme   The temperatures were <u>extreme</u> in July.

20. moment   The car stopped a <u>moment</u> and then drove away.

21. compose   The man is trying to <u>compose</u> a song.

22. riding   They like <u>riding</u> their horses.

23. mermaid   A <u>mermaid</u> is part fish and part woman.

24. fiber   You need lots of <u>fiber</u> in your diet.

25. bonnet   The pioneer woman wore a sun <u>bonnet</u>.

DSA Form B: Derivational Constancy Feature List

1. politician   The <u>politician</u> was hoping to be reelected.

2. collide   Watch where you're going so you don't <u>collide</u> with someone.

3. expression   He reads with a lot of <u>expression</u>.

4. assurance   With <u>assurance</u> he said, "I'll be there."

5. inedible   That piece of old fruit is <u>inedible</u>.

6. persuasion   The salesman used <u>persuasion</u> to sell the vacuum cleaners.

7. design   I like the <u>design</u> of that house.

8. submissive   The dog was <u>submissive</u> to its owner.

9. prohibition   At one time there was a <u>prohibition</u> against all drinking of alcohol.

10. irresponsible   It is <u>irresponsible</u> to leave your homework at home.

11. consumption   The company's <u>consumption</u> of water is tremendous.

12. definite   She gave him a <u>definite</u> answer.

13. disposition   That cat has a playful <u>disposition</u>.

14. eternity   It seemed like an <u>eternity</u> until his birthday.

15. solemn   Their faces were <u>solemn</u> as they left the room.

16. inspiration   The artist had a sudden <u>inspiration</u>.

17. stability   The <u>stability</u> of the broken shelf was questionable.

18. suppress   The woman tried to <u>suppress</u> her cough during the play.

19. proclamation   The king's herald read the <u>proclamation</u>.

20. accumulate   Dust will <u>accumulate</u> if you don't clean regularly.

21. persistent   Sometimes you have to be <u>persistent</u> to get something done.

22. hasten   We must <u>hasten</u> to get there on time.

23. disruption   The hot-air balloon caused quite a <u>disruption</u>.

24. muscle   He pulled a <u>muscle</u> in his left leg during the race.

25. immobile   The car was <u>immobile</u> when it ran out of gas.

DSA Form B: Letter Name Answer Card

1.	pa <u>th</u>	E	16.	ri <u>ch</u>	D
2.	ca <u>mp</u>	E	17.	t <u>u</u> b	C
3.	l <u>a</u> p	C	18.	hu <u>nt</u>	E
4.	<u>dr</u> op	D	19.	<u>th</u> is	B
5.	<u>t</u> op	A	20.	<u>y</u> es	A
6.	r <u>i</u> p	C	21.	<u>sp</u> ot	B
7.	<u>c</u> ut	A	22.	<u>tr</u> ot	D
8.	<u>sh</u> op	B	23.	fi <u>sh</u>	E
9.	<u>ch</u> in	D	24.	<u>cr</u> ib	B
10.	va <u>n</u>	A	25.	<u>j</u> ob	D
11.	w <u>e</u> t	C			
12.	ne <u>st</u>	E			
13.	<u>gl</u> ad	B			
14.	h <u>o</u> t	C			
15.	di <u>g</u>	A			

DSA Form B: Within Word Pattern Answer Card

1. br <u>o</u> k <u>e</u>   F

2. b <u>ur</u> n   G

3. p <u>i</u> n <u>e</u>   F

4. sp <u>oi</u> l   J

5. sc <u>are</u>   G

6. <u>qu</u> een   I

7. c <u>u</u> b <u>e</u>   F

8. <u>scr</u> ub   I

9. sl <u>i</u> d e   F

10. st <u>or</u> m   G

11. tr <u>ai</u> n   H

12. bri <u>ck</u>   I

13. gr <u>ow</u> l   J

14. p <u>ea</u> ch   H

15. d <u>aw</u> n   J

16. t <u>igh</u> t   H

17. ca <u>tch</u>   I

18. m <u>ou</u> nd   J

19. sh <u>ee</u> t   H

20. sh <u>oo</u> k   J

21. r <u>oa</u> st   H

22. d <u>ir</u> t   G

23. ri <u>dge</u>   I

24. fr <u>a</u> m <u>e</u>   F

25. cl <u>ear</u>   G

DSA Form B: Syllable Juncture Answer Card

1. ca <u>bb</u> age*   L
2. conc <u>er</u> n   N
3. ta <u>ping</u>**   K
4. adv <u>i</u> c <u>e</u>   M
5. st <u>ur</u> dy   N
6. th <u>ir</u> ty   N
7. mount <u>ai</u> n   O
8. tail <u>or</u>   O
9. spo <u>tted</u>**   K
10. refr <u>ai</u> n   M
11. sol <u>ar</u>   O
12. sha <u>ll</u> ow*   L
13. ski <u>pping</u>**   K
14. cont <u>ai</u> n   M
15. dimp <u>le</u>   O

16. p <u>ur</u> chase   N
17. p <u>a</u> rade   O
18. gra <u>bbed</u>**   K
19. extr <u>e</u> m <u>e</u>   M
20. m <u>om</u> ent*   L
21. comp <u>o</u> s <u>e</u>   M
22. ri <u>ding</u>**   K
23. m <u>er</u> maid   N
24. f <u>ib</u> er*   L
25. bo <u>nn</u> et*   L

*A vowel must follow the underlined letters. One must also *precede* the underlined letters in words 1, 12, 25.
**A *single* vowel must precede the underlined letters.

DSA Form B: Derivational Constancy Answer Card

1. politi <u>c</u> ian**   Q

2. <u>coll</u> ide   T

3. expre <u>ss</u> ion**   Q

4. assur <u>ance</u>   S

5. ined <u>ible</u>   S

6. persua <u>s</u> ion**   Q

7. desi <u>gn</u>   P

8. submiss <u>ive</u>   S

9. pro <u>h</u> ibition*   P

10. <u>irr</u> esponsible   T

11. consum <u>pt</u> ion**   Q

12. de <u>fin</u> ite   R

13. dis <u>pos</u> ition   R

14. etern <u>ity</u>   S

15. sole <u>mn</u>   P

16. in <u>spir</u> ation   R

17. <u>sta</u> bility   R

18. <u>supp</u> ress   T

19. pro <u>clam</u> ation   R

20. <u>acc</u> umulate   T

21. persist <u>ent</u>   S

22. ha <u>st</u> en   P

23. disrup <u>t</u> ion**   Q

24. mu <u>sc</u> le   P

25. <u>imm</u> obile   T

*A vowel must precede and follow the underlined letter.
**A correct vowel (or consonant) must precede and follow the underlined letter(s).

Words by Feature, Form B

LN Stage

A	B	C	D	E
5	8	3	4	1
7	13	6	9	2
10	19	11	16	12
15	21	14	22	18
20	24	17	25	23

WW Stage

F	G	H	I	J
1	2	11	6	4
3	5	14	8	13
7	10	16	12	15
9	22	19	17	18
24	25	21	23	20

SJ Stage

K	L	M	N	O
3	1	4	2	7
9	12	10	5	8
13	20	14	6	11
18	24	19	16	15
22	25	21	23	17

DC Stage

P	Q	R	S	T
7	1	12	4	2
9	3	13	5	10
15	6	16	8	18
22	11	17	14	20
24	23	19	21	25

PART II

◆◆◆

Fostering Children's Word Knowledge

CHAPTER 3

◆

Planning Appropriate Instruction

Blind sorts are challenging and fun.

Students reinforce their knowlege of homophones with a game of concentration.

Chapter at a Glance

◆

This chapter addresses the how-to of word study. Ideas for developing and using word sorts are presented, as are techniques for classroom management and organization. The strategies are aimed at furthering students' knowledge of how words work so that they can become more skilled readers and writers. Because attitude plays a fundamental role in learning, the last portion of the chapter is devoted to ideas for instilling students with a love of words. Word play, language-appreciation activities, and "history mysteries" (the stories behind words), arouse students' (and teachers') interest in learning about words.

WORD SORTING: GETTING STARTED

◆

As previously pointed out, fluent reading and writing depend on a well-developed knowledge of spelling patterns and their relationship to sound and meaning (Adams, 1990; Perfetti, 1992; Snow, Burns, & Griffin, 1998). Although children's word knowledge is enhanced by their reading and writing experiences, teacher-guided instruction and practice facilitate students' detection of patterns in words and help them internalize their understandings. For some children, such explicit support is not only an aid to word learning but also a necessity.

Effective instruction does not rely on memorizing rules (Hanna, Hanna, Hodges, & Rudorf, 1966), nor does it need to be dry and boring. The instructional approach discussed in this and later chapters taps into a learning activity that is central to the way we make sense of our everyday world—categorization, the grouping together of objects, experiences, and ideas by common characteristics. We separate work "to do" from the "done" pile, sort knives, forks, and spoons into different drawer compartments, distinguish deciduous trees from evergreens by their falling leaves, and compare the merits and demerits of a seaside vacation with those of a mountain retreat. Through categorization we create order out of the world around us. Generalizations formed about the traits that define particular groups enable us to assimilate new concepts and experiences into existing understandings (Gillet & Kita, 1979). In word sorting, children categorize words by sound, spelling pattern, and meaning (Barnes, 1989; Bear, Invernizzi, & Templeton, 1996; Morris; 1982). Unlike more traditional approaches, where students are passive receivers of knowledge, word sorting actively engages students in manipulating words written on cards into groups and in testing hypotheses of how words go together.

Determining the Categories

Word sorts make it possible for students to reflect on the characteristics of a certain orthographic feature by examining words with and without the feature. As they look at the way words are alike and different, students discover spelling patterns that represent particular sounds and meaning. Various types of sorts are discussed in this chapter; closed sorts, open sorts, blind sorts, writing sorts, speed sorts, word hunts, and concept sorts. Some rely on words, and others on pictures, but they all involve categories. When a spelling feature is first introduced, there may be just two categories, but as subtler aspects of the feature are explored, additional columns are added so that there may eventually be four or five.

Students are generally guided to their discoveries about word features with a *closed sort*. During a closed sort, students match words to like categories identified by key words. Once the matching is complete, they analyze the common characteristic(s) of each category and try to develop a generalization that explains why certain words are grouped together. Typically, a closed sort contrasts one or two new word elements with features that are already known. For example, when long vowels spelled *a–consonant–e* (*aCe*) are introduced, a logical contrast is short vowels (for example, *short a* words [*bat*] and *long a* words [*bake*]). This contrast makes an especially good starting point. It not only allows children to draw on their already established knowledge of short vowels; it also provides a clear contrast that makes it easier for students to focus on the characteristics of long vowels. By comparison, consider the greater difficulty of grasping the concept of "long vowelness" if presented with the categories *aCe* and *ai* (*make* and *rain*), or even *aCe* and *iCe* (*make* and *bike*). Both of these examples prevent students from using what they know, and they make it difficult to tell just what a long vowel is. Although categories should be obvious at first, in time they may become less distinctive and more complex. For example, an appropriate follow-up to the above categorization with *short a* and *aCe* would be a sort that expands the concept of long *a*, such as one that adds a new long *a* pattern to the categories already examined:

Short *a*	Long *a*	
cat	rake	rain

When students become comfortable with these patterns, other columns may be added, perhaps *ay* and *ei*, further extending their understanding. This type of scaffolding prevents students from becoming frustrated by new concepts and helps ensure successful learning for everyone.

Both sight and sound associations need to be integrated into a student's orthographic knowledge. Efficient writing and reading depend on students' ready access to these stored associations. When writing, students must be able to draw on their memories for the stored *visual* patterns that relate to the sounds they wish to write. When reading, students are presented with the visual cues but must be able to make appropriate *sound* matches. Therefore, when possible, it is desirable to develop sorts that contain sound as well as visual contrasts. Many categorizations, like the one below, allow students to sort the same set of words first by sound, then by pattern, and finally by sound and pattern simultaneously. Although more difficult, this last type of sort is definitely worth working up to. Because it requires students to integrate their knowledge of sound and pattern, carryover in reading and writing is more likely.

	Sound sort				Pattern sort	
got	globe	how		got	globe	flow
stop	flow	now		stop	bone	how
fox	bone	down		fox	hose	now
rob	throw			rob		throw
	hose					down

	Sound and pattern sort		
got	globe	flow	how
stop	bone	throw	now
fox	hose		down
rob			

Teachers and students often come upon words that do not fit a particular sound or pattern. These should not be avoided. Exceptions promote students' thinking and discourage overreliance on either visual or sound clues. For example, if *done* and *come* were included in the sound and pattern sort just presented, students might fail to attend to the vowel sound and think the words should go with *globe*, *bone*, and *hose*. Actually, these two words do not fit any of the categories in this sort; they belong in a special column for exceptions. Teachers refer to this category by various names, including *oddballs, cuckoos, other,* and *miscellaneous,* and they often label it as ?. Even if no exceptions have been included in the sort, the category should be available to students. Much can be learned by listening to students' explanations about why they have placed a given word in this special column. This information makes it easier to help students clear up misconceptions.

Contrasts that take students from the known to the new and from the simple to the more complex promote active student participation in the learning process. As your students examine words through sorting activities and on their own, encourage them to think and talk about their observations and to ask questions. Help them make generalizations about the categories. Questions like "How are all of these words alike?" and "Why did you put these words together in this column, but leave the others over here?" help students zero in on the common characteristics of features. This approach encourages sensitivity to differences in dialect and to fragile understandings. Teachers listen to what students have to say and clarify and expand on their understandings, rather than provide them with a list of rules.

In addition to engaging students in closed sorts with predetermined categories, you may want to invite them to freely explore a set of words and come up with their own classifications. These *open sorts* are an enjoyable alternative for students, and they afford teachers insights about how students think about words. Although the resulting categories may resemble those that students have recently been examining, this is not always the case. Categories based on word length, parts of speech, meaning, and common letters are other possible outcomes. For example, one open sort led to the following two categories: *wave, man, rain, same, can,* and *train, tap, game, fast, shake.* Rather than sorting the words by sound or spelling pattern, this child grouped the words according to those with letters that are "long and tall" (*t, p, g, f, h,* and *k*) and those that are not.

Selecting Words

Ideally, words for study come from the children's reading and writing. However, because exemplars from these sources are sometimes limited, supplemental listings of words are provided in Appendix 1. When selecting words from these or other sources, keep in mind that students need to be able to read the words being used. Automatic recognition allows students to put their mental energy into examining sound, pattern, and meaning relationships rather than struggling to decode the words themselves. Because it is impossible to know in advance whether students *can* read all the words, it is a good idea to have them identified at the start of a session so that problem words may be omitted. For beginning readers with limited sight vocabularies, pictures may be substituted for words or used to supplement known words, so that they too can analyze word elements and reflect on their properties. Picture sorting is most appropriate for students at the emergent, letter name, and early within word pattern stages, where the primary focus is on sound. Pictures may be categorized by initial consonant sounds, blends, digraphs, and vowels (see Figure 3-1). When pictures are used, they should clearly depict the words and be relatively free of extraneous and distracting detail.

Another consideration for choosing words is their sophistication relative to the students' level of maturity and the likelihood that students will use them in their writing. Words included in the supplemental listings are intended for use across a broad range of ages. Therefore, it is important to keep particular students in mind, and not just the focused spelling feature. For example, suppose the within word pattern feature *other long vowels* is targeted for study and the pattern being introduced is long *a,* spelled *ai.* Words like *strait* and *hail* fit the pattern and may be identifiable by students, but are they good choices? If the words are intended for older children, they probably are; if they are to be used with first or second graders, there probably are better choices, like *train, nail,* and *paint.*

As noted above, exceptions to categories should not be avoided. However, when added to sorts, they should be used sparingly so that they do not confuse students. I like to use them the same way I use cayenne pepper—to spice things up a bit, but not to overwhelm the palate.

FIGURE 3-1. A picture sort with *s, t,* and *st.*

At times, teachers may want to invite students to add some of their own findings to the pool of words being studied. Ordinarily, these are words that have been collected and recorded in a notebook as part of a previous week's study. Students enjoy the opportunity to provide input and are careful to contribute words that fit the spelling patterns being explored.

A final consideration for word selection is how many words to choose. *There is no right number.* Because students compare and contrast words with and without a particular feature, they simply need enough examples of each category type to distinguish similarities and differences. This may mean 3 to 4 words per category, or it could mean 10. Individual teachers must decide on the number that seems best for their particular situation. A total of 10 to 25 words for two to five categories is common.

In general, students should already know how to spell about half of the words they will be using. In order to ascertain whether this is the case, teachers may opt to periodically give beginning-of-the-week quizzes on the words.

ESTABLISHING A ROUTINE

◆

Word study activities comprise but a small part of students' reading and writing time, but this time is *very important.* Although there is no *one* way to carry out word study, it is important to consider what will work best for you and your students before you begin so that you can establish a routine. When the situation is predictable, students are able to function more independently and more time can be spent on learning.

The day-by-day schedule I have used at various grade levels and with a full range of student abilities is built around a Monday through Friday routine but could easily fit other time frames. I begin the week with a small group "word walk." The purpose of this teacher-guided instructional time is to help students discover the sound, pattern, and meaning characteristics of words. Throughout the week I provide opportunities for students to practice sorting the words into categories so that their understandings begin to be internalized. I also provide experiences that allow them to apply what they are learning to other words in different contexts. Small group instruction is balanced with paired, individual, and cooperative activities. The routines shown in Figure 3-2 are just two of many possibilities.

weekly goals

Teachers who aren't used to working with flexible groups sometimes wonder about the logistics of managing the rest of the class when the instructional focus is on a small group. From the intermediate grades on, most students are able to work cooperatively or independently on assigned tasks (such as, process writing, silent reading, response journals, and word study notebooks) as the different word study groups meet. A clear understanding of teacher expectations and student options is important. In the primary grades, teachers often use a *circle, seat, and center* approach for scheduling time to meet with flexible small groups. This format easily accommodates three small groups and enables children to pursue varied activities. *Circle* refers to teacher-guided reading, writing, or word study instruction. During *seat* time, children typically write in journals (recounting their weekend news, for example) or complete theme-related work from one of their studies. *Centers* (located at a table, a counter, or a space on the floor) may include reading or browsing a book in the classroom library, listening and following along to a tape-recorded story, solving a math or science problem, drawing or painting, using the computer, or enjoying a word study game. Posted charts, such as the one shown in Figure 3-3, help students know when they will be doing what. Velcro attachments make it easy to switch the symbol cards around from day to day.

Regardless of how word study time is structured, explicit instruction should occur at the start of each exploration of new words. Other activities are a matter of personal choice but should give students opportunities for practice and application. Some, such as word hunts, are most appropriate after students have become familiar with the categories under study. The list of activities described below is not extensive. Just a few basic ideas are needed to get going (and even to sustain a successful program). The list may be expanded or adapted over time.

Many of the activities involve students in sorting word cards. Word cards are made by printing the week's words on small rectangular pieces of paper or index cards. Because the cards can be freely manipulated, students are able to actively test out ideas and change their categorizations as needed. Using a template, such as the one shown with long and short *a* words in Figure 3-4, makes it easy to provide each student with a personal set of word cards. Word cards can be created on the computer using a spreadsheet or with a specially designed program like *Cardmaker* (Taylor, 1996a). The latter produces word cards

A Sample Schedule for the Primary Grades

Day 1 20 minutes	Day 2 10 minutes	Day 3 15 minutes	Day 4 15 minutes	Day 5 15 minutes
Teacher-guided word or picture walk (closed sort) Small groups	Be-the-Teacher Small groups	✓ Buddy blind sorts Partners	✓ Picture or word hunts and recording Partners or small group	✓Assessment: Quiz Partners, small groups, or whole class

Possible follow-up or homework activities—Times will vary

Cut and paste picture sort; writing sort Independent	Draw and label or write and draw Independent	Student choice or SAW activity Partners or independent	Rhyme time or change-a-letter Partners or independent	Games Partners or independent

✓ Depending on your students, you may be able to have all students carry out these activities at the same time.

A Sample Schedule for the Intermediate Grades

Day 1 20 minutes	Day 2 10 minutes	Day 3 20 minutes	Day 4 15 minutes	Day 5 15 minutes
Teacher-guided word walk (closed sort) Small groups	Buddy sorts (answer key provided) Partners	✓ Word hunt and recording Cooperative small groups	✓ Speed sorts or blind sorts Small groups or partners	✓ Assessment: Quiz Partners, or whole class

Possible follow-up or homework activities—Times will vary

Writing sort and word walk log entry Independent	Write and draw Independent	SAW Independent	Computer sorting or student choice Partners or independent	

✓ I have all students carry out these activities at the same time.

FIGURE 3–2. Weekly word study schedules.

FIGURE 3–3. Chart showing a possible rotation of activities for primary students during small group instructional time (groups are identified by color).

for students and a sorted copy for the teacher in one step. When using the former approach, set the margins to 0 to avoid leftover paper when the words are cut apart.

In preparation for each group's exploration of words, I put together sorts that address a need demonstrated by the DSA results and that reflect the previously discussed considerations for word and category selection. Once categories and words are determined, I print or type the words in a random order on the template. Copies of the template are then made and placed in a predictable location—on desktops, in mailboxes, and so on. (For primary-age children, to avoid card confusions, use different colors of paper for each group.) When the children arrive on Monday, they cut apart the words and store them in a manila envelope or plastic bag. To aid identification, they may put their initials or a personal mark on the back of each card. In anticipation of the upcoming word walk, students frequently begin looking for likely categories as they cut their words apart.

A Word Walk: Introducing the Sort and Building Vocabulary

Once the first small group has gathered, I hold up each card and ask students to identify the words. Words that aren't recognized are discarded. (Knowing all the words is less critical for students at the syllable juncture and derivational constancy stages, but students should still be familiar with most of them.) I follow up on several of the words by

flap	paint	place
shape	said	sack
train	blame	brain
have	crack	grade
mail	rain	shade
mask	fake	sail
nail	pail	?

FIGURE 3-4. Word card template with long and short *a*.

asking students to tell me what they mean. This is a valuable strategy for getting children to expand their use of language. At the beginning of the year, for example, when asked to tell what a *desk* is, students commonly respond, "It's a *thing* that you sit at," or "It's where you work." We discuss other words that could be referred to by these definitions and establish guidelines that help students elaborate on their responses. Naming the basic category to which the word belongs (for example, *people, animals, furniture, actions*) and avoiding the word *thing* are two worthwhile criteria. Students view the activity as challenging and fun and soon come to know and use many words.

After the week's words have been read and discussed, I model the sort. I begin by placing a key word for each of the categories in front of me, being sure to read the words as I lay them down. Different key words may be necessary, depending on whether the sort is focused on sound, pattern, or sound and pattern. Students who have already examined the words at their seats may be given an opportunity to share their hypotheses about the categories at this time. I usually respond to their ideas with "Well, let's see if you're right," and proceed with modeling the sort.

Taking a word from the stack, I pronounce it and try matching it with each of the key words, being sure to read both the new word and the key words aloud. After due consideration, I place the word under its appropriate column and continue in a similar manner with several of the remaining words, each time reading the new word and its matching key word. As the columns start to take shape, students begin to detect the word elements that are common to each. When they're ready to join in, they take a turn at categorizing the words, being sure to say the word and its match. If a word is misplaced, I usually say something like "Actually _____ goes under _____" and move the word to the right column. If you wish, you may allow the error to pass until the sort is complete; then have it located and recategorized. I do this only if students are well into the routine of word sorting, and only one or two errors are involved. When students place a word in the oddball category, I like to ask why they chose that column. Their responses not only reveal much about their understanding but also can make you aware of pronunciation differences due to dialect. I usually show a sensitivity to such variations in speech by permitting students to leave the words where placed during a sound sort, but I also tell them that many people would put the word in a different category and show them which one. Once the sorting is complete, the categories are discussed and identified. Figure 3-5 highlights the steps of a word walk.

To follow up, before sending this group back to their seats and meeting with the next group, I often have the children use their word cards to practice the sort as I watch and assist. They follow the same procedure modeled in the group sort and then review their work by reading through the lists. When they're ready, I check the work with them. If an error or two exists, I usually name the column and ask them to try to find the out-of-place words. If time allows, the columns may be resorted using the problem words as key words (Barnes, 1989).

Another way to follow up is with a card game. One set of the word cards is shuffled and dealt to the players. Although individuals may end up with different numbers of cards, this does not matter because the game is not approached as a competition. Students who are holding key cards begin the play by laying them down. Then the next player, following a clockwise rotation, selects a word, reads it and the matching key word, and places the word in a category. If it is the appropriate category, play continues with the next person. If not, group members call out, "Hold it," and the card goes back into the student's hand until it can be correctly played. If no one catches the error (which rarely happens), I do the calling out. Once all cards are sorted, students read through the lists and identify the features. They then return to their seats, and I meet with the next group.

Although I may spend twenty minutes with each group on this first day, the time is well spent. Students learn to distinguish the categories and sort their words. They may be slow and deliberate in completing the process, but that is to be expected. As the week progresses and students have more opportunities to practice and work with the features under study, they will begin to internalize their understandings and become more fluent in sorting.

Sorting Variations

The many sorting variations discussed in this section enable students to practice, apply, and extend understandings they acquire during the initial teacher-guided instruction. The activities may be structured in different ways, depending on student needs, other de-

This word sort with long and short *a* focuses on sound and pattern. The new pattern being explored is *ai*.

1. **Have the students bring their word cards to the small group area.** A circle formation works well. Students set their cards out of the way. You need a set of the words; these may be template-size or larger.

2. **Hold up each word for the students to identify.** Say, "Let's see if you can tell me what each word is. Be sure you say the word loud enough so I can hear everyone." Students read the words in unison. Discard unknown words.

3. **Stop and discuss a few of the words.** Ask, "Who can tell us what this word means? Remember, try to use words that will really help us understand it." Prompt discussion with comments such as "Does anyone have more to add?" Wow! How did you learn that?" Refine understandings as needed, and acknowledge student insights.

4. **Introduce the sort by placing key words in front of the students as category headers.** (Before laying the word cards down, you may want to begin with comments like "Does anyone have ideas about this week's sort? What do you think we're working on? What makes you think so? Well, we'll soon find out.") Then direct attention to the category headers. "Our key words for this week are *flap, wake,* and *braid* [point to each.] Today when we sort, I want you to think about the way the word sounds *and* the way it looks."

5. **Model the sort until students catch on.** Take the stack of cards, and say, "I'm going to sort some of the words, but as soon as you can, I want you to show me where the rest go. Ready? My first word is *state. State—flap...*, *state—wake...*, *state—braid.* [Hold the card under each key word as you say it.] *State* goes with *wake.* [Place the new card under the key word.] *Crack—flap.* [Place the card.] *Nail—state...*, *nail—braid; nail* goes under *braid.* Where does *fast* go? Good job! And how about this word?" [Hold up *train....*]

6. **Correct mistakes as needed.** Move incorrectly placed cards to the correct category with an accompanying comment like "*Train* does sound like *wake,* but even though we are thinking about the way the word sounds, we're also paying attention to how it looks. *Train* goes with *braid.*" When students place words in the oddball column, say, "Tell us why you put that word there." This can be informative. Be sensitive to differences in dialect.

7. **Discuss the completed categories.** Encourage students to analyze the results with comments like "Now that we have placed all of the words, check over the categories, and see if you can make any discoveries about our sort. What do all of the words in each column have in common that makes them different from words in the other columns?" Questions of this type help students form their own generalizations about words.

FIGURE 3–5. Steps for a guided word walk.

mands for teacher time, and so on. For example, sorting practice can be carried out without the teacher by pairing students with partners in the same group. When this technique is used, list the buddy-pairs on the board or a chart (see Figure 3-6), so students can inform the next pair of their turn. Sorts are practiced at a designated table or floor area. When finished, students check their categories (frequently using an available answer key) and record the sort in their word study notebooks.

If supervised practice is needed, students may sort their words in a small group as the teacher watches. Or they may participate in a Be-the-Teacher activity in which students work in pairs or triads and take turns sorting their words and "being the teacher." Designated teachers support sorters as needed and provide feedback. Young students especially enjoy the added responsibility and independence associated with this activity. Teachers also find the procedure interesting (and sometimes quite enlightening), as the apprentices take their roles seriously, often imitating techniques modeled during the word walk—even phraseology and mannerisms! Once sorting is completed and any problems are cleared up, students record the categorized words in their notebooks (or glue in pictures when these are used, labeling as much of each word as they can).

Writing Sorts

In a writing sort, words are written down under appropriate categories, headed by key words. Because the classifying is done on paper, the cards themselves may not be sorted at all. Writing sorts are usually completed as an independent activity but may also be carried out with a partner or in a small group. They are sometimes combined with a blind sort.

Blind Sorts

This type of sort is especially useful in reducing students' reliance on visual cues. As the name suggests, students are not allowed to see the words to be sorted but must

<u>Sorting Schedule</u>

William – Natalie
Drew – Tracy
Jessie – Lindsay
Spencer – Steven
Hanna – Elizabeth
Susan – Miranda
Nathan – Taylor – Dana

FIGURE 3-6. Sorting schedule for buddy-pairs.

depend on sound and their knowledge of the associated pattern to determine word placement. Even when teachers take care to incorporate sound and pattern contrasts into a sort, students sometimes focus primarily on the visual information. For example, consider a sort with short *a* (*pat*) and short *i* (*pit*) contrasts (or one with short *a* [*tap*] and *aCe* [*tape*]). Students can easily end up with correctly sorted columns by merely putting words with *a* in one column and words with *i* in the other (or those with *e* on the end in one column and the rest in another). Teachers who overlook the importance of balancing attention to pattern *and* sound are often puzzled by students' failure to transfer their *apparent* fluency with the features under study to their reading and writing. In actuality, the students may have acquired little understanding of the features. Since the task did not require them to make pattern–sound and sound–pattern relationships, the information was not integrated in their word knowledge. Blind sorts encourage students to balance visual clues with phonological information and should be a part of the weekly routine. Substituting pictures for a few words in an all-word sort or adding an exception or two (for example, *done* or *some* in a sort with *o–consonant–e* words) may also be effective.

To complete a blind sort, buddy-pairs work together. The key words are placed in front of one of the buddies, while the other buddy calls out the remaining words. Without looking at the word, the first buddy judges where the word belongs and points to the appropriate category. Inaccuracies are corrected, and completed cards are stacked under their matching key words. Once all of the words are placed, the roles reverse.

Blind sorts may also be written. In a written blind sort, instead of pointing to categories, students write the words under the right key word. This kind of sort may be done in small groups as well as partnerships. Some teachers use blind written sorts at the end of the week to evaluate students' understandings.

Speed Sorts

This form of sorting is practiced after students are able to accurately categorize their words. The added focus on speed helps students work toward automaticity with the features under study. Speed sorts are frequently done with buddy-pairs; students alternate between sorting and timing with a stopwatch. When this is the case, each student sorts twice, trying to increase his or her speed on the second attempt while maintaining accuracy. Software programs are becoming available that enable you to enter students' words and have them practice their sorts on the computer, with or without a timed component (Taylor, 1996b).

A variation of the speed sort that is highly motivational is Beat-the-Teacher. It may be carried out by small groups or as a whole class activity by having students meet with their respective groups at a cluster of desks or floor area. Both speed and accuracy are important. As students practice categorizing their words, the teacher circulates, sorting each group's words while being timed by a student equipped with a stopwatch. The teacher's times are recorded, and the stopwatches are reset. Students then attempt to sort their words correctly and beat the teacher's time for their group. Several trials are run. After each, partners check the sort and re-collect each other's words in scrambled fashion. Record-breakers receive a special privilege or recognition later in the day. Fifteen minutes is ample for a three-group teacher rotation and provides the students with considerable sorting practice.

Word Hunts

During a word hunt, students search through material they are currently reading to find additional words with the features being studied. Hunting is limited to pages that have already been read so that *skimming* to find words is not confused with *reading for meaning*. Because the activity encourages students to apply and extend their understandings, it is best reserved for the middle or end of the week.

Word hunts may be done in small groups, pairs, or individually. I especially like having students complete the activity in cooperative groups. They enjoy the peer interaction, and the collaborative effort promotes discussion and clarification of ideas. If possible, use a teacher-guided activity to introduce the procedure to the entire class at once. A couple of modeling sessions precludes later problems.

The categories should highlight word elements that all students understand so that all can participate and give their attention to the process. For a cooperative word hunt, each group needs a colored marker and piece of chart-sized paper at least 3 feet by 2 feet, with the key words written across the top and circled (Figure 3-7). Students bring a trade book or textbook they are reading to the group location. A recorder is chosen to call on students as they find words and to write their contributions under the appropriate category. Because every student is expected to contribute at least one word, it is helpful to note the finder's initials in pencil. Disagreements that arise concerning a word's placement are resolved through discussion or with the aid of a dictionary.

short a	long a		?
clap	shade	rain	
fact	named	paint	hair
grandmother	save	rainbow	was
had	age	gain	say
sandals	made	brain	said
family	take		
back	sale		

FIGURE 3-7. Results of a cooperative group word hunt.

Word hunts continue for about fifteen minutes. The goal is for students to find at least 10 words, with a minimum of 1 word per category. Although exceptions should be recorded, these are not counted in the number. When words like homophones or derivationally related pairs are the hunt's focus, I set different expectations. If one of the pair is found—such as *read* or *compose*—the other one is determined through discussion— *red* or *composition*—and both words are then recorded.

As the hunt progresses, I circulate from group to group making comments and questioning students about their placement of certain words in order to understand their reasoning and to clear up any confusion. When students are through searching, we briefly discuss their findings, and they record the words under category headings in a notebook, as in Figure 3-8.

Although this activity may be done as homework, I prefer to have students complete it at school so that I can interact with them. Also, when word hunts are done at home, well-

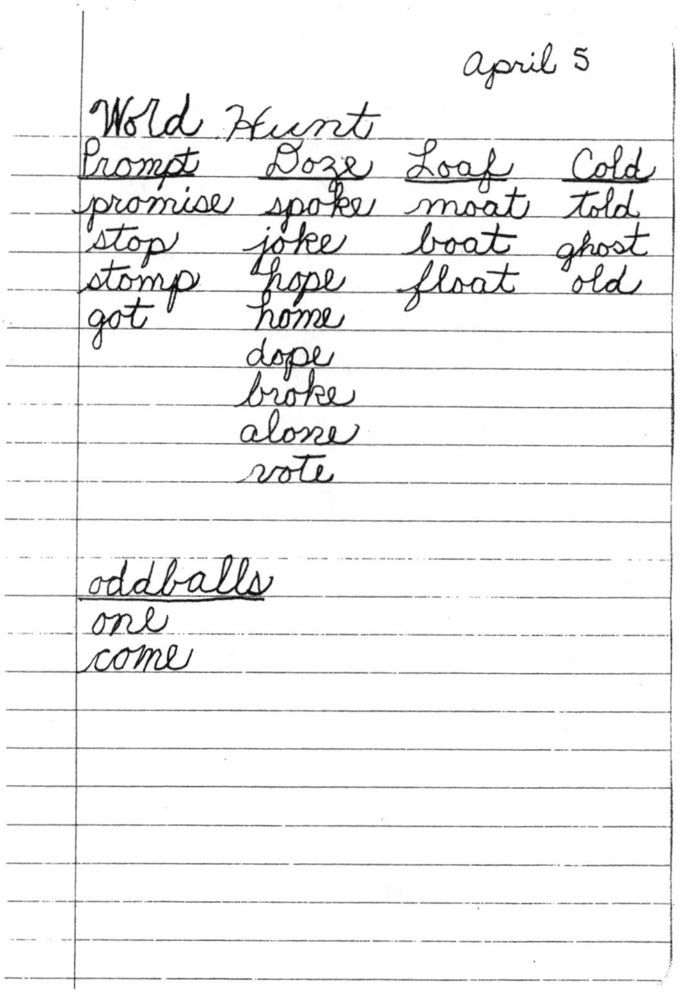

FIGURE 3-8. Notebook recorded word hunt.

intentioned family members frequently try to help by coming up with the specified number of words. One variation that I have found worthwhile is to have the students hunt for words in their own writing—in process writing pieces as well as response journals.

Beginning readers frequently engage in word hunts using catalog pictures or the collections of known words in their word banks. They also try to find words with particular features by hunting through a typed copy of a recently read story. Consecutive searches may be carried out with the same copy, each one focusing on a different word element (for example, short *a* words one time, and short *i* the next). Found words are underlined, and often a new color is used for each search to highlight feature differences. Dictated experience stories, poems, and rhymes provide additional material for word hunts. If children collect and number these in a personal ring binder, they are readily available for word hunting as well as for choral and repeated readings.

Sometimes it's fun to carry out the word hunt as a "reading the room" activity. Students look for words with the appropriate sounds or patterns anywhere in the room—bulletin boards, mailboxes, magazines, and so on. Even the names of objects can be recorded (for example, *sharpener* [*r*-controlled vowel] or *desk* [short *e*]). Primary grade teachers sometimes collaborate with their upper-level colleagues and have the students work as buddy-pairs. One half of each class works in each room, with the older students acting as supportive scribes.

Concept Sorts

Through content areas like social studies and science and their reading of children's literature, students are exposed to many new concepts. Categorization tasks can help them come to terms with these new ideas by highlighting various traits of the concepts through pictures or words. Pictures are useful for younger children not only because they enable those with limited literacy development to be active learners, but also because they are less abstract than words (see Figure 3-9). Students with more advanced literacy understandings often develop concept sorts out of vocabulary culled from their reading. The concept sort below shows how several fourth graders organized words from a science study under "earthquakes" and "volcanoes." Later, they reexamined the two-syllable words and categorized them according to the spelling feature they were currently exploring—namely, those with an open first syllable (long vowel sound) and those with one that is closed (short vowel).

Concept sort		Spelling-related sort		
Earthquakes	Volcanoes	Open syllable	Closed syllable	?
faults	magma	emit	magma	faults
tectonics	fissure	crater	tremor	vent
tremor	igneous		Richter	
Richter	emit		fissure	
magnitude	crater		tectonics	
	vent		magnitude	
			igneous	

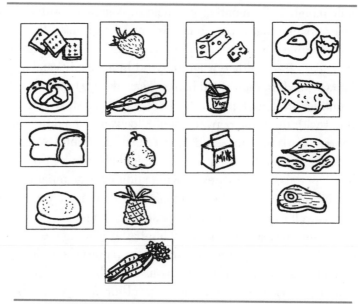

FIGURE 3–9. Basic food groups: A concept sort with pictures.

A variation of the concept sort that students enjoy uses neither pictures nor words but the students themselves. In the "yes/no" game, based on the concept attainment model (Bruner, Goodnow, & Austin, 1956), students try to discover a feature that is unique to some members of the class. Begin the activity by choosing a focus characteristic. Hair and clothing color are fairly obvious and work well with younger children; with older students the feature can be more difficult to detect—collar type, sleeve length. A student with the feature is called forward and stands in the "yes" area. At this point, it's helpful to discuss what the mystery feature might be. Next, identify a student without the feature, and ask that person to stand in the "no" area. Again, discuss possibilities in light of the new information. Proceed with more students, being sure to balance membership in the two groups and to continue discussion as needed. When you think some of the students have caught on, ask for volunteers who think they know which category they fit in. Verify their responses, and have them join the appropriate group. Although students may identify the feature at any time, waiting until the end gives everyone plenty of opportunity to figure it out.

The Word Study Notebook

Word study notebooks are a place where students record their sorts, word hunt results, and other activities they engage in as they study words. A spiral notebook, composition book, or even a three-ring binder serves the purpose well. The notebook provides a wonderful record of a student's explorations with words over the course of the year. It enables student, parents, and teacher to trace the child's journey to more sophisticated understandings about words and to celebrate progress.

If desired, specific expectations may be defined for notebook activities. These are typed and glued into the notebook for the students' reference. They address topics like handwriting, spelling, sentence writing, use of time during partner and collaborative activities, and methods of evaluation. As the students progress, changes in the criteria can easily be made by adding a new page to the notebook.

Although you are likely to ask students to complete specific activities in their notebooks, it is a good idea to give them choices as well. Options for these times may be listed on the first page of the notebook under the heading "Word Study Activities." As activities are introduced, they are added to the list for students' ready reference. The word hunts, writing sorts, blind written sorts, and open sorts that have already been described should be included in the listing. A few additional possibilities follow. Because some activities are more appropriate for certain stages, recommended stages are listed in parentheses after the title.

Discovery Log (Late LN, WW, SJ, DC)

Although certain notebook pages can be designated for recording discoveries about words throughout the year, I like to have students make log entries on the same page they use to complete an activity. For example, after a word walk, I often ask students to do a written sort at their seats. Below the sort, they write a sentence or two describing what they learned on the walk (Figure 3-10). Entries can address findings related to the meanings of words as well as to spelling features. Students sometimes choose to make entries on their activity pages and recorded open sorts as well.

Draw and Label (LN)

Students draw pictures that relate to the key letters and sounds they are studying. They label the pictures with as much of the word as they can, then either draw a blank line for the rest of the word or use invented spelling to finish it.

Change-a-Letter (LN, Review for WW)

This activity can be carried out in small groups, with a buddy, or individually. Students are given a word with a consonant–vowel–consonant (CVC) pattern as a starting point. They are allowed to change one word element at a time in order to create a new word. The initial element, known as the onset, is the easiest for students to alter (see Example 1 below). Because the rest of the word stays the same, students need only apply their knowledge of beginning consonants (or consonants, blends, and digraphs, if they are ready) to form a new word. Changes are usually made from consonant to consonant (*cap/map*) or from one blend or digraph to another (*flap/trap*), but they can also be made by replacing a single consonant with a blend or digraph and vice versa (*tap/slap* or *snap/zap*). Students who have studied different families of words with the same vowel, like *ap, at, ag,* and *an,* are ready to change either the initial or the final element. This is more challenging (see Example 2) but does not require students to discriminate between vowel sounds since the vowel remains constant. Finally, once students have explored several families of words with different vowels, they are ready for the most challenging version of the activity (see Example 3), which allows them to change any portion of the word—beginning, ending, or middle vowel. When students reach a roadblock and cannot think of a

November 15

Word Sort

Open	Closed		
VCV	Doublet	VCCV	Oddball
Shiloh	dinner	window	river
detour	reddish	whisper	
notice	follow	hundred	
reason	rabbit	morning	
season	supper	wander	
protect	wallet	gristmill	
	coffee		

Discoveries

1. The long vowel sound in an open syllable can be spelled with two vowels like reason and season.
2. In a VCCV pattern when there are three consonants two go together like gristmill and hundred.
3. Words with VCV can be closed—river.

FIGURE 3-10. Syllable juncture word sort and discovery log entry, based on words from the first two chapters of *Shiloh* by Phyllis Reynolds Naylor.

next word, the activity ends. Lists for the challenging versions can get quite lengthy due to the greater possibilities for generating words.

Example 1: Easy	Example 2: More challenging	Example 3: Most challenging
cat	cat	cat
bat	cap	cut
fat	clap	nut
sat	flap	not
hat	flag	spot
rat	bag	spit
flat	wag	pit
mat	tag	pot
	tan	hot
	fan	hat
	plan	that

Write and Draw (Late LN, WW, SJ, DC)

For this independent activity, students choose *some* of their words to use in sentences and draw pictures of *some* of the others. Before students begin, model how to write an interesting sentence that really illustrates the meaning of the word. Notice the difference in the paired examples below:

> I <u>heard</u> you.
> I <u>heard</u> my dog bark when a car pulled slowly up my driveway.
> He <u>bragged</u> to his friends.
> He <u>bragged</u> to his friends about his new ten-speed bicycle saying, "It cost three hundred dollars!"

If the idea of "painting pictures" with words hasn't been dealt with during process writing, now is a good time to introduce it. Children's literature abounds with examples of descriptive language— "snapshots" and "thoughtshots" (Lane, 1993)— that can be used. You may want to encourage self-evaluation of the sentences by having students star their best one. Letting them decide whether to use one or two of their words in a sentence also adds to the activity. However, advocating the use of more than two of the week's words in a given sentence often leads to sentences that lack meaning. The same result commonly occurs when teachers ask students to use their words in a story or paragraph. Use these options with caution.

Sentence writing also affords students an opportunity to experiment with techniques they are learning in writing-related minilessons. They may try out different types of punctuation; use carefully selected adjectives, verbs, and adverbs; create a particular mood; and so forth. During write and draw, students should give special attention to spelling the week's words correctly. They should do the same with words that have features they already know. Inventions are appropriate for other, more difficult words.

Regardless of age, most students enjoy the drawing component of this activity and put considerable effort into making the word meanings clear (see Figure 3-11). Also, many students who have difficulty with reading and writing excel when it comes to drawing and appreciate the opportunity to express themselves visually. Use of color (crayons or colored pencils), detail, and appropriate size should be discussed.

Rhyme Time (All)

Students generate rhyming words based on words from their weekly list or from the list of rhyming units below. This activity might aptly be called "rime time" for the *rime* of the word—namely, the vowel and what follows it—is usually maintained and only the beginning of the word changes. For example, *wage → page → stage*. When weekly word study words are used, partners begin by agreeing on a starting word from their list. Once it is recorded, the students write down as many rhyming words as they can, using a timer or other device to insure that each partner has an equal chance to record words. When the time is up or both students have run out of words, partners check their lists for words that are correct and unique to their list. As one buddy reads off the

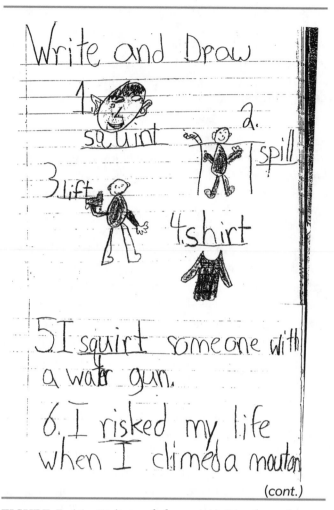

(cont.)

FIGURE 3–11. Write and draw activities by primary-grade and intermediate-grade students.

list, the students place a check mark (✓) by every shared word. Each of the remaining words earns one point. A point is subtracted for an incorrectly spelled word. Words that rhyme but do not share the starting word's rime, such as *read* below, receive double points, provided they are correctly spelled. An expert or the dictionary is used to settle questions. Three to four rounds are played, with a new focus word each time. This activity is most appropriate for work with single-syllable words. Rhyme time may also be done individually; if points are kept, the same scoring system is used but there are no shared words.

Example 1	Total points
Student 1: *judge:* smudge ✓budge ✓grudge ✓fudge nudge	2
Student 2: *judge:* ✓fudge ✓budge ✓grudge trudge	1

Wordstudy

1-2 The <u>plumber</u> made the pipes much <u>sturdier</u>.

3. The <u>banister</u> was made of wood.

4-5. The <u>sale</u> was a <u>disaster</u> because when the <u>consumer</u> got there the products were all gone.

6-7. When the <u>composer</u> lit the light he caused it to <u>flicker</u>.

cucumber   prettier

Hey Y'all

FIGURE 3-11. (*cont.*)

Example 2
Student 1: *seed:* ✓feed ✓speed deed <u>read</u>   3
Student 2: *seed:* need ✓feed ✓speed bleed   2

Some rimes are more common than others. Wylie and Durrell (1970) developed a list of 37 rimes that occur in nearly 500 primary-grade words. Words with these rimes are especially good choices for rhyme time since they occur in many polysyllabic words as well. Syllable juncture and derivational constancy students can use the list of rimes to generate polysyllabic words with syllables that rhyme. For example, the rime *ap* might lead to words like, *apple, capsule, caption, aptitude, evaporate, chaperone, dilapidated;* and *ide* to such words as *bona fide, confide, dioxide, divide, insecticide, provide.*

Rimes

ack	ail	ain	ake	ale	ame	an
ank	ap	ash	at	ate	aw	ay
eat	ell	est	ice	ick	ide	ight
ill	in	ine	ing	ink	ip	it
ock	oke	op	ore	ot	uck	ug
ump	unk					

Word Operations (All)

In this activity, students add, subtract, or add and subtract word elements to make a new word. They choose 5 to 10 words to "operate" on, record them in their notebooks, and write the new word after each. If you wish, you may have them underline the alterations. Examples for each stage are shown below.

LN: camp → cramp lost → list set → sent plump → lump
WW: sport → short—fur → fir real → rail pounce → pound
SJ: planned → planed pillow → pillows respect → disrespect
DC: accuse → excuse magical → magician carnivore → herbivore
confidential → confident

SAW—Sort, Alphabetize, and Write (WW, SJ, DC)

Although students may complete this activity at school, I have often incorporated it into sorting that is assigned for homework. Once the children have a clear understanding of their week's categories, a copy of the word card sheet may be sent home for them to practice sorting. After their last practice, students arrange each column of words in alphabetical order, write down the sort, and return it to school. A number of benefits result from this approach: Sorting is practiced; alphabetical ordering is made easier through manipulation of the word cards; and assignment checking is simplified because students have their words in a like order.

Game Applications

Games described in this section may be applied to word features at any of the spelling stages.

Folder Games

Folder games reinforce students' knowledge of the spelling feature they are exploring and are quick and easy to make. Use medium-sized stick-on labels to create the path, and add a little pizzazz or relate the game to a particular theme by adding student drawings and cutouts from gift-wrap paper. Usually, words or letters that highlight the orthographic features being studied are recorded on the path spaces (initial consonants, blends, digraphs, short vowels, long versus short vowels, open and closed syllables, stressed syllable, roots, and so on) and other words or pictures with the features are included in a draw pile. During play, students draw cards from the stack, identify the word or picture, and move to the closest match on the path. *Words Their Way* (Bear, Invernizzi, & Templeton, 1996) includes a fine assortment of folder game ideas developed by classroom teachers.

Card Games

Many card games—Go Fish, Rummy, and Concentration, for example—lend themselves to word study adaptations. In each of these, students seek matches with like word features. Variations can be devised to accommodate most features, including blends, word families, vowel patterns, homophone pairs, or roots. When making cards for this type of game, be sure to keep in mind the fact that the children will be holding the cards. Words should be written in the center of the card as well as in the upper left corner to insure visibility (see Figure 3-12).

Concentration is a card game that can easily be played with a partner or as a trio, using one student's word cards. A deck of 16 to 20 cards is shuffled and placed face down in a four-by-four or five-by-four array. Play may focus on the particular features under study, and only those matches count; or players may simply try to identify a common word feature in the turned-over cards—initial or final consonant, vowel pattern, number of syllables, stress, syllable structure, meaning. The approach should be agreed on before the game begins. In either instance, player 1 starts by turning over two cards and tries to recognize a shared characteristic. If a property is identified and accepted by the other player(s), the two cards are set aside, and another pair is turned over. Player 1 continues until two cards are drawn that cannot be categorized. These cards are returned to the array, and the next player takes a turn. The game ends when no other matches can be made. If the week's features are the focus, the person with the most cards wins. If more open sorting has been allowed, patterns currently under study may still be emphasized by using the following scoring system and awarding points after each play: (1) a pair of words with a pattern under study earns 2 points, and (2) all other pairs receive 1 point. The player with the highest total wins.

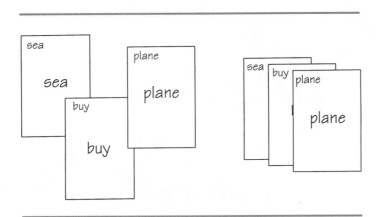

FIGURE 3-12. Homophone rummy cards.

Mini-Sorter

This activity takes time to make, but it is well worth it (see Figure 3-13). I have used it at various grade levels, and students give it rave reviews. It is highly motivational, versatile, and self-checking. Cards with words or pictures that focus on word elements the children are investigating are dropped into the mini-sorter. Students match their word (or picture) to the appropriate key word or letter labeled on the front of the mini-sorter. They then poke a small plastic or wooden rod through the corresponding hole and check the accuracy of their response by pulling up the card. If the answer is correct, the card is easily removed, because the corresponding hole on the card has been cut away. However, when the match is incorrect, the card stays put, and the student must try again.

Mini-sorters can be made of different materials and to any specifications. Mine are made of lightweight wood (paneling) and accommodate about 20 4-inch × 6-inch index cards. Matting board sold at frame shops is also a good material. In addition to the front and back, you need spacers for the inside that will give depth and create the slot—a bottom and two side strips. If matting board is used, you may want to glue together two or more like strips to create a deeper slot that will hold more cards—¼ to ½ inch of depth works well.

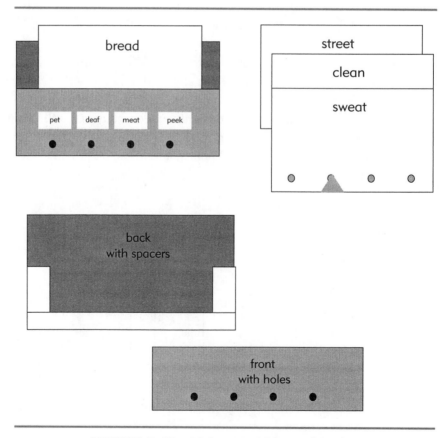

FIGURE 3-13. Mini-sorter with word cards.

To make the mini-sorter:

1. Cut the pieces.
2. Drill or punch holes into the front panel.
3. Assemble the sorter sandwich-style—first the back, then the inside pieces, and finally the front, gluing the pieces together as you go. Be sure the adhesive is appropriate for the material used.
4. Add a stick-on label above each hole for the key words.

To prepare the mini-sorter cards:

1. Place a blank card into the slot, being sure to leave room to wiggle it back and forth slightly.
2. Stick a pin through each hole in the sorter so an impression is made on the card.
3. Remove the card, and punch a hole at each mark.
4. Use this card as a model to mark the holes on your set of word or picture cards.
5. Punch holes at the marks.
6. On each card, write a word (or glue a picture) that fits your category headings.
7. Cut away the correct hole on each card.
8. Put the cards in the slot, and you're ready to go.

A short piece of wooden dowel or a plastic stirring rod, like the kind sold in the beverage section of the grocery store, works well for selecting answers.

Weekly Evaluations

Observation

You can learn much about students' progress during the week by observing them in the various activities. Sorting that was likely slow and cautious when the feature was newly introduced should be rapid and require little effort by the week's end. Anecdotal notes of these and other observations, including word hunt participation and indications of feature knowledge being exercised in reading and writing, provide a record of what is learned. For some teachers, notations of this type and a periodic reassessment with the DSA suffice for evaluation. Others choose to also give an end-of-the-week quiz on some of the words.

Quiz Options

My experiences with giving a Friday word study quiz have been positive. Although my observations give me a clear idea of how students are doing, I find that the students them-selves like having a quiz. It provides tangible evidence that their sorting efforts paid off. Also, the quiz is an easy way to let parents know that spelling is receiving attention. Quizzes may be teacher-dictated or completed in buddy-pairs.

Several formats for an end-of-the-week assessment are possible. Some teachers use a traditional spelling test format. Others have students write the words under key words as they are called out (blind written sort). When the latter procedure is used, credit is usually awarded for correct category placement and for correct spelling (one point for each). Sometimes additional words not in the week's sort are included in the dictation. These may be review words from previous weeks or new words with like patterns that are included to see how well students can generalize their learning. Nonsense words can be used for the latter. For example, to evaluate within word pattern students' transfer of the *dge* pattern, the nonwords "padge" and "widge" might be included in the dictation.

Regardless of how you structure the quiz, I recommend randomly selecting about 10 (or half) of each group's words for the quiz. This is sufficient to assess students' understanding and saves time. The quiz should take no more than 10 to 15 minutes and, when teacher-dictated, can be given to several groups simultaneously.

This process is facilitated if each group has a name. When groups are first organized, have the students choose a name. Even though the makeup of groups changes during the year, the names usually remain the same. For ease and consistency, I sometimes limit name choices to a particular theme, such as animals, colors, or athletic teams. With each group's word card template in hand, I begin the end-of-week dictation in the following manner, moving from one word card sheet to the next, calling out the words I've selected:

> "Turquoise Group, number 1 is *plant*. The boy set the *plant* down on the table. *Plant*.
> "Blue Group, number 1 is *tailor*. The *tailor* was supposed to sew up the man's shirt. *Tailor*.
> "Scarlet Group, number 1 is *expression*. She had a surprised *expression* on her face when she saw the present. *Expression*.
> "Turquoise Group, number 2 is *wave*. The ocean *wave* came crashing onto the shore. *Wave*.
> "Blue Group, number 2 is. . . ."

Dictation continues with the remaining words. This format enables you to move along quickly without rushing the students. I have used it successfully with students from second grade on up.

A third approach to the quiz employs a bingo-like format and is highly motivating. For "Spello," students are given a blank three-by-three or four-by-four template, such as the completed one shown in Figure 3-14, on which to write their words. If desired, one of the spaces may be designated as "free." Each dictated word is recorded on a blank card and placed in a container. After the dictation, tokens are passed out, and a game of Spello is played. The rules for bingo are followed with one exception. When a player has covered a horizontal, vertical, or diagonal row and calls out "spello," in order to win the appropriate words must be marked with a token *and* each of the covered words must be correctly spelled. After the game, all responses are checked.

Transfer to Writing

This also needs to be considered when evaluating students. However, it should be noted that until they have a firm grasp of a particular feature, students are not likely to use it

SPELLO		
met	deaf	beach
bread	FREE	street
meant	cream	weed

FIGURE 3–14. Spello quiz.

with consistency in writing. This is why children need many opportunities to work with their words so that the words become overlearned and can be recalled automatically.

Some issues pertaining to carryover relate to teacher expectations. Students need to realize that you expect them to correctly spell words that have easy features as well as what I call no-excuse words. The latter includes the current week's words as well as words that are "print-handy"—for example, the title of a book a student is reading, the names of its main characters, the present month of the year, and so on. In order to help weaker spellers develop a sense of "looks right" for high-frequency words like *who, friend,* and *from,* four or five of these words (as well as theme-related words) may be displayed at one time on a highly visible area of the wall, so that they are readily accessible for students to copy. I am selective about the words I choose and keep a watchful eye on students' writing to be sure they are spelling the words correctly.

When teachers set realistic expectations for correct spelling (and, remember, *realistic* means taking into consideration developmental differences) and are consistent in their follow-through, students rise to the occasion. I remember being dismayed a number of years ago by the poor quality of spelling I was getting in students' literature response journals. Even good spellers were misspelling easy words. When I reflected on the matter, I realized that I was at the root of the problem. I had communicated to students my interest in *what* they wrote but had not set a standard for *how* they spelled it. Their journal entries were filled with interesting reflections about characters and events *and* with careless errors. We discussed the matter, and I explained that I planned to highlight words that they should have caught through proofing. These would need to be corrected. Words that I knew were difficult for them at this time would be overlooked. I suggested that they proof their journal entries for spelling from the bottom up in order to avoid being distracted by the content. Within a week, I noticed a dramatic improvement. When I complimented them on the change, their response was, "You should have told us sooner; we didn't know it mattered"!

LEARNING TO LOVE WORDS

◆

Modeling with Literature

Arousing students' general interest in words should be a part of word study. Although sensitizing children to the sounds and meaning of language can be accomplished in many ways, one of the best practices is teacher modeling. When teachers show a curiosity about words and an appreciation for language, students begin to attend to language more closely and seek opportunities to share their own discoveries about words.

Read-aloud time is a prime time for celebrating the wonders of language. Rhymes, similes, metaphors, personification, alliteration, carefully crafted sentences, and more abound in children's literature today. Images like those that follow deserve a pause—a chance for children to share their impressions or to savor the language. The first two illustrations are from Chris Van Allsburg's *The Polar Express*:

> It [the train] was wrapped in an apron of steam. (p. 3)

> We climbed mountains so high it seemed as if we would scrape the moon. But the Polar Express never slowed down. Faster and faster we ran along, rolling over peaks and through valleys like a car on a roller coaster. (p. 9)

Natalie Babbitt's vivid descriptions in *Tuck Everlasting* give the reader a sense of being right there, looking at the scene:

> On the left stood the first house, a square and solid cottage with a touch-me-not appearance, surrounded by grass cut painfully to the quick and enclosed by a capable iron fence some four feet high which clearly said, "Move on—we don't want *you* here." (p. 6)

In Karen Hesse's *Out of the Dust*, readers can almost feel the hot, dry winds of 1934 recorded in the diary of 14-year-old Billie Jo:

> On Sunday,
> winds came,
> bringing a red dust
> like prairie fire,
> hot and peppery,
> searing the inside of my nose,
> the whites of my eyes.
> Roaring dust,
> Turning the day from sunlight to midnight. (p. 46)

There is no shortage of examples; students just need to have them brought to their attention. Doing so will not only heighten their sensitivity to language but will also help them to construct meaning with text that is rich in description or symbolism. Without such guidance, many students will simply read or skip over the words, unaware of what they have missed.

Poetry is another channel for fostering appreciation of language. Again, there is no scarcity of wonderful choices. Jane Yolen's poetic lullaby, *Nocturne*, is well worth sharing with students of any age. Repetition, rhyme, alliteration, similes, metaphors, and rich images fill its pages. Young children enjoy the rhythm and repetition; older students find a special appeal in Yolen's novel compound words: "In the night, in the velvet night, in the wraparound blacksurround velvet night" (p. 13). Two other books that celebrate the sounds of language in a similar fashion are *In the Tall, Tall Grass* by Denise Fleming and *Listen to the Rain* by Bill Martin Jr. and John Achambault.

The use of onomatopoeia (words that sound like what they mean) in poetry and stories seldom fails to capture students' interest. Children enjoy the special "sound effects" of these words and once aware of them often begin incorporating similar words into their own writing. Soon after hearing Patricia Polacco's *Thunder Cake* read with its "CRACKLE, CRACKLE BOOOOOOOM, KA-BOOOOOM" and "KA-BANG BOOOOOOOOAROOOOM," seven-year-old Abigail (refer to Figure 1-6) considered the quieter sounds of weather in her "Drip, Drop Tiddle Top" poem about rain (Figure 3-15).

Students readily associate alliteration (repetition of beginning sounds) with tongue twisters and show an eagerness to tie up the oral muscles of their friends with sentences like this third grader's: "Allie Alligator added an amazing amount of ants to his awful apple pie." Chris Van Allsburg's alphabet book, *The Z Was Zapped: A Play in 26 Acts*, is an excellent catalyst for students to write their own alliterative sentences in the form of an alphabet play (see Figure 3-16). Three other books students will enjoy are *Aster Aardvark's Alphabet Adventure* by Steven Kellogg, *Animalia* by Graeme Base, and the alphabet pop-up, *Alpha Bugs*, by David Carter.

Students also enjoy plays on word meanings. Primary-age students are often first introduced to this through books like Peggy Parish's series featuring Amelia Bedelia, an amusing character who interprets language literally; when asked to "draw the blinds," she sets about sketching them. Another book that appeals to kindergartners as well as intermediate-grade students is *Dog Breath* by Dav Pilkey. The story recounts a family's attempt to rid their dog, Hally Tosis, of her offensive breath. Although a "breathtaking" mountaintop view does not do the job; nor does an exciting movie leave her "breathless," in the end the situation is resolved and everyone is glad to have Hally around. Older students with sufficiently advanced vocabulary appreciate the abundant word play in *The Phantom Tollbooth* by Norton Juster as well as in Elizabeth Hass's series of books featuring Incognito Mosquito, Private Insective. Although word play is not the central focus of Andrew Clement's *Frindle*, words are. The main character's trials with his teacher over a newly coined word—*frindle*—make this book a favorite with many intermediate-grade readers. *Donovan's Word Jar* by M. DeGross also focuses on words, their magic, and their power. The book provides a wonderful springboard for children to collect their own interesting words.

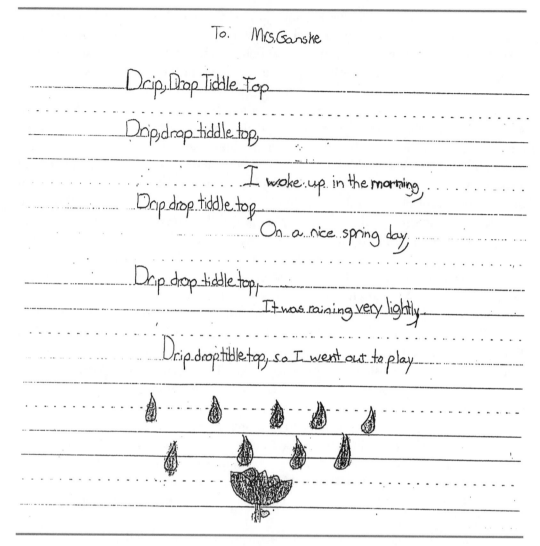

FIGURE 3–15. Seven-year-old Abigail's rain poem.

In kindergarten and first-grade classrooms morning messages are usually composed as a group so that students can benefit from teacher modeling. Many teachers in grades beyond these write a morning message on the chalkboard as a greeting to students when they arrive. These typically contain highlights of the upcoming day or logistical information about where to put homework or how to spend the before-school time. The message is a good place to highlight an interesting word that students will be exposed to that day. It is also an ideal spot to remind students of an unusual or important word from the previous day. For example, if E. B. White's *Charlotte's Web* is being read aloud, a natural beginning to the morning message might be:

Dear Class   or   *Dear Class,*
    Salutations! Today we. . . .   *This is going to be a radiant day!*

FIGURE 3-16. Sample from a primary grade version of *The Z Was Zapped: An Alphabet Play in 26 Acts.*

I also like to foster an interest in words by modeling use of the dictionary. All too often, children are taught how to navigate the dictionary but fail to see it used for authentic purposes. Instead, assigned words are looked up, definitions copied, sentences devised, and the dictionary is placed back on the shelf. However, when a teacher regularly shows curiosity about a word in the read-aloud or one encountered elsewhere, students themselves begin to wonder and ask about new words they come upon. Regardless of the grade level, in addition to whatever student dictionaries may be available, it is a good idea to keep a collegiate dictionary in the classroom for questions about unusual words. Nicknamed "Big Red" by a former student, my collegiate dictionary was a welcome resource in the classroom and received considerable use.

Words Have Histories Too

Because English is a living language, one that is changing, students of all ages enjoy hearing the stories behind some of the words. Few students have ever considered that words have histories, just like people and nations. The meaning of a word today may differ greatly from its original meaning. Most college and high school dictionaries include etymology in each dictionary entry. Here the word's history is traced back to its root and to the meaning of that root. Some dictionaries such as *The American Heritage Dictionary of the English Language*, have a special word history entry every few pages that describes in a paragraph just how a particular word came to have its present meaning.

Numerous wordbooks also provide this information. They sometimes have limited printings, so finding a certain one can be difficult. One of my favorites, which has gone out of print but is well worth seeking in used bookstores, is *Where in the Word: Extraordinary Stories behind 801 Ordinary Words* by David Muschell. The stories are written in a lively style and cover words from *dandelion* to *smorgasbord*. Two more readily available resources are *The Merriam-Webster New Book of Word Histories* and *Words Can Tell: A Book about Our Language* by Christina Ashton. The former contains the stories of 1500 words and claims to be "the most up-to-date concise history of English words and how they have evolved." Although the latter includes only over 50 words (such as, *salary, gossip, bangs, sirloin, coconut*), it also contains an interesting section on how our language developed and is written in an easy-to-understand style. Figure 8-1 in Chapter 8 lists additional resources.

As a fifth-grade teacher, I always enjoyed sharing the story behind the word *school* with my students during the first week of class. After explaining that word meanings change over time just as people do, I would ask them to tell me what they thought *school* originally meant. Students often related the word to schools of fish and hypothesized that the meaning connection resulted from the fact that both deal with groups. As soon as I informed them that the word first meant *leisure*, laughter inevitably followed. I asked the students to explain how they thought this connection came about. Speculation soon produced an apt explanation: only well-to-do individuals with leisure time had the opportunity to attend school. Others had to work. This introduction to word histories succeeded in awakening the students' interests in words and caused them to view words as more than just letters and meaning units on a page.

Young students enjoy hearing the stories of words, too. I once watched a group of primary-age students spend their recess scouting around the playground for dandelions after they learned that *dandelion* means "tooth of lion" in French and that the plant is so called because its sharply indented leaves resemble a row of big teeth. Their shouts of "It REALLY does look like that!" drew in older students who were soon enlightened by the discovery.

Eponyms are words with special stories; they are named after people and places. *Guppies in Tuxedos: Funny Eponyms* by Marvin Terban includes the stories behind many common words (*sandwich, tuxedo, bikini, OK, America*, days of the week, and months of the year). This book also provides a list of additional resources on eponyms and word play.

Playing with Words

Hink Pinks

Using a short clue, students try to guess these two-word rhyming phrases. Depending on the students, easy (such as, unhappy father = sad dad) or more sophisticated clues and rhyming phrases (such as, pastel basin = pink sink, or breakable violin = brittle fiddle) may be used. Students love coming up with their own creations with which to challenge their classmates (and the adults). Bruce McMillan's photo-illustrated book, *One Sun: A Book of Terse Verse*, provides a good introduction to hink pinks. The terse verses are presented on facing pages—one with the rhyme, the other with an accompanying illustration. Although there are no clues, when using this book I like to show the photo to students, create my own clue, and then have them predict what the terse verse is before showing the text page. For example, for WET PET I might say damp dog, or for SMALL BALL I might say tiny sphere.

Hink pinks can be included as an option for the word study notebook. Using one of their words for the week in each rhyming pair, students try to come up with as many hink pinks as they can. A study of long and short *e* patterns might yield the following:

A wimpy high-pitched cry = weak squeak
A thin 13-year-old = lean teen
A true bargain = real steal
Head robber = chief thief
Finest exam = best test
Used penny = spent cent

Themes under study are another good source for hink pink creations. You may want to try your hand at the following hink pink related to the theme of this book: "a brief categorization of words." The solution appears at the end of the chapter.

Making Words

Like word sorts, *Making Words* (Cunningham & Cunningham, 1992) engages children in an active, hands-on approach and reinforces their knowledge of spelling patterns. In the activity, learners make words using letter cards. The teacher chooses a word and provides students with its letters but does not disclose what the word is. Students begin by building words with just two letters, then three, and work up to a final word that uses all of the letters. It works well to use a theme-related word for this activity—author's name, character's name, topic being studied, a special word featured for the day, or the like. For example, the word *radiant* from *Charlotte's Web*, included in the morning message described earlier, could be reused here (see Figure 3-17).

The activity can be completed in a number of different formats—whole class, small group, cooperative groups, buddy-pairs, and independent. Each group or individual needs a set of letter cards. Modeling can be done using note-card–sized letters and a pocket chart. Or, if a piece of magnetic tape is attached to the back of each card (available at craft stores and teacher supply stores), the cards can be manipulated directly on most chalkboards. Older students like the challenge of discovering and making the new words; younger children may need to be told what words to make and given guidance in building them. Each new word is recorded on the board or in a personal notebook. Out of the seven letters in *radiant*, a group of second graders made fifteen other words—*at, an, it, in, ant, rat, ran, tin, tan, rid, rain, dart, dirt, train,* and *drain.*

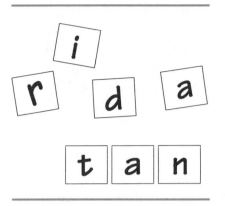

FIGURE 3-17. A making words
activity, using the word *radiant.*

Much can be learned about students' word knowledge during this activity by observing their involvement and facility with relating patterns to sounds. As a follow-up, words from the completed list can be sorted by sound and/or pattern or can be used to read and spell rhyming words. For example, a teacher might ask: *"If rain is r-a-i-n, how is stain spelled?"* Proper nouns can easily be included in the word-making by simply writing the uppercase form of the letter on one side of each card and the lowercase on the other.

You may want to add making words to the list of word study activity options. Whether in small groups, with a partner, or independently, students usually enjoy selecting words from their weekly list and building words. The number of words chosen will depend on the complexity of the words. Students at the early stages may work with three or four; those at the upper stages may have their work cut out with just one or two. To add the element of mystery into the final word, buddies may choose their partners' words and write down the letters. A ready supply of blank letter cards should be kept for this activity; magnetic letters could be an option.

Camouflage

This vocabulary-reinforcing and vocabulary-building activity (Cecil, 1994) is a favorite of older students, but I have used it successfully even with second graders. It was originally designed for individual oral responding. However, I also like to use the activity with cooperative teams and have students write their responses. Each team (or student) is given a different word to "smuggle" into a paragraph (or an oral response) that answers a specific question, such as *What do you like to do for fun? What time of year do you enjoy the most? Where is a fun place to visit? What food is your favorite?* or *Who is a special person in your life?* The words used for the activity should be *slightly* more difficult than words within the students' normal speaking vocabularies. The object is for each group to camouflage the special word so well that fellow students cannot guess it. Teams quickly learn that the best way to fool their classmates is to think of other advanced words to include in the response as distractions. This was the tactic used by a group of fourth graders when they attempted to conceal the word *satisfy* in their paragraph about a favorite food:

> Of all the different food groups, our favorite is vegetables. Although each veggie is tasty and very delicious, the one that seems to *satisfy* our appetites the most is corn. It is scrumptious! Try it.

When the paragraphs are completed, teams take turns reading aloud their paragraphs. After each reading, members of the other teams reach a consensus about what they think the hidden word is and share their decisions. If more teams fail to come up with the correct word than do guess it, the presenting group wins. This same procedure applies when the activity is carried out on an individual basis. Thus, there is no limit to how many groups (or individuals) can win.

LOOKING AHEAD

◆

This chapter provides "how to" information. This same focus continues in Chapters 4 through 7, which address instructional considerations for the letter name, within word pattern, syllable juncture, and derivational constancy stages of spelling development. You will notice that the format is different. The chapters are designed as a practical resource, a guide that you can often refer to as you plan instruction for your students. When you're ready to teach a group of children about *r*-controlled vowels, you simply turn to that section in the within word pattern chapter (Chapter 5), read the accompanying information, and choose appropriate sorting contrasts from the charted information for your students. Page numbers for supplemental words that may be needed in the sort are indicated in a small gray box—first the targeted feature, then contrasting features in parentheses. If another group of children is ready for prefixes and suffixes, you turn to that part of the syllable juncture chapter (Chapter 6) to find support for teaching the feature. In this way you can plan timely instruction for all students.

(Solution to the hink pink: a brief categorization of words = *a short sort*.)

CHAPTER 4

◆

Letter Name Word Study

A student tracks print in a big book.

A picture sort with initial consonant sounds.

Chapter at a Glance

Literacy Development of Students at the Letter Name Stage:
   An Overview
Orthographic Features Explored
   Initial and Final Consonants: Feature A
   Initial Consonant Blends and Digraphs: Feature B
   Word Families and Short Vowels: Feature C
   Affricates: Feature D
   Final Consonant Blends and Digraphs, Including More
      Word Families: Feature E

◆

Early letter name spellers write words by representing only the most prominent sounds (K for *cat* and BP for *bump*). However, as their concept of word stabilizes and they are able to accurately fingerpoint to memorized text as they read, they start to include a vowel in each stressed syllable (BODR for *butter* and TABL for *table*). As discussed in Chapter 1, a *letter-naming* strategy is used. Rather than choosing letters on the basis of letter-sound associations, children often base their decisions on the sound and feel of the letter's name. This accounts for spellings like JREP for *drip* and YAT for *wait*. As the latter word illustrates, letter name spellers represent only the sounds they hear.

Because these novice spellers have just recently achieved a concept of word, their sight vocabularies (words they can recognize automatically) are limited. For this reason, pictures play a major role in word study activities at this stage. They enable children to increase their understandings about letters and sounds without being restricted by print. Words are used, but usually only when they are *known* (see Figure 4-3). Eventually, as students acquire a stronger sight vocabulary, words replace the pictures.

Instruction for letter name spelling concentrates on one-syllable words and addresses single consonants, blends, digraphs, and short vowels. During this stage, students learn to recognize the CVC (consonant–vowel–consonant) pattern as a short vowel signal. Whether the C stands for one consonant or more, when there is just one vowel in the middle, the vowel sound is usually short, as in *pat, let, bit, hot, cup* and *fast, tent, trick, clock, bump.*

Much of word study at this stage is approached through *onsets* and *rimes*. Onset refers to the initial element of a syllable—m̲at, sl̲ug, ch̲imp—and rime to the vowel and any consonants that follow it—m̲a̲t̲, sl̲u̲g̲, ch̲i̲m̲p̲. Onsets and rimes are the easiest units of sound for children to detect in single-syllable words (Treiman, 1992). Because they are less abstract for children than are individual phonemes (/sl/ + /ŭg/, rather than /s/ + /l/ + /ŭ/ +/g/), they are often used to help letter name spellers expand their knowledge of letter–sound relationships. Students enjoy putting onsets and rimes together to make words, and they can record the results in their word study notebooks. Small glazed tiles work well (see Figure 4-1); they can be written on with a permanent marker and are available at many teacher supply stores.

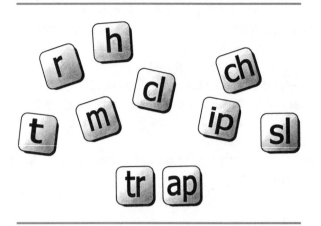

FIGURE 4-1. Making words with onset and rime letter tiles.

Children use their orthographic knowledge when they read and write. In order to become more skilled at both reading and writing, students need much support and many opportunities to exercise what they know. Poems, dictated experience stories, and pattern books provide support during reading, as do choral, echo, and partner-reading. Support in writing is chiefly given through the use of patterned stories and a helpful "scribe." When children write their own versions of a favorite pattern book, they have fewer words to figure out how to spell than when they write a completely new story. Teachers usually provide the repetitious part of the story on a handout so that students need only complete the phrases with personally chosen words to make their own story.

Story-writing based on personal experience or imagination is usually carried out as a joint venture. Students write part of the story and dictate the rest to a more experienced writer—teacher, student, or parent. This type of collaborative writing can also serve as a means for modeling how to write and spell words. The morning message affords an opportunity to involve the whole class in this. Students dictate possible sentences and share ideas about how they think words are spelled as the teacher refines their understandings and writes the sentence. Figure 4-2 shows the type of comments a teacher may use during the modeling. Payne and Schulman (1998) and McCarrier (1999) offer additional ideas for shared writing with kindergarten, first, and second graders.

INITIAL AND FINAL CONSONANTS: FEATURE A

◆

Letter name word study begins with initial consonants. The sequence that follows takes into consideration letter frequency (initial and final word positions), shape, and sound. It is merely a suggested order. Children need to work with what they know, and the collection of known words in their word banks may dictate other possibilities. If you choose to use other letter contrasts, be sure to consider possible shape and sound confusions.

- "Jenna would like our first sentence to be *Today is our play*. Let's all say the first word—*Today*. Who can tell me how that word starts—*t-t-today*?"
- "Good, Mia, *today* does begin with a *t*, a capital *T*, because it's the first word in the sentence [writes *T*]. And you're right, Devan, the little word *to* is part of this word, so the next letter is an *o* [writes *o*]. *Today*, *d-d-day*. What does the *day* part start with?"
- "Dana and Darrell, you both said it—*d*. *Day* starts with the same letter as *Darrell* and *Dana* [writes *d*]. Good going! *Today*, *a-a*. What sound do we hear at the end of *today*?"
- "You're right, Keisha. It is an *a*—*Today* [writes *a*]. Those are all the sounds we hear, but there is also a *y* after the *a* that I'm going to add on [includes the *y* and points to the word *today* while reading it]."
- "Now how about *is*? Can anyone spell **is**, *i-is* for me? Good remembering. *Is* was in our sentence yesterday, and it's spelled *i-s* [writes the word]. We now have *Today is* [points to each word]. What about *our*? This word is kind of tricky. Does anyone know how to spell *our*? [No one volunteers.] It starts with *ou* [writes *ou*]. Listen to the ending—*ourr*. Say it with me now—*ourr*. What letter makes that sound?"
- "That's right. Wow! A lot of you knew that. It is an *r* [writes the *r*, then points to each word and reads it]. Our last word in the sentence is *play*. Let's say it together—*play*. What sound do you hear at the beginning of **p-p**-*play*?"
- "Good job, Tony. *Play* does start with *p* [writes *p*]. What comes after the *p*? Listen carefully and say it with me—*pl-ay, pl-ay*?"
- "Yes, there is another *a*, Katie, but before I write it, I'm going to put a line, because there's one more letter before the *a* [draws a short line after the *p* and then writes *a*]. *Pl-ay*, *play*. That's right, Jeremy, we need an *l* where the blank is [writes the *l*, erases the blank, then says '*p-l-a*']. And just like we did with *today*, I'm going to add a *y*, because *today* and *play* rhyme with each other [writes a *y*, and adds a period]. Now let's read the sentence together as I point to the words—*Today is our play*. What else should we write? Does someone have another sentence?" Modeling continues with another sentence.

FIGURE 4-2. Teacher modeling of writing during the morning message.

Initially, it is best to avoid letter combinations that physically resemble each other (*m, n; b, d, p, q;* and *f, t*) as well as those that have similar sounds (*g, j; c, s, z; d, t; b, p; f, v;* and *w, y*). After such letters have been examined separately, they can be studied as a group. The letter *x* has been omitted from the suggested sequence, because the letters *ex-* generally produce the "eks" sound, and *x* as a beginning consonant nearly always has the sound of /z/, as in *xylophone*. *Q* is introduced here but is examined in greater depth as a complex consonant in Chapter 5.

Bb bat	*Mm* man	*Ss* sun	
Bb bed	*Mm* mug	*Ss* sad	*Rr* rat
Tt top	*Nn* nut	*Pp* pig	
Tt ten	*Nn* nap	*Pp* pan	*Gg* gas
Dd dig	*Hh* hat	*Ll* leg	
Dd dog	*Hh* hug	*Ll* lip	*Cc* can
Ff fox	*Ws* wet	*Jj* jog	
Ff fan	*Ws* web	*Jj* jug	*Kk* king
Yy yes	*Vv* van	*Zz* zip	*Qq* queen

Words:
pp. 201–203

Although two different sorts are suggested for all but the last consonant group shown in the chart, many students may be able to handle four letters at a time; others may do better with just two. It is unlikely that letter name spellers will need to examine all of the consonants in all of the groups. Adjustments should be made where necessary. Final consonants are not likely to require a systematic study, but when they do, the same basic sequence as that for initial consonants may be used. When students are ready for exceptions, you may want to consider including a letter from the next contrast in the sort (such as a picture of a _rake_ when exploring *B, M,* and *S*).

Because pictures are used extensively at this stage, let's take a look at how a "picture walk" with *b, m, s,* and *r* might progress. Other feature studies with pictures would be approached in a similar way.

The modeling procedure for a picture walk is basically the same as that described in Chapter 3. Pictures, too, should be identified before the children begin to work with them. What may be perceived as a hill in one region of the country, may be considered a mountain elsewhere. Likewise, a picture construed by one child as a mat may be viewed as a futon by another. Problem pictures can be eliminated, or children may be allowed to categorize them in the oddball category if they don't fit the sounds being compared. Once the pictures have been recognized and any special words discussed, you are ready to begin the sort. If you are building on letters from the previous week (for example, *b, m,* and *s*), you may want to ask the students to recall these letters. Then continue as follows:

1. Head the columns with letter cards for each of the sounds (see Figure 4-3). Both uppercase and lowercase forms of the letters should be used in the early part of this stage. Choose a key picture card for each sound. As you put the picture cards down under their corresponding letters, say the name of the letter and the pic-

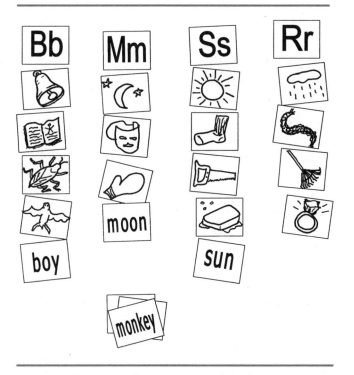

FIGURE 4-3. *B, M, S, R* picture sort with known words at the bottom.

ture, stretching out the sound for emphasis (*B—bbell, M—mmmoon, S—sssun,* and *R—rrrain*).

2. Shuffle the remaining cards and say something like "We're going to listen carefully to the sound at the beginning of these words, so that we can decide which group to put them in. Watch me; I'm going to do a few, and then I want you to help with the rest. *Mmmask* begins like *mmmoon,* so I'm going to put it under the *m* and the picture of the moon. *Bbook* starts like *bbell,* so I'll put it here under the *b* and the bell picture." The amount of modeling needed will depend on your students. As soon as they catch on, invite them to take a turn. When a mistake occurs, correct it by moving it and saying something like "*Rrrope* goes under *rain* because it starts with an *r.*"

3. When all of the cards have been sorted, ask the students to tell you how all of the words are alike in each column.

4. Before sending the students back to their desks, have them individually practice the sort with their sets of cards, or do the practice in the game-like fashion described in Chapter 3. When students finish sorting, have them name the pictures in each column as a self-check to see if they are sorted correctly. If there are misplaced cards that are not detected, tell the student(s) how many, and see if they can find them. If further guidance is needed, tell them the column location.

Word bank words may also be included in the group sort if everyone can identify them. Because the children have probably been engaged in similar reading experi-

📖 Literature Links

Collins, B. (1993). *Six sick sheep: 101 tongue twisters*. New York: Morrow. This book of tongue tanglers is geared towards 5– to 7–year-olds.

Lobel, A. (1994). *Away from home*. New York: Greenwillow. An alphabet book that uses the repeated format of *child's name, action, location,* to describe children's travels around the world. For example, "Paul painted in Paris."

Rosenbloom, J. (1999). *The tongue twisters*. New York: Sterling. An A to Z book filled with hundreds of wacky rhymes, phrases, and sentences for ages 9 to 12.

Schwartz, A. (1972). *A twister of twists, a tangler of tongues*. New York: Harper & Row. Guaranteed to give students' tongues a workout; this book has long been a favorite of all ages.

FIGURE 4-4. Books that repeat initial consonant sounds.

ences, their banks of sight words are likely to contain some common words. For example, prior to this sort they may have read easy pattern books like *The Bicycle* (Cowley) and *Sunshine, Moonshine* (Armstrong) and added words like *boy, bear, bicycle, sun,* and *moon* to their word banks. Or, if appropriate, while exploring *b, m, s,* and *r,* students may concurrently be reading *Monkey See, Monkey Do* by Marc Gave, a pattern book that includes numerous words with the target letters. Known words may be included in the initial sort or saved for later in the week. Rather than moving back and forth between pictures and words, I recommend saving the shuffled word cards for the end of the sort, as shown in Figure 4-3.

Tongue twisters are an enjoyable way to reinforce students' understanding of initial consonants. After hearing a few read aloud (see Figure 4-4), students are usually eager to write their own, using the consonants they've been studying. They dictate the sentences and provide the spelling for the initial consonant and any other sounds they hear, and an older student or the teacher fills in the missing parts. The sentences can be rewritten on chart paper or sentence strips for later rereading. Children love letting alliterative phrases like the following "trip" off their tongues:

B̲ored Baby Bobby blew big bubbles,
M̲any maids madly mopped muffin messes,
S̲even silly sailors sent soldiers some salami,
R̲ed robots rattled round rough roads.

INITIAL CONSONANT BLENDS AND DIGRAPHS: FEATURE B

◆

Blends are consonant units made up of two-letter or three-letter sequences (only two-letter sequences are dealt with at this stage). In two-consonant blends, each of the consonants is heard as the blend is said. For example, say and listen to the word *spot* (/s/ +

Digraphs

s	*h*	*sh*
sit	hop	shop
c	*h*	*ch*
cup	hit	chin
t	*h*	*th*
tap	hot	think
sh	*ch*	*th*
ship	chip	them
w	*h*	*wh*
wag	him	whip

Words:
p. 204
(pp. 201–203)

S-Blends

s	*t*	*st*	
sat	tub	stop	
s	*p*	*sp*	
sub	pen	spin	
st	*sp*	*sk*	*sn*
step	spin	skin	snap
sc	*sm*	*sl*	*sw*
scab	smell	sled	swim

L-Blends

sl	*fl*	*pl*	
slip	flag	plug	
bl	*cl*	*fl*	*gl*
blob	clap	flip	glad

R-Blends

cl	*fl*	*cr*	*fr*
clam	flat	crib	frog
cr	*br*	*gr*	*pr*
crab	brag	grab	prop
d	*r*	*dr*	
dot	ran	drum	
t	*r*	*tr*	
tan	rub	trap	
dr	*tr*	*br*	*gr*
drag	trip	brush	grass

/p/ + /ŏt/). By contrast, consonant digraphs make just one sound, often a new sound (/ch/ and /sh/. Initial consonant blends and digraphs may be studied together. Some teachers prefer to start with blends because known consonant sounds can be discerned in them; others prefer digraphs because they produce a single sound just like the consonants recently studied. Regardless of which is chosen, it is a good idea to contrast the blend or digraph with its initial consonant counterpart (*s, sh* or *s, st*). The second consonant that makes up the blend or digraph may also be included (*s, h, sh*). It is not necessary to break every blend or digraph down into its component parts for comparison. Observe your students; if they're catching on to the process, introduce two or three new blends at a time. If they seem to be having difficulty, continue to use the single consonant(s) and the blend.

S-blends are a good starting point for the study of blends, because their sounds are somewhat easier to isolate and stretch out during the blending. Be sure to model the process for students, using a rime the children know—"ssssssnnnnaap." It's helpful to use words that remain real words when the additional blend letter is dropped (*snap/nap, scat/cat, spit/pit, spin/pin, spot/pot, stop/top, stub/tub, brag/rag, clip/lip*). That way you can highlight the difference the blend makes in their sound. Also, show students the difference. Write *snap* on the board and ask them what part you should erase to change the word into "nap." The process of blending is easy for some, more difficult for others. You may find it helpful to use a visual. I've often sketched a slide on the chalkboard and written the letters of the word going down it. As I orally blend the letters of the onset (*sn*) and move into the rime of the word (*ap*), I move my hand down the corresponding portion of the slide.

When working with digraphs, reserve *wh* for last. A limited number of one-syllable words begin with *wh*, and it is difficult (even for many adults) to discern a difference in sound between *wh* and *w*.

The study of blends and digraphs can easily be interwoven with the study of word families and will expand the number of words that can be used for that feature study. For literature links, see Figure 4-5.

WORD FAMILIES AND SHORT VOWELS: FEATURE C

◆

Word families are groups of words that share a common rime. Because the words *flap, cap, snap,* and *strap* all have the *ap* rime, they are part of the *ap* word family. Rimes like *ap* that are found in many words are known as *phonograms*. There are many phonograms. The 37 most common are listed in the "rhyme time" activity in Chapter 3.

Phonograms and word families are a good way to gradually introduce students to short vowels. Because the words differ only in their onsets, word cards can be used in place of pictures. Once students can read a phonogram, they can apply their knowledge of consonants to read many words in the family. Johnston (1999) suggests introducing students to word families with the same vowel after children are fairly secure in their knowledge of initial and final consonants. Because rimes are used, the focus is not on the the vowel, and students can rely on their knowledge of consonants for reading and sorting words. As understandings about blends and digraphs develop, the families can be ex-

 Literature Links

Although most books have words with blends and digraphs, here are a few selections that students and I have especially enjoyed.

Blends

Cutting, B., & Cutting, J. (1996). *Are you a ladybug?* Bothell, WA: Wright. This is the easiest of the three books listed for *s*-blends and, as its title suggests, employs a question-and-answer format. It includes words with *sn, sl, sp* and *s*. Its fine illustrations are an added plus.

Gelman, G. (1977). *More spaghetti, I say!* New York: Scholastic. This is the most challenging of the three books with *s*-blends, but is sure to excite young readers with its "'More spaghetti, I say! I love it! I love it. I love it. I do. I love it so much!' 'More than me?' 'More than you.'" Such an attitude is sure to spell problems with a friend, and it does. *St, sp, sl, sk,* and *s* are included. This book also has numerous words with *th*.

Preller, J. (1994). *Wake me in spring*. New York: Scholastic. Bear is ready to hibernate, and Mouse is sad that he won't see him for a while. The text, which is repetitive and rhyming, highlights the *sl, sn, st, sk* blends and the contrasting consonant *s*.

Cowley, J. (1998). *The scrubbing machine*. Bothell, WA: Wright. This story features the popular Mrs. Wishy-Washy who rents a machine to clean her house. The machine works so well it cleans *everything* in its path. This book supports the study of *l*-blends and *r*-blends (*dr* and *tr*).

Digraphs

Cowley, J. (1998). *Dishy-washy*. Bothell, WA: Wright. All chaos breaks out when Mr. Wishy-Washy sets out to wash the dishes. Although the /sh/ sound abounds in this easy text, it is either at the end or in the middle of the word.

Milgrim, D. (1994). *Why Benny barks*. New York: Random House. This is a story many readers will relate to—what is it that makes dogs bark, sometimes incessantly? It includes words with the *wh* digraph and its phoneme components. It also provides a good review of the consonants *b, m,* and *s*. Although it does employ rhyme, this is a fairly challenging book.

Shaw, N. (1991). *Sheep in a shop*. New York: Houghton Mifflin. Sheep go shopping and find so many things they like that to pay the bill they clip their wool. This story is strong on rhyme. Although few different *sh* words are used, they are used often. There are other books in this series.

Bacmeister, R. (1988). "Galoshes." In *Sing a song of popcorn: Every child's book of poems*. New York: Scholastic. This ever-popular poem about Susie's "galoshes" that make "splishes and sploshes" emphasizes the /sh/ sound. It also includes several *s*-blend words.

FIGURE 4-5. Consonant blends and digraphs.

panded to include words with these as well. As always, be sensitive to students' needs so that you will know if you should pick up the pace or slow it down. Add, delete, or consolidate sorts as needed.

There is no best vowel with which to begin. Have students thoroughly examine the various phonograms associated with whatever vowel is chosen. Word families that highlight short *a* are listed first below. If you begin with *a*, the *at* family is a good choice. It is common and will therefore appear in much of the text the children are reading. Alice Cameron's *The Cat Sat on the Mat* provides a good introduction. (See Figure 4-6 for other literature connections.) The book can be read aloud and then reread with choral or echo reading. As a follow-up, students can find and record *at* words from the story. These can be displayed on charts to be compared to other families of words and added to the children's individual word banks.

Word Family Study—Same Vowel				Words: p. 205
at fat				
at bat	*an* can			
ad sad	*ag* tag	*ap* cap		
it kit	*in* win	*ip* lip	*ig* pig	
ob rob	*op* hop	*ot* not		
ed red	*en* ten	*et* pet		
ub rub	*ug* bug	*un* fun	*ut* cut	

When students begin to examine word families across different vowels, as in the following group of contrasts, the focus shifts from the rime to the short vowel.

Word Family Study—Different Vowels			
ap cap	*ip* dip	*op* top	
at cat	*et* get	*ot* hot	
ag tag	*ig* wig	*og* jog	*ug* rug
an fan	*en* men	*in* pin	*un* run

Literature Links

Word Families

Foster, K., & Erickson, G. (1991). *The bug club*. Hauppauge, NY: Barron's. <u>ug</u>. Bugs are definitely on the move in this story.

Foster, K., & Erickson, G. (1991). *The sled surprise*. Hauppauge, NY: Barron's. <u>ed</u>. Two kids build an unusual sled.

Gregorich, B. (1996). *Jog, Frog, jog*. Grand Haven, MI: School Zone. <u>og</u>. A dog takes the pleasure out of Frog's jog.

Wildsmith, B. (1982). *Cat on the mat*. New York: Oxford University Press. <u>at</u>. Several animals join a cat on a mat until it becomes crowded and the cat chases them away.

Short Vowels

Coxe, M. (1996). *Cat traps*. New York: Random House. A cat tries getting a snack by setting traps. All short vowels are represented.

Foster, K., & Erickson, G. (1993). *What a day for flying*. Hauppauge, NY: Barron's. A cat and a fish are hot-air ballooning when the cat's hat blows off. This book has numerous representations for each of the short vowels.

FIGURE 4-6. Word families and short vowels.

After working with phonograms that end in a single consonant, students may be ready to try those that end in a blend or digraph, such as *ack, ick, ock,* and *ang, ing, ung*. Suggested contrasts and supplemental word lists for these rimes are included in the "Final Consonant Blends and Digraphs" section. Flip books like the one shown in Figure 4-7 are easy for students to make and reinforce children's knowledge of phonograms.

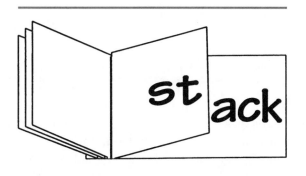

FIGURE 4-7. A flip book for the *ack* word family.

Short Vowels	Words:

Compare short *a* and short *i* words.

Compare short *e* and short *o* words.

Compare words with short *a*, short *i*, and short *u*.

Continue to examine short vowels, comparing two or three at a time. Gradually, create sorts that contain the more difficult contrasts of *a/e, e/i, i/o,* and *o/u.* If desired, use pictures as well as words in the sorts. When students are ready for an added challenge, include an oddball like *was* or *fur.*

Words: pp. 206–207

To extend students' understanding of short vowels, return to words that have different phonograms but the same vowel, such as *at, an, ag,* and *ap.* Have the children sort the words into families and then collapse the families into a single category. Read through the list of words together, and have the students take note of what the words have in common. If their comments do not include something like "the /ă/ sound," isolate the vowel sound in several words by separating off one word element at a time, beginning with the onset and moving on to the final consonant: *fat → at → a, clap → ap → a,* and *bag → ag → a.* Do the same with another contrasting vowel, and then compare words with the two vowels as in Figure 4-8. Avoid contrasting easily confused vowels initially—*a/e, e/i, i/o, o/u*—but do work up to these. Blind sorts (discussed in Chapter 3) can be incorporated into short vowel work so that students attend to sound as well as to visual cues.

AFFRICATES: FEATURE D

◆

dr	*d*	*j*	
drop	dog	jug	
ch	*h*	*tr*	*t*
chap	had	trap	ten
ch	*dr*	*tr*	*j*
chip	drag	trip	jog

Words: pp. 201–204

Single consonants, blends, and digraphs that can produce an affricate sound (*g, j,* letter name *h, dr, tr,* and *ch*) have been included in the sections on "Initial and Final Consonants" and "Initial Consonant Blends and Digraphs." A review is included here for students who are still confusing them and would benefit from further reinforcement of this feature. Pictures may supplement the words used. For literature links, refer to Figure 4-5.

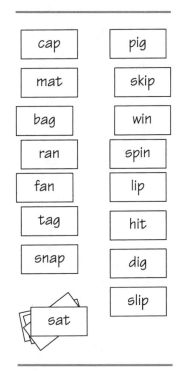

FIGURE 4-8. Short *a* and short *i* sort.

FINAL CONSONANT BLENDS AND DIGRAPHS, INCLUDING MORE WORD FAMILIES: FEATURE E

◆

Most of the suggested contrasts for this feature focus on the final blend or digraph, not on specific rimes. If you wish to begin with rimes, you can have students examine the word families first (*ash, ish, ush*), and then collapse them into the final element (*sh*), as was done with short vowels. Rimes with final *ck* are among the word families introduced during this feature; it is again featured at the within word pattern stage under "Complex Consonants" because it is often confused with other /k/ endings.

Consonant blends and digraphs with an *m* or *n* preceding the final consonant are especially difficult for students—*bump* and *land*. As noted in Chapter 1, the sound of these preconsonantal nasals is obscured by the consonant that follows, making it easy for novice spellers to overlook them in their spelling. It is usually not until the end of the letter name stage that students begin to consistently include nasals before another consonant. For literature links, see Figure 4-9.

Digraphs		
ch	*th*	*sh*
much	bath	dash

Words:
pp. 208–209
(pp. 201–203)

Blends			
t	*st*	*ft*	
mat	best	raft	
m	*p*	*mp*	
hum	dip	lamp	
d	*t*	*nd*	*nt*
kid	pet	hand	rent
mp	*nt*	*nd*	*st*
pump	dent	sand	list

Word Families Ending in Two Consonants			
ack	*ick*		
sack	kick		
eck	*ock*	*uck*	
neck	rock	duck	
ang	*ing*	*ong*	*ung*
bang	king	song	hung
ank	*ink*	*unk*	
bank	pink	junk	
all	*ell*	*ill*	
ball	tell	hill	

📖 Literature Links

Final Blends and Digraphs

Hoff, S. (1992). *Stanley*. New York: HarperCollins Children's Books. The other cavemen are skeptical of Stanley's interests in art and plants, but when he builds himself a house, they change their minds. This book has 64 pages, each with 1 to 4 lines. It includes many words with the preconsonantal nasal *n*.

Most, B. (1992). *There's an ant in Anthony*. New York: Morrow. Anthony goes in search of other words with *ant* once he finds it in his name. 32 pages.

FIGURE 4-9. Final consonant blends and digraphs.

CHAPTER 5

◆

Within Word Pattern
Word Study

Students practice sorting their words by pattern.

Chapter at a Glance

◆

As a result of their increased orthographic knowledge and additional experiences with print, students at the within word pattern stage of spelling development are usually well on their way to becoming fluent readers and writers. While letter name spellers are likely to read only about 50 words per minute, students at the within word pattern stage typically read close to 100. They read in a phrased way, often silently. Children frequently find the newly opened world of chapter books particularly engaging and read for longer sustained periods, following the adventures of their favorite character. Writing, too, is less taxing. Students write words with greater ease and are able to channel more effort into expressing their ideas.

As discussed in Chapter 1, there are also changes in spelling strategy at the within word pattern stage. Sound is no longer perceived as *the* source of information for spelling words. Rather, students' growing sight vocabularies call into question their previously held notions about how the spelling system works. They realize that *plate* is associated with the spelling *p-l-a-t-e*, not PLAT, and bridge, with *b-r-i-d-g-e*, not BRIJ. By the within word pattern stage, students have a fairly firm grasp of the use of short vowels in single-syllable words. However, other types of vowels, particularly long vowels, and complex consonants present new challenges that must be sorted out.

Many of the pattern complexities encountered at this stage result from the fact that English is a cosmopolitan language, a language shaped by many other languages. One of the strongest influences on the patterns of our language was the Norman French conquest of England in 1066. During the years following the invasion, there was a tremendous influx of French vocabulary into the existing English language. Estimates suggest that approximately 40 percent of modern-day English has French origins. Merging of the two languages led to various spelling and pronunciation changes that so altered Old English that it became a new language—Middle English. Numerous vowel patterns were added, including *oi, oy, ou, au, ie*, and *ee*, and pronunciation of particular patterns sometimes varied from word to word, as in *sneak, head,* and *great*. Scribes of the time also contributed changes. For example, in order to eliminate confusions related to the use of the letter *u*, which was identical to *v* and if doubled formed *w*, scribes often substituted an *o* in words where the /ŭ/ sound was followed by a *v* or the graphically similar *n* and *m* (Scragg, 1974). This explains unusual spellings like *come, some, son, ton, dove, love, shove*.

Despite the complex nature of English spelling patterns, within word pattern spellers do learn to master their use in single-syllable words, a prerequisite for study at later stages. Instruction at the within word pattern stage focuses on long vowel patterns, *r*-controlled patterns, abstract vowel patterns, and complex consonants. Words are sorted by sound and pattern, and pattern is linked to meaning as students explore homophones and the *ed* past tense meaning unit.

To assist students' reading of polysyllabic words, you can take a few minutes several times a week to engage the whole class in reading a few "whoppers." Although some students in the group may have automatic recognition of the words and others may be just starting to read, everyone will soon feel they have something to contribute to the solving of these word mysteries. Write a two-syllable word on the board (or a longer word when students are ready), like *fever*, *sideways*, or *hammock*. The current read-aloud is a good source for words. Next, model how to break the word into chunks in order to recognize known parts. Vary the complexity of the word elements you highlight—the sound of a single consonant, a vowel pattern, or a meaning unit (such as a prefix or suffix). Whenever possible, draw an analogy between the new word and a known word. For example, you might call students' attention to the recognizable word *ham* in *hammock* and then go on to point out that *ock* produces the same sound in *lock* and *block*. Since *m* is pronounced as /m/, the last part of the word must be *mock*—*ham-mock*. Students enjoy the challenge of reading bigger words and the sense of accomplishment that accompanies recognition.

LONG VOWELS WITH VC*e*: FEATURE F

◆

a can	*a*C*e* cane			
a mask	*a*C*e* flake		**?** car, have	Words: p. 213 (pp. 206–207)
i wig	*i*C*e* line			
i him	*i*C*e* prize		**?** give	
a crash	*i* dish	*a*C*e* gate	*i*C*e* pipe	
o spot	*o*C*e* globe			
o trot	*o*C*e* broke		**?** from, done	
u plus	*u*C*e* cube			
o shop	*u* dust	*o*C*e* cone	*u*C*e* use	

Vowel–consonant–*e* (VC*e*) is the easiest of the features examined at this stage. Most students quickly realize that adding a silent *e* to the end of a CVC pattern makes the vowel say its name (*mad* versus *made*), in other words, changes it to a long vowel. Introduce the feature with pictures that contrast the long and short sounds of a particular vowel. If you don't plan to have students spell the words at week's end, you can

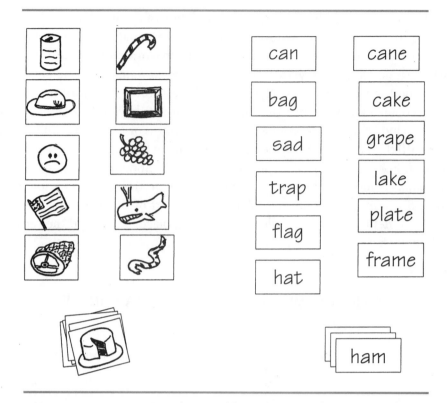

FIGURE 5-1. Comparing short and long *a*: Sorting by sound and then by pattern.

include pictures with several different patterns in the long vowel category. If accurate spelling is an expectation, I recommend limiting the long vowel pictures to those with a VC*e* pattern and moving from the picture sound sort directly to a pattern sort with words, as shown in Figure 5-1. The initial use of pictures helps children discriminate the two sounds. Keep in mind that you want students to use visual cues but not to rely too much on the patterns they see, and the *e*-marker is a strong visual cue. Unless students can clearly differentiate the sounds of long and short vowels, they may attend primarily to visual differences in the words and fail to associate the sound with the pattern. As previously discussed, such students are likely to seem adept at categorizing their words (a task they accomplish by merely looking to see which words have a final *e* and which do not), but demonstrate little transfer to writing. Because the sound–pattern connection was never really made, the absence of the visual cue during writing leaves the student at a loss. The blind sorts discussed earlier help learners maintain a balance between pattern and sound; the use of pictures and the inclusion of an exception or two are also helpful (see Figure 5-2).

You will notice the absence of a long and short *e* contrast in the sorting sequence above. In single-syllable words, *eCe* words are rare. Other long *e* patterns are addressed in the section on "Other Common Long Vowel Patterns." Literature links for this spelling feature are listed in Figure 5-3.

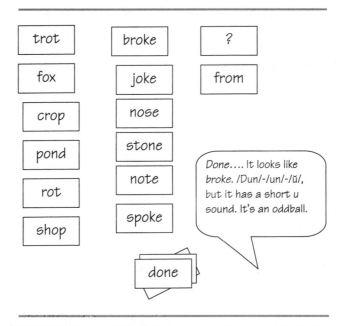

FIGURE 5-2. Short and long *o* word sort that includes exceptions.

📖 Literature Links

Most books that are accessible to early within word pattern spellers contain a variety of long and short vowel patterns. The two titles listed below highlight short vowels and the VCe long vowel pattern.

Marshall, E. (1981). *Three by the sea.* New York: Puffin. While at the beach, three kids try to tell the most interesting story. Each story, which features a cat and a rat, is better than the last. This short chapter book includes numerous examples for each of the short vowels, as well as a few for the VCe pattern.

Hoban, L. (1981). *Arthur's Funny Money.* New York: HarperCollins. Arthur needs to earn money to buy a T-shirt and cap, so he washes bikes. Violet needs help learning how to use math, so they work together. This book includes many words with *a*Ce and *i*Ce, as well a few with *o*Ce. There are several short vowel examples for *a*, *i*, and *o* also.

FIGURE 5-3. Short vowels and VC*e*.

R-CONTROLLED VOWELS: FEATURE G

◆

With Short Vowel Patterns

a dash	*aCe* plate	*ar* card	? warm	**Words:** p. 214 (pp. 206–207, 213)
i clip	*iCe* dime	*ir* bird		
o blob	*oCe* poke	*or* horn	? your	
u club	*uCe* tube	*ur* burp		
ar dark	*or* fork	*ir* dirt	*er* her	

R-controlled (or -influenced) vowel patterns are the source of numerous spelling errors. Some of students' difficulties stem from the fact that the /r/ sound includes a vowel. As a result, spellers sometimes omit the vowel in words like *bird* and *girl*—BRD and GRL—even though they include vowels in other words. Students also confuse the different patterns, especially *er*, *ir*, and *ur*, which sound alike (SKURT for *skirt*). Reversed letter order is another type of problem (for example, FRIST for *first*). Incorrect spellings of this type may look right to students because of the many *r* blend words they are accustomed to seeing in print.

You can help students catch mistakes by making them more conscious of how the reversed letter order affects the word's pronunciation. Choose an *r*-controlled word, like *bark*, from the list of paired words below, and write it on the chalkboard. Then have students analyze its sounds—*bark → ark → ar*. Do the same with the blend + vowel word—*brat → at → a*. Discuss and compare the results. Encourage students to proofread spellings that involve *r* to be sure they've written what they intended.

bark/brat   perk/press   bird/brim   corn/crop   burn/brush
dart/drat   term/trend   girl/grid   torn/trot   curd/crud

The series of contrasts outlined above assumes that students have had experiences with the VC*e* feature (F). The sequence could also include a contrast of short *e* and *er*, if desired. Teachers sometimes introduce this feature by sending students on a search for words with vowel + *r*. Each new word is written on a blank word card. Once students are through hunting (in books and stories in progress, on charts and bulletin board captions, and so on), they do an open sort with the cards to see what they can discover. Findings are shared and discussed. Students should realize that vowels are influenced by the "bossy *r*." Depending on the words they gather, students may also notice that different patterns produce the same sound—*her*, *girl*, *turn*.

With Long Vowel Patterns

					Words:
ar arm	*aCe* take	*ai* rain	*are* care	*?* where, are	p. 214
ar smart	*are* share	*ai* trail	*air* air	*?* warm	pp. (213–217)
er fern	*ea* seat	*ee* teeth	*ear* clear	*?* heart	
er clerk	*ee* sleep	*ear* near	*eer* cheer	*?* learn, earth	
ir skirt	*iCe* ride	*igh* night	*ire* tire	*?* trip	
or short	*oCe* those	*oa* toast	*ore* score	*?* roar, work	

Note. No sort with *ure* is included because there are few single-syllable words with this pattern.

The series of sorts above is a difficult one. It is intended for use *after* a study of the "Other Common Long Vowel Patterns" feature (H). I have found that dividing the study of *r*-controlled vowels into two parts—(1) those with short vowel patterns, and (2) those with long—makes it easier for students to grasp this complex feature. The inclusion of short *r*-controlled vowels in this series provides a good review. The sound-alike nature of many of the *r*-controlled patterns complicates learning to spell them. Students can sometimes use meaning as a help, since many of the words are homophones (*bare/bear* and *dear/deer*). They also need to realize that the vowel pattern is going to be the tricky part of the word, the one that will require their attention.

OTHER COMMON LONG VOWEL PATTERNS: FEATURE H

◆

This sequence, like others I've suggested, is recursive in nature. A new element is introduced in each sort, but previously examined features are returned to again and again as the basis for comparison. This not only provides a scaffold upon which children can build new understandings, but also ensures that earlier learnings are reviewed. By contrast, traditional approaches tend to give students one chance to come to terms with a particular vowel and often expect them to do so without the benefit of a contrasting sound. For example, the focus one week may be on long *a*, with *aCe*, *ai*, *ay*, *ei*, and *ey* words all included in the list. The next lesson may be a study of long *e* with several different patterns. The following year the issue of long vowels may be revisited at the beginning of the year but with several, if not all, long vowels in a single lesson. I have found that children not only need opportunities to contrast patterns and sounds; they usually need more than one week to study a particular vowel.

				?	
a crab	*aCe* grade	*ay* play	was, ball		**Words:** pp. 215–217
a plant	*aCe* shake	*ay* stay	*ai* chain	? said, want	(pp. 206–207, 213)
a dash	*aCe* state	*ai* paid	*ei* eight	? they, wash	
e desk	*e* he	*ee* keep		? these, flew	
e kept	*ee* need	*ea* beat		? great, break	
e rest	*ee* sweep	*ea* peach	*ie* chief	? lie, friend	
e melt	*ee* green	*ea* reach	short *ea* bread	? steak, been	
i mix	*iCe* drive	*y* sky		? live (2 sounds)	
i trim	*iCe* wipe	*y* why	*igh* light	? tie	
i limp	*iCe* dime	*igh* right	*iCC* find	? gym	
o got	*oCe* stove	*oa* float		? done, move	
o plop	*oCe* bone	*oa* soap	*iCC* hold	? some, gone	
o slot	*oCe* chose	*oCC* most	*ow* blow	? toe, lose	
u plum	*uCe* June	*ue* glue	*ui* fruit	? push	
u crust	*uCe* rule	*ue* glue	*ew* drew	? none, does	

The above sequence for long vowel study could easily be done with a different order of vowels. The *e* patterns are especially complex due to the two ways of spelling short *e*. The final *e* sort can be reserved for later, if necessary; however, students usually enjoy the challenge of this "demon" sort. It is best approached by having students sort by sound first, then by pattern, and finally by sound and pattern, as shown in Figure 5-4. Words for the short *ea* pattern are listed at the end of the column of long *ea* words in the supplemental word lists.

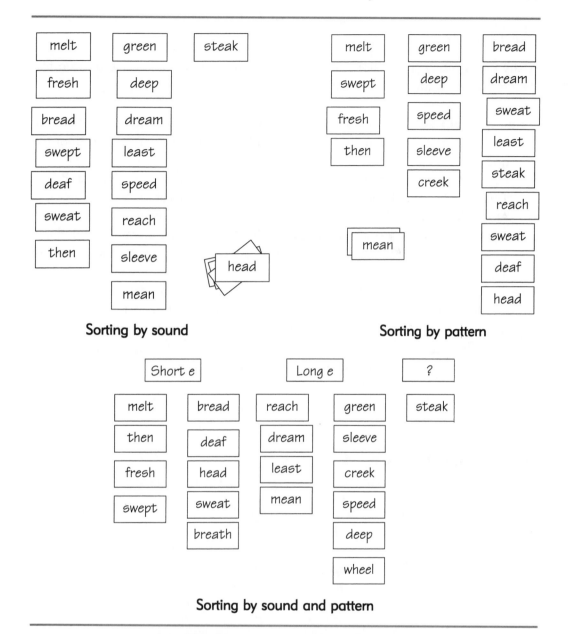

FIGURE 5–4. Comparing short and long *e*.

COMPLEX CONSONANT PATTERNS: FEATURE I

◆

This section discusses several complex consonant patterns, including triple-letter blends; spelling variations for final /k/, /ch/, and /j/; hard and soft *c* and *g*; and silent consonants. The different aspects of this feature do not need to be explored consecutively; rather, they should be chosen as needed. A few favorite literature links are included in Figure 5-5.

📖 Literature Links

Poetry offers many connections to spelling features being studied. Here are a few favorites for work with complex consonants.

Prelutsky, J. (1984). *The new kid on the block.* New York: Scholastic. "I've Got an Itch," a short poem students will relate to, includes words with final *tch* and *ch.*

Sierra, J. (1998). *Antarctic antics: A book of penguin poems.* New York: Harcourt Brace. This is a wonderful book of poems that will be enjoyed by students of all ages. "I Am Looking for My Mother" is a good choice when studying final /k/. Baby Penguin can't tell which mother is hers, so she decides to listen and identify her mother's sound. Is it "ECK, ICK, EEK, AWK, or ACK"? Many words with final *k* and *ck* are included.

Silverstein, S. (1996). *Falling up.* New York: HarperCollins. "The Gnome, the Gnat, and the Gnu" is a humorous poem that has silent *g* in words where it should be as well as where it shouldn't (such as, *gknock, gnodded,* and *gnice*).

FIGURE 5–5. Complex consonant patterns.

Triple-Letter Blends

k kite	*qu* quake	*squ* squid		Words: p. 218 (pp. 202, 204)
st stem	*str* strike	*th* thank	*thr* throb	
sp spend	*spl* splash	*spr* spring		
sc scab	*scr* scrape	*sh* shed	*shr* shrink	

Triple-letter blends are of two types—those in which each consonant sound is heard, like *str* (/s/ + /t/ + /r/) and *scr,* and those that are a blending of a digraph and a consonant, as *thr* (/th/ + /r/) and *shr.* When you look for words to contrast with triple-letter blends, you may want to browse the within word pattern section of the lists of supplemental words in order to find more challenging words than those listed with the letter name consonants, blends, and digraphs.

Final /k/ Sound

ck	ke		?	Words:
black	bake		speak	p. 219
ck	**ke**	**k**		
sick	poke	week		
ck	**ke**		**k**	
clock	hike	park	sneak	
		milk	look	

Although *ck* was introduced in "Final Consonant Blends and Digraphs" in Chapter 4, it is dealt with more intensely as a part of this feature. Spellings for the final /k/ sound are often confused by the within word pattern speller, making this an optimum time for instruction.

In single-syllable words, the *ck* spelling is used with short vowel words, except when the final /k/ sound is preceded by another consonant (*milk, bank, perk*). Then the ending is just *k*. Most long vowel words end with *ke*. Those that end with just *k* are mainly long *e* words, which is not surprising since there are very few single-syllable words with *eCe*. Words with abstract vowels (*shook, stalk*) also end in just *k*. Have your students begin sorting by vowel sound. Then ask them to subdivide the sound columns by pattern. Once they realize when each ending should be used, they can sort by sound and pattern simultaneously.

Final *tch* and *dge*

tch and *ch*				Words:
ch	**tch**			pp. 219–220
coach	ditch			
VVch	**Cch**	**tch**	**?**	
beach, pouch	belch	match	much	
dge and *ge*			
---	---	---	---
dge	**Vge**	**Cge**	
edge	page	large	

In most short vowel words that end with /ch/, the final phoneme is spelled *tch*. The words *much, rich, such,* and *which* are exceptions. Long vowels, abstract vowels, and the consonants *l, n,* and *r* signal the use of *ch* (*beach, couch, bench, belch, birch*). While this may seem complex at first, it's really quite straightforward: Other than the exceptions noted above, when you hear a short vowel sound use *tch*, unless you also hear a consonant sound before the /ch/, you then use *ch*. Final *dge* and *ge* follow the same principle. Begin a study of either pattern by having students sort the words by vowel sound. The first sort above focuses on just the vowel sound; the second adds on the influence of a consonant preceding the final /ch/ (see Figure 5-6). If needed, the study of *ge* and *dge* could also be broken down into two sorts.

Hard and Soft *c* and *g*

c (*a, o, u*)	c (*e, i, y*)	s	
came	cent	say, soak, surf	**Words:** pp. 201, 220
g (*a, o, u*)	g (*e, i, y*)	j	(pp. 202, 203)
game	germ	jar, joke, just	

The soft sounds of *c* (/s/) and *g* (/j/) occur when these consonants are followed by *e, i,* or *y*. The hard sounds (/g/ and /k/) result when *a, o,* or *u* follow the consonants. Although there are exceptions (*get* and *give*), the principle holds true for many single-syllable words as well as for many polysyllabic words. This is an important principle for students to grasp not only for their reading and writing at this stage, but also because an understanding of hard and soft *c* and *g* is necessary to accurately spell words at later stages. For example, is it *knowledgable* or *knowledgeable*; *invincable* or *invincible*?

Silent Consonants

Students at the within word pattern stage also become aware of silent consonants (*know, write, limb*). These may be examined separately or may be included in appropriate vowel pattern sorts. Regardless of which **Words: p. 220** route is chosen, students need to be aware that the silent letter adds a tricky element to the word that they need to remember. Many of the *kn* and *wr* words have homophones and will receive attention during that study as well.

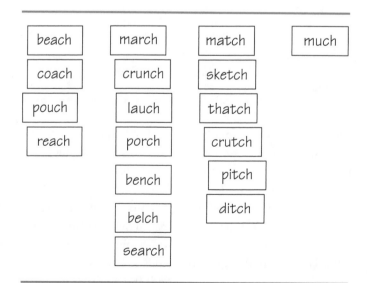

FIGURE 5-6. A *ch* and *tch* sound and pattern sort.

ABSTRACT VOWELS: FEATURE J

◆

o slop	oy boy	oi coin			Words: pp. 221–222 (pp. 206–207, 217)
ew stew	long oo tooth	short oo book		? sew, truth	
ow crow	ou /ou/ shout	ow /ou/ town		? could, though	
long oo spool	ou /ou/ sound	ow /ou/ now	ou (long oo) group	? bought	
a draft	al salt	aw crawl	au haunt	? laugh, watch	

This feature deals with abstract vowels, vowels other than those influenced by *r* that are neither long nor short. It is often the last feature to be mastered at the within word pattern stage. As with other spelling feature studies, many different comparisons could be planned. Most of those listed above highlight a new word element by contrasting it with what students already know—namely, long and short vowel patterns. Then finer distinctions are made. Students compare words with the same sound but different patterns (*caught, raw, talk* or *shout, howl*), or they contrast words with the same pattern but different sounds, like *foot* and *moon* (see Figure 5-7).

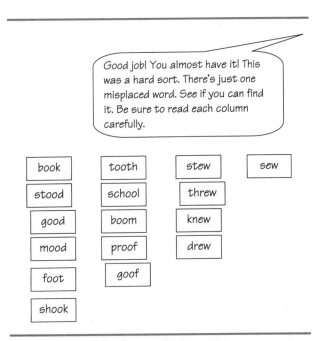

FIGURE 5-7. Sound and pattern sort with abstract vowels that includes a misplaced card.

As students work with abstract vowels, help them form generalizations about the sound-alike patterns. For example: "When the vowel sound is heard at the end of the word, notice which spelling pattern is used."

/oi/	/ou/	/ô/
boy	brow	draw
joy	cow	jaw
soy	how	law
toy	wow	saw
(not *oi*)	(not *ou*)	(not *au*)

Be sure to use the assessment results and students' writing to guide you in determining which abstract vowels your students need to study. Eliminate the sorts they already know.

OTHER FEATURES FOR STUDY

◆

Sounds of the *ed* Inflectional Ending

/ĭd/	/d/	/t/	?	Words:
lifted	sailed	crushed	grew, spoke	p. 223

Although the issues of *e*-drop and doubling before an inflectional ending (such as *ed* or *ing*) are addressed at the syllable juncture stage, it is appropriate for within word pattern spellers to gain an understanding of *ed* as a past tense meaning unit. Spellers at this stage still typically write many *ed* words by sound (TRAPT = *trapped*, DOTID = *dotted*, HUMD = *hummed*). Having students contrast words with the various *ed* sounds will help them realize that, regardless of its pronunciation, we usually use *ed* to show that an event occurred in the past. Study of the *ed* meaning unit can be done at any time during this stage, provided that students are beginning to use it correctly—TRAPED, DOTED, HUMED. See Figure 5-8 for literature links.

Homophones

An analysis of the spelling errors in nearly 20,000 compositions written by students in grades 1 to 8 showed *homophones*, words that sound alike but have different spellings and different meanings, to be the most common source of spelling problems (Cramer & Cipielewski, 1995). Unlike most misspellings, which are nonwords (COWCH for *couch*), homophone errors are typically real words, just the wrong choice (PEACE for *piece*).

📖 Literature Links

Although most easy chapter books contain words with all three pronunciations of the *ed* meaning unit, the Henry and Mudge series by Cynthia Rylant is particularly useful for connecting literature to this spelling exploration. There are several books in the series, including *Henry and Mudge: The First Book*, *Henry and Mudge and the Long Weekend*, and *Henry and Mudge and the Wild Wind*. The last one is my favorite for this feature study. It has four chapters, each about 10 pages in length, and is packed with exemplars to choose from for sorting or for students to find during a word hunt.

/t/		/d/		/ĭd/	
flapped	walked	rippled	whined	started	headed
looked	asked	whistled	turned	nodded	lifted
switched	dropped	called	grumbled		
sniffed	missed	wagged	followed		
laughed		whispered	grabbed		
		crawled	cleared		
		played	frowned		
		grinned			

Be sensitive to differences in dialect when exploring this feature; /t/ and /d/ are articulated in similar ways, and students in some regions may have difficulty discerning a difference.

FIGURE 5–8. The many sounds of the *ed* meaning unit.

Some of the word confusions can be blamed on carelessness and lack of attention to proof-reading. Because homophone errors look right, they are easy to overlook. Even computer spell-checking programs gloss over them. That's because *meaning* is the critical issue with homophones. In order to correctly spell these sound-alikes, students need to have a firm understanding of which meaning to associate with which spelling pattern, and many students lack this.

A few troublesome homophones can be learned with the help of mnemonics. For example, the words *there, their,* and *they're* are often confused, especially the first two. To help children keep these words straight, point out that the correct spelling for *there* is the one that contains the word's opposite—*here*. Memory devices are also helpful for such pairs as *heard* (we hear with our *ear*) and *herd*, *piece* (we get one from *pie*) and *peace*, and *meat* (what we *eat*) and *meet*.

Although mnemonics provide worthwhile reminders for some homophones, children learn to master most homophones through repeated opportunities to explore and work with them. One possibility is to have students collect homophones from their reading and writing and compile them into a personal or class book. The word entries can include illustrations as well as definitions or sentences. This activity draws students' attention to word meaning *and* spelling and is great fun. In fact, one year my students became so engrossed in a study of homophones that their word hunting led them to create a reference book of more than a hundred homophone pairs for their use and that of future classes! Everyone got involved collecting words, drawing illustrations, writing sentences, designing the cover, and figuring out how to organize such a wealth of information. The class thought alphabetical order seemed like a logical approach to making the book user-friendly until someone pointed out that some homophones begin with different letters (*I, eye* or *you, ewe, yew*). The students finally resolved the issue by alphabetizing each pair by the word most familiar to third graders (*I* and *you*). Finished pages (see Figure 5-9) were arranged in a large three-ring notebook so that additional finds could be added in the future. The book was (and still is) greatly enjoyed.

Games are also a good way to reinforce homophone meanings. Through the frequent use of homophones, students come to internalize the spelling–meaning connection and apply their understandings in their writing. Although many games can be adapted for use with homophones, over the years card games have been my students' favorites. Two of their top choices have been Concentration and Homophone Rummy. One of the rules of the game should require students to provide a meaning or sentence for the words in order to score.

For Homophone Rummy, students need a deck of at least 36 homophone cards, more if the number of players exceeds three. Because several cards are held at a time, write the word in the upper left corner as well as on the center of the card (refer to Figure 3-12 in Chapter 3). Each player is dealt six to eight cards; the remaining cards are placed in a draw pile. Students take turns drawing and discarding, with the objective of collecting and playing as many pairs as possible. In order to lay down a pair, students must demonstrate an understanding of the meaning of each word. If the player can't or if the meaning given is incorrect, the player must pick up the cards. A discard is then made, ending the player's turn. Discards are placed in a line so that they are visible. Players may choose a card from this line when it is their turn rather than drawing from the pile. The selected card must be playable, *and* all cards following it in the line must also be picked up. The game proceeds in like fashion until someone runs out of cards. The player who has played the most cards wins.

If desired, word sorting may be incorporated into the study of homophones. Below are the beginnings of two possible sequences that reinforce vowel patterns from the within word pattern stage. The first set has students categorizing homophone pairs by long vowel sound across different vowels (short vowels could be approached in a similar fashion). The second approach focuses on sound also, but one vowel at a time.

While students are exploring this spelling feature, you may want to introduce them to some of the many books written on homophones and word play (see Figure 5-10). Give a short book talk on a few favorites to whet students' appetites for reading them. Since children love humor and riddles, little else is needed, other than time to read and share them with their friends.

deer

I saw a deer in the little woods.

dear

Dear, Mrs. Cleary

Love, Diane

The head of my letter is Dear Mrs. Cleary.

FIGURE 5-9. Page from a third-grade homophone book.

Different-Vowel Comparisons		
a	*i*	*u*
ate, eight	right, write	blew, blue
e	*o*	
meat, meet	know, no	

Same-Vowel Comparisons		
short *a*	long *a*	*r*-controlled
rap, wrap	mail, male	hair, hare

Words:
pp. 224–225

Contractions

Words:
p. 226

Contractions are words that are made up of two or more words, with some letters removed and replaced by an apostrophe (*I'm, there's, o'clock* = *I am, there is, of the clock*). Students need to understand the principles underlying contraction-making so that they know where to put the apostrophe when they write contractions and so they can understand their meanings when they read (for example, *he's* = *he is* or *he has* and *they'd* = *they had* or *they would*). Contractions are best examined by families so that students can see the consistencies, for example the *not–n't* family and the *will–'ll* family. It's helpful to have students think of the apostrophe as a placeholder, marking the spot where the letters were omitted.

📖 Literature Links

Gwynne, F. *The king who rained* (1970), *A chocolate moose for dinner* (1976), and *A little pigeon toad* (1988). New York: Simon & Schuster. This group of books features a young child who pictures what she hears her parents discussing. For example, one sentence indicates that big bills are coming in the mail. The accompanying picture depicts three tall birds standing behind the mailbox with their bills protruding out the front. Homophones and words with multiple meanings are presented. Students are often eager to create their own examples after reading a book in this series.

Parish, P. (1963). *Amelia Bedelia*. New York: Harper & Row. One of a series featuring the ever-popular Amelia Bedelia, a maid who takes everything literally.

Presspon, L. (1997). *A dictionary of homophones*. New York: Barron's. A good resource for homophone study.

Schwartz, D. M. (1999). *If you hopped like a frog*. New York: Scholastic. This stimulating picture book highlights 12 similes like "strong as an ant" and "scurry like a spider." The author describes what the phrases would mean for us if we really had those abilities and explains how he used math to get the answers. This book is sure to arouse students' interest to find out about other similes—"If you ate like a horse, how much would you eat?"

Terban, M. (1987). *Mad as a wet hen! And other funny idioms*. New York: Clarion. This illustrated book gives the stories behind common idioms, like "hold your horses" and "straw that broke the camel's back."

Terban, M. (1991). *They hay! A wagonful of funny homonym riddles*. New York: Clarion. Kids love riddles, and the nearly 100 presented in this book are solved with two to four sound-alike words. For example, the answer to "When the bells **ring out** loudly, **take the skins off** the bananas" is *peal/peel*.

Terban, M. (1992). *Funny you should ask: How to make up jokes and riddles with word play*. New York: Clarion. After reading some of the homophone riddle books listed, students will be ready to write their own.

Terban, M. (1993). *Eight ate: A feast of homonym riddles*. New York: Clarion. More homophone riddles for students to puzzle over and savor. For example, "What is a smelly chicken? A foul fowl."

Viorst, J. (1994). *The alphabet from Z to A with much confusion on the way*. New York: Atheneum. Viorst piques the reader's curiosity about homophones through an ABC format that plays on within word sounds and patterns.

FIGURE 5-10. Homophones and word play.

CHAPTER 6

Syllable Juncture Word Study

*Speed sorting on the computer is a fun way to work
toward automaticity with e-drop and doubling.*

Chapter at a Glance

Literacy Development of Students at the Syllable
    Juncture Stage: An Overview
Orthographic Features Explored
   Compound Words
   Doubling and *E*-Drop with *ed* and *ing*: Feature K
   Other Syllable Juncture Doubling: Feature L
   Long Vowel Patterns in the Stressed Syllable: Feature M
   R-Controlled Patterns in the Stressed Syllable: Feature N
   Abstract Vowel Patterns in the Stressed Syllable
   Unstressed Syllable Vowel Patterns: Feature O
   Plurals and Possessives
   Prefixes and Suffixes
   Polysyllabic Homographs and Homophones
   Final /k/ Revisited

◆

Most syllable juncture spellers read and write with fluency, ease, and confidence. Their knowledge of patterns in single-syllable words is secure, enabling them to process words of this type automatically. Although they still have much to learn about how words work, especially polysyllabic words, by this stage, word recognition no longer poses a major challenge for students during reading. Instead, attention can focus on comprehension and the use of strategic knowledge for monitoring understanding. Meaning becomes increasingly important in writing, too, as students experiment with different genres, write for varied purposes, and become more aware of their audience.

Through their reading, writing, and content area studies, students encounter more sophisticated vocabulary and more complex spelling patterns. Although students have been reading and writing polysyllabic words for some time, it is at the syllable juncture stage that these longer words become the center of instruction. Students' solid grasp of sound–pattern relationships in single-syllable words prepares them to negotiate the new issues that are inherent in words of more than one syllable. For example: How do meaning units like prefixes and suffixes combine with base words? How are syllables within a base word joined? How does syllable stress, or accent, influence spelling and pronunciation? By resolving questions like these, students enhance their ability to efficiently read and write more difficult words.

COMPOUND WORDS

◆

The study of compound words is a good way to introduce students to the syllable juncture stage and to words of more than one syllable. Because compounds are composed of intact words, the juncture and stress issues that dominate this stage are not problematic, nor are the vowel pattern issues.

There are many ways to approach the study of compounds. One activity students enjoy involves the use of two or three key words on cards, such as *book*, *head*, and *night*, and a stack of other single-syllable word cards. The challenge is to see how many compounds can be formed and recorded. Include a couple of possibilities for words that, like *headdress* and *nighttime*, result in a double consonant when the compound is made, so that students realize that compounds really do contain two separate words. That way, when students try to spell a word like *granddaddy* or *earring*, even though it may not look right, they will know there needs to be two consonants in the middle. As students work with the meanings of compounds, many will enjoy drawing pictures of the literal and actual meaning of the two words, such as the example for *shoebox* shown in Figure 6-1.

book	head	night
bookcase	headache	nightgown
bookend	headband	nightmare
bookshelf	headlight	nighttime
bookworm	headline	
	headdress	
	headphone	
	headway	

Words:
pp. 229–231

Some compound words are hyphenated (*baby-sit, forty-five*). Many of these are adjectives, and some are comprised of several words: a "*down-in-the-mouth* look," or "*step-by-step* directions." Students enjoy creating their own hyphenated compounds and using them to describe story characters and settings—"For the third day in a row, the little girl wore her *kick-a-lot* shoes to school. She was determined to take care of the *red-headed* bully." I introduce this type of compound to older students during a writing workshop minilesson. After presenting a few examples, I have partners pick a character or setting from our current read-aloud and generate their own descriptive compounds to share. See Figure 6-2 for compound word literature links.

Students need to learn to use the context to determine whether words should be written as a compound or as separate words. For example, compare: "A *runaway* horse and carriage careened down the street," and "The boy decided to *run away*," or "Train is *one way* you can travel," and "She drove her car down the *one-way* street."

Since compound words are used to introduce students to the study of polysyllabic words, this is a good time to make sure they know what is meant by a *syllable*. All syllables have at least one vowel and are easily identifiable by their beat. By clapping the syllable beats, students can readily identify four-, five-, and six-syllable words. In fact, students love demonstrating their expertise by handling the challenge of all challenges:

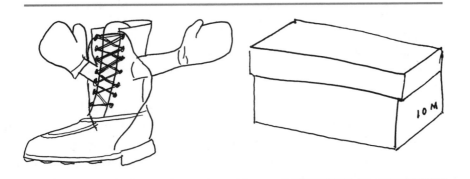

FIGURE 6-1. Fun with words: Illustrating the literal and actual meanings of compound words.

📖 Literature Links

Maestro, B., Maestro, G. (1992). *All aboard overnight: A book of compound words*. New York: Clarion. This is an easy text with numerous compound words; it can serve as a springboard for students' own stories with compound words.

Terban, M. (1989). *Superdupers! Really funny real words*. New York: Clarion. Learn the definitions and origins of unusual compounds like *whippersnapper*, *helter-skelter*, and *claptrap*.

Yolen, J. (1997). *Nocturne*. San Diego: Harcourt Brace. This picture book tribute to nighttime with its wonderful examples of descriptive compounds—"quiltdown, quietdown velvet night"—will stimulate students to create their own compounds.

FIGURE 6–2. Compound words.

supercalifragilisticexpialidocious! Figure 6-3 describes another way to have students apply their knowledge of syllables. (See "Other Features for Study" for a possible follow-up study to compound words.)

DOUBLING AND *E*-DROP WITH *ED* AND *ING*: FEATURE K

◆

base + *ing* (no change) asking, mailing	**e-drop + *ing*** shaking		Words: pp. 232–233
base + *ed* (no change) lifted, rained, touched	**e-drop + *ed*** liked	**?** ate, slept	
base + *ing* (no change) meeting, missing	**e-drop + *ing*** hoping	**double + *ing*** hopping	
base + *ed* (no change) spilled, fooled	**e-drop + *ed*** shaded	**double + *ed*** hugged	
no change greeting, melted	**e-drop** smiling, graded	**double** planning, jogged	

In order to correctly spell words with inflectional endings, like those targeted in this feature, students need to know how to spell the *base word*, the word to which the ending is added, and they need an understanding of the *e*-drop and doubling principles. For example, in order to spell *taking*, a student must know that the base word is *take* not *taik* and must realize that the final *e* is nearly always dropped before adding *ed* or *ing*. The *e*-drop principle is dynamic and applies not only to inflectional endings like *ed* and *ing* but to other vowel-initiated suffixes as well (*hiker*).

📖 Literature Links

Connect students' syllable-learning to reading and writing by introducing or revisiting the haiku poetic form. This type of Japanese verse is written with a total of seventeen syllables—three lines with five, seven, and five syllables respectively. Although most poetry anthologies include at least a few haiku poems, *Cool Melons—Turn to Frogs! The Life and Poems of Issa* is a beautifully illustrated book devoted entirely to haiku. Issa (1763–1827), a Japanese poet, wrote more than 2500 poems during his lifetime. His best-loved haiku are included in this work. Although the strict syllable count is not always preserved due to the translation, the simplicity and charm of the poems are. Poetry, biographical information, watercolor paintings, and Japanese renderings of the haiku in the margins make this an inspiring book. After sharing some of Issa's poems, invite students to write and illustrate their own haiku.

Gollub, M. (1998). *Cool melons—Turn to frogs! The life and poems of Issa.* New York: Lee & Low.

For other types of poems that focus on syllables, refer to this fine resource:

Padget, R. (1987). *The handbook of poetic forms.* New York: Teachers and Writers Collaborative.

FIGURE 6–3. Attending to syllables with haiku poems.

Students usually have more difficulty with the issue of doubling consonants to mark short vowels, what Henderson called the core principle of syllable juncture spelling (1990, p. 68), than with *e*-dropping. As you will see in the feature discussion on "Other Syllable Juncture Doubling," the doubling principle applies to syllable junctures within words ("Put *butter* on the bread" not *buter*) as well as to the juncture between a base word and a suffix ("He *planned* to go on his trip" not *planed* to go). However, its use is most consistent in the latter case. Even though there are few, if any, exceptions to doubling the final consonant before adding an ending to a single-syllable word (this does not consider alternative past tense forms like *eat/ate* and *keep/kept*), it may be worthwhile to teach students the simple "1-1-1 check" as a mnemonic for dealing with this spelling issue. When they're ready to add an ending that starts with a vowel to a base word, students simply ask themselves the following three questions:

Does the word have 1 syllable?
Does the word have 1 vowel?
Does the word end with 1 consonant?

If the answer to all three questions is "yes," the final consonant should be doubled. If the answer to any of the questions is "no," it should not. (Note that polysyllabic base words require special consideration when adding inflectional endings. These issues are discussed in Chapter 7.)

There are various ways to approach the study of this feature; a description of one I've often used is detailed below. It is based on the third sort in the sequence suggested above so that a word walk with all three categories—*no change, e-drop,* and *doubling*—can be addressed.

When you create the word sort, it is helpful to construct a double set of word cards for yourself—one with the inflectional ending, and one with just the base word. This will enable you to visually refresh students' memory of how the base word is spelled, if necessary. After the students have read and discussed the words with the *ed* or *ing* ending, let them know that they're going to help you sort the words according to vowel sound—*short, long,* and *other*. Some students may be able to carry this out with minimal modeling if they have thoroughly studied these sounds at the within word pattern stage. However, you should demonstrate with at least a few examples.

When the sort is complete, have the students help subdivide the categories by pattern—CVC and CVCC for the short vowels and CVC*e* and CVVC for the long and other or abstract vowels (see Figure 6-4). If necessary, use a marker to highlight the pattern on your set of words. After the new categories are formed, have students reflect on what change (if any) was made in the base word when the ending was added. Ask them to consider whether the change was consistent across words of a certain type. They should notice that in some cases no change was made; in others either the final *e* was dropped or the final consonant was doubled. If they don't realize the connection between sound and pattern and whether a change was made, draw their attention to *hoping* and *hopping* and discuss the differences. You may also want to ask them how a word like *fanning* would be pronounced if it had just one *n* (*fa•ning*—long vowel sound).

Next, reshuffle the cards and model categorizing the words according to *no change, e-drop,* or *double*. Most students should feel confident about adding their contributions early on. (If time is short, this part of the word walk can be saved for a follow-up session the next day.) After the categorizing, discuss each column and the principles at work (see Figure 6-5). As you talk about the *e*-drop principle with students, keep in mind that suffixes like *ed* and *er* are meaning units. These are added to the base word intact. It is misleading and incorrect to tell students to "just add *d* or just add *r*."

When you, or you and your students, choose words for this feature, be sure to include a word or two like *miss*. Words of this type appear at first glance to belong in the "double" column due to their double consonants. They cause students to think more about the base word to which the ending is added and to rely less on visual cues. This type of thinking will aid students in applying their understanding of this feature to their writing.

It is best to revisit the issues of *e*-drop and doubling periodically with students during word investigations. Additional reinforcement may come from a game, such as the popular self-checking one described in Figure 6-6. After an initial study of *ed* and *ing* endings, you can extend students' understanding of base words, *e*-drop, and doubling through work with prefixes and suffixes (see "Other Features for Study").

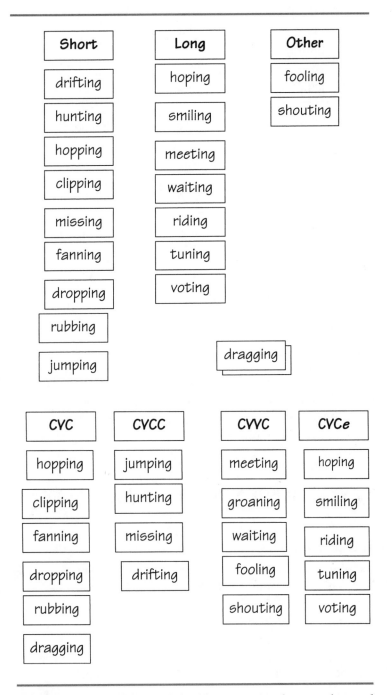

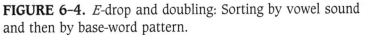

FIGURE 6–4. *E*-drop and doubling: Sorting by vowel sound and then by base-word pattern.

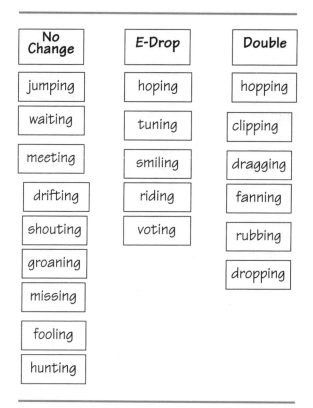

FIGURE 6–5. *E*-drop and doubling: Sorting by inflectional ending change.

OTHER SYLLABLE JUNCTURE DOUBLING: FEATURE L

◆

Across-Syllable Patterns

VCV open	doublet (VCCV)			Words:
clover	dipper			pp. 234–235
VCV open	VCCV	doublet		
glider	scarlet	pillow		
VCV open	VCCV	doublet		
fever, hoping	index, athlete	wedding, middle		
VCV open	VCCV	doublet	?	
Friday, beaver	dentist	classic	comic	
VCV open	VCV closed	VCCV	doublet	
meter	planet	enjoy	sudden	

Although it is not essential, I find that some understanding of the *e*-drop and doubling principles (feature K) is helpful for students as they explore across-syllable patterns. It means that they already know that the way one syllable is spelled may affect the spell-

REACH THE PEAK

The game is designed for two players and may be played without teacher-direction after its initial introduction.

Materials
Game board, two playing pieces, and 24 word cards prepared as follows.

Preparation
Write words like those below on the front side of 20 of the cards.

peep

No change	E-drop	Double
peep play walk	hope slope grade file	plan dot tap grip
float wait	tape tune wave	stop pin step slip

Keep the word cards in categories, and set up the backside of the cards as shown below.

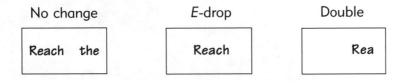

No change	E-drop	Double
Reach the	**Reach**	**Rea**

On the remaining four cards, write: **(e-drop)**, **(double)**, **(no change)**, and *ing* (or *ed*). The backside of each of the four remaining cards will look like this:

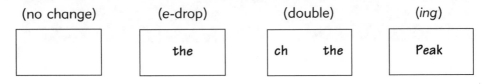

(no change)	(e-drop)	(double)	(ing)
	the	**ch the**	**Peak**

Procedures
1. Shuffle the stack of 20 word cards, and place it word-side-up on the game board. Spread the four remaining cards face-up between the two players. Game pieces are placed at start.
2. Player 1 takes the first card and determines what change, if any, is needed before the *ing* ending is added. The base word, change indicator, and *ing* cards are then lined up in a row.

pin	(double)	ing

(cont.)

FIGURE 6-6. Reach the peak: A game for reinforcing inflectional endings.

3. To check the answer, Player 1 turns over the three cards. If the response is correct, the cards will read

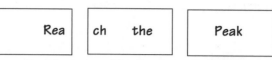

and Player 1 moves up one space. No move is made for an incorrect answer.
4. Players continue alternating turns until each has had ten plays. The goal is to correctly add endings to all ten words and thus reach the peak.

Variations

1. Use half of the cards for an individual player.
2. Require players to write down the spelling of their words each time in order to provide the teacher with a written record and to give the players practice in writing the words.
3. Substitute nonsense words for the real base words in order to increase the challenge for expert players.
4. Choose your own title and theme. Be sure the chosen title is a three-word phrase ("Off and Running").

FIGURE 6–6. (*cont.*)

ing of another and that consonant doubling is a means of maintaining a short vowel sound. During their study of this feature, students examine similar issues. However, the focus is on syllable junctures *within* a base word, rather than between a base word and an ending. Two types of syllables are relevant to this study—*open* and *closed*. Open syllables typically end with a long vowel sound (<u>pa</u>•per, <u>sea</u>•son, <u>ho</u>•ping); closed syllables end with a consonant and have a short vowel sound (<u>en</u>•ter, <u>but</u>•ter, <u>hop</u>•ping). Closed syllables are usually followed by another consonant (see Figure 6-7).

The pattern, or structure, at the syllable juncture is either VCV (<u>ro</u>•<u>bot</u>) or VCCV (<u>mar</u>•<u>ket</u>). *Doublets* (<u>dip</u>•<u>per</u>) are a special type of VCCV pattern. The vowel in these patterns is usually a single letter, but can be two letters that act as a single unit, as in *season*. The same is true of consonants. Blends and digraphs are considered as one unit, not as two distinct letters. That is why *ba*•*ther*, despite its appearance, has a VCV structure. When students first hunt for words with VCV and VCCV patterns, they often miscategorize such words and are not quite sure of how to deal with words that have three consonants at the juncture (<u>ath</u>•<u>lete</u>). When this happens, suggest that they try pronouncing the word as if it is divided between the consonants as well as if the consonants are

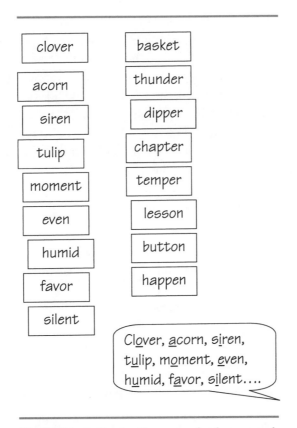

FIGURE 6-7. Sorting words by sound: Identifying open and closed syllables (and checking the results).

acting together as a single unit (<u>bat</u>•<u>her</u> and <u>ba</u>•<u>ther</u> or <u>bath</u>•<u>er</u>) to see which way sounds like the real word. This soon clears up the matter.

Words with final *le* also raise questions. In words like *bubble*, the *l* does not form a blend with the *b* but is linked with the *e*. The preceding consonant plus the *le*, however, do constitute the final syllable (<u>bub</u>•<u>ble</u>—doublet).

A basic knowledge of across-syllable patterns can aid students in spelling and pronouncing words. For example, a student wanting to spell *cider* hears an open first syllable. The long *i* sound of the open syllable provides a clue to the word's spelling. In English, when a syllable ends with a long vowel sound the consonant that follows is not doubled. Unfortunately, this principle is not as reliable when it comes to words with short vowels. Although two consonants usually follow the vowel (*blizzard*), over time the influx of words from other languages into English has given us words like *habit* and *robin*, words with a VCV pattern but a closed syllable. It is important for students to realize that, when learning to spell words with closed syllables, they need to attend carefully to whether there is one consonant or two.

An awareness of syllable juncture patterns also helps students identify unfamiliar words in their reading. Being able to approach an unknown word one syllable at a time makes the task of decoding the word much easier. The VCCV pattern presents fewer difficulties than its VCV counterpart. Although digraphs and blends may be tricky at first, students soon learn to divide between consonants. By contrast, the VCV pattern is sometimes divided before the consonant and sometimes after, depending on whether the syllable is open or closed (<u>to</u>•<u>ken</u>, <u>top</u>•<u>ic</u>). When they encounter such words, students should first try making the syllable division before the consonant and applying a long vowel sound. If this does not result in a familiar word, the syllable should be considered closed and the division made after the consonant. Such flexibility in reading unknown words with a VCV pattern is important. I have frequently observed students at the syllable juncture stage puzzle over words that could easily have been identified if the students had had some understanding of the way syllables are joined.

Syllable Stress

Moving from Structure Study to Stress Study			Words: pp. 234–235
VCV open pi<u>ra</u>te, be<u>yo</u>nd	**VCCV** ca<u>ctu</u>s, en<u>jo</u>y	**doublet** r<u>a</u>bbit, <u>a</u>tta<u>ck</u>	
stress 1 pirate cactus rabbit		**stress 2** beyond enjoy attack	

After students have gained an understanding of the patterns that extend across syllable boundaries, they are ready to learn about syllable stress, or accent. A good way to introduce the study of stress is with first names—*KATH•y*. Students enjoy using their names and can quickly tell if someone is stressing the wrong syllable. *Homographs*, words spelled alike that have different pronunciations and different meanings (*OB•ject* and *ob•JECT*), also work well. Additionally, they provide an opportunity to link pronunciation to meaning. Polysyllabic homographs tend to be accented on the first syllable when used as nouns and on the second when used as verbs. For further information, see the section on homographs under "Other Features for Study."

Identifying the stressed syllable in words other than names and homographs is difficult for some students. There are several techniques that can help with this. "Chin-drop" is one approach well worth sharing with students. It does not work with all words or with all students, but it does with many. Students simply make a fist with their dominant hand and hold it just in front of the chin with the thumb extended (bottom up) and *almost* touching the underside of the chin. When a word is pronounced, the chin will drop slightly more with the stressed syllable, tapping the thumb. (Try it with the following words: *bacon, perform, famine, demand*.) Another strategy that works with some students is having them use the word orally in a sentence. Over time you can also help students notice that (1) the stressed syllable often has a long vowel sound— *con•TAIN*; (2) prefixes and suffixes are rarely stressed— *dis•PLEASE* and *REAL•ly*; (3) in two-syllable words, the first syllable is usually accented; and (4) syllables with a schwa vowel (sounds like "uh" but is not a short *u*) are *not* stressed. For example, compare the sounds of *a* in the following two words: *fa•TIGUE* and *PA•tient*. If all else fails, students should consult a dictionary to identify the stressed syllable. With experience, most students soon become quite adept at recognizing this emphasized part of the word.

When students are ready to examine stress in other words, select words that vary in the placement of the stress, and have your students categorize them according to first-syllable or second-syllable stress. At first, expect the task to be completed slowly, deliberately, and with mistakes; speed and accuracy will come as the students gain competence. Once they can do this with ease, give them words with more than two syllables to determine the stress. The 50 states are fun to use and enable word study to be integrated with social studies.

After students have had many opportunities to explore the stress in words, you may want to have them try a few highly challenging sorts, such as sorting by sound (stress) and pattern (across-syllable structure) simultaneously. The final categories might be:

Sorting by Structure and Stress Simultaneously				Words: pp. 234–235
open VCV 1 vacant	**open VCV** 2 polite	**VCCV** 1 custom	**VCCV** 2 contain	
open VCV 1 program	**open VCV** 2 decide	**VCCV** 1 pencil	**VCCV** 2 observe	**doublet** 1 worry

LONG VOWEL PATTERNS IN THE STRESSED SYLLABLE: FEATURE M

◆

a tablet	*aCe* bracelet	*ai* afraid	*ay* decay	**Words:** **pp. 236–241**
a perhaps	*aCe* escape	*ai* failure	*ay* maybe	open *a* labor
e effort	*ee* freedom	*ea* creature	*ie* belief	
e suggest	short *ea* leather	*ee* degree	long *ea* repeat	
e engine	*ee* asleep	*ei* ceiling	open *e* fever	
i kitchen	*iCe* excite	*igh* highway	*iCC* behind	
i chimney	(short) *y* symbol	*iCe* iceberg	(long) *y* hydrant	open *i* minus
o lobster	*oCe* compose	*oa* goalie	*oCC* postage	
o beyond	*oCe* erode	*ow* bowling	open *o* locate	
u pumpkin	*uCe* perfume	open *u* student		

Through this feature, students extend their within word pattern knowledge of vowels. Nearly all of the vowel patterns presented, except for those that are open, have already been studied. Even the open patterns are not entirely new as students have likely worked with words like *he, me, she, go, so, ho* at the previous stage. What is new is the context—namely, polysyllabic words. Since students are familiar with most of the patterns, several are contrasted at a time. Because there are often many different ways to represent a particular vowel sound, students will need to be particularly attentive to patterns during their exploration of this feature. As with all of the features, you should choose the sorts that are most appropriate for your students. Some individuals will need to complete only a few of the sorts listed; others may benefit from more extensive work with specific patterns or with a particular vowel.

A rudimentary knowledge of stress will be helpful to students, since they need to be able to identify the vowel pattern in the *stressed* syllable, and that syllable may not be the first. It is especially valuable when working with words that contain more than one of the patterns in a sort (*be̲lief* and *com̲pose*). For information on introducing syllable stress, see the section on homographs under "Other Features for Study."

R-CONTROLLED VOWELS IN THE STRESSED SYLLABLE: FEATURE N

◆

With Long and Short Vowel Patterns					Words: pp. 242–245
ar harvest	*are* declare	*air* chairman		**?** parent	
ar margin	*air* dairy	*ar* baron		**?** cherry	
er thermos	**short** *ear* early	**long** *ear* weary	*er* heron	**?** severe	
ir thirsty	*ire* desire				
or forest	*ore* ignore	*ur* purple	*ure* secure	**?** courthouse	

R-controlled vowel patterns continue to be troublesome for students at the syllable juncture stage because of their sound-alike nature. Here, too, just as with some of the other features at this stage, students must learn to recognize that this part of the word requires their attention and is particularly important to remember. Having students categorize their words by sound before moving on to examine pattern *and* sound contrasts will increase their awareness of which patterns they will be likely to confuse (see Figure 6-8).

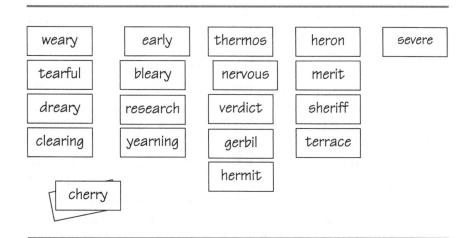

FIGURE 6–8. *R*-controlled patterns in the stressed syllable: A sound and pattern word sort.

ABSTRACT VOWELS IN THE STRESSED SYLLABLE

◆

long oo cartoon	short oo woodland	oi avoid	oy loyal	? jewel, steward	Words: p. 246
ou /ou/ county	ow /ou/ coward	au faucet	aw sawdust	? disown, lower	

As with other vowel patterns in the stressed syllable, students should already be proficient with the use of abstract vowels in single-syllable words. However, they may need reinforcement on their use in polysyllabic words. The contrasts above are just two possibilities. Redefine, limit, or expand the sorts according to your students' needs. If your students are already using this feature correctly in their writing, omit it; don't plan instruction around it just because it's here.

UNSTRESSED SYLLABLE VOWEL PATTERNS: FEATURE O

◆

Vowel patterns in unstressed syllables are some of the most difficult to spell due to the fact that sound provides no clue to the pattern. Each vowel (*a, e, i, o, u*), as well as combinations of vowels, can result in a schwa /ə/, or unstressed sound. Although this is again an aspect of the word that students must learn to focus their attention on, meaning does sometimes provide a clue to the spelling. As a result, this is a good place to integrate grammar with word study. I find books like *Many Luscious Lollipops: A Book about Adjectives* from Ruth Heller's series on parts of speech (see Figure 6-9) to be particularly helpful and interesting to students. What's more, the concepts presented in striking pictures and limited text progress from the simple to more difficult, making it possible to stop when ideas become too complex or begin in the middle and continue to the end.

I often begin the study of unstressed syllables by showing students a few words that have the same vowel pattern but a different stress. Words with *ain* work well for this. Some examples are *contain, regain, complain, explain, refrain* and *captain, certain, bargain, villain, curtain*. The stress on the *ai* in the first group provides the speller with a clear sound and narrows the possibilities for its representation to *ane, ain,* and possibly *ein*. By contrast, the unstressed context for the second set of words gives the speller little clue; there are many possibilities, including *an, en, in, on,* and *un,* none of which is correct. Although there are many ways to draw students' attention to the relative ease with which the first five words can be spelled compared to the last five, one especially effective way is to dictate words from both groups in random order and ask students to spell them. Discuss the responses when finished. Students are usually amazed to find that the same spelling pattern is used in all of them. This is a good time to point out that the unstressed syllable is definitely one that requires careful consideration.

📖 Literature Links

Heller, R. (1988). *Kites sail high: A book about verbs*. New York: Putnam & Grosset. From—"Verbs tell you something's done. Roses BLOOM and people RUN"—to a presentation of the "moods" and "voices" of verbs, this book runs the gamut.

Heller, R. (1989). *Many luscious lollipops: A book about adjectives*. New York: Putnam & Grosset. Articles, demonstratives, possessives, comparatives, superlatives, and more types of adjectives are covered.

Heller, R. (1990). *Merry-go-round: A book about nouns*. New York:Putnam & Grosset. Concrete nouns, abstract nouns, compound nouns, and how plurals are formed are addressed.

Heller, R. (1991). *Up, up and away: A book about adverbs*. New York: Putnam & Grosset. Ruth Heller's many examples clearly demonstrate the use of adverbs, a part of speech that is difficult for some students to grasp.

FIGURE 6–9. Books that highlight parts of speech.

Final /ər/				Words: pp. 247–249
er noun (person) miser	**er noun/verb** (concrete) toaster, litter	**er adj./adv.** (comparison) cheaper		**?** doctor, author
er noun (person) trooper	**er noun** (concrete) poster	**or noun** (person) sculptor	**or noun** (concrete) parlor	**?** simpler
er noun (person) archer	**er adj./adv.** (comparison) quicker	**or noun** (person) sponsor	**ar adj.** (concrete) stellar	**?** sugar, beggar

Final /ən/			
en adj. golden	**en verb** sharpen	**on noun** button	**?** chicken, raisin

Final /əl/		
al adj. legal	**el** angel	**le** angle

Here are several meaning clues and other helpful hints for spelling unstressed syllables:

1. *Final /ər/*. Words pertaining to people (agentive nouns) tend to end with either *er* or *or*. Examples: *baker* and *governor*. Adjectives are *er* (comparisons) or *ar*. Examples: *bigger* and *rectangular*.

2. *Final /ən/.* Verbs end in *en* as do most adjectives. Examples: *deafen, sharpen, wooden,* and *swollen.* If the word is a noun, your best guess is *on,* as in *ribbon, lesson, bacon,* and *melon.*

3. *Final /əl/.* Words ending with *al* tend to be adjectives. Examples: *coastal* and *bridal.* When deliberating between *el* or *le,* it's helpful to consider that many more words end with *le* than with *el.* (Word hunts can make this apparent.) The letter that precedes the "ul" should also be considered. The consonants *b, c, d, g, k, p, t,* and *z* typically team up with *le* (*bubble, uncle, needle, beagle, twinkle, staple, title,* and *fizzle*). Another possible aid to spelling the final syllable is letter-sound knowledge. For example, remembering that a *g* or *c* followed by an *e, i,* or *y* has a soft sound (/j/ or /s/), leaves the speller with little doubt about which ending (*el* or *le*) to use for words like *angel, parcel, bugle,* and *circle.*

Schwa Vowels				Words: p. 250 (pp. 236–241)
open a bacon	**schwa a** patrol	**open i** migrate	**schwa i** gossip	
open e legal	**schwa e** velour	**open o** notice	**schwa o** atom	

The above two sorts highlight the schwa as a single vowel, rather than as a common syllable pattern (*er, or, en, on, el, le*). There is not a rule that determines the spelling. However, having students examine the schwa in a variety of contexts will increase their awareness of how to pronounce syllables that contain a schwa and will sensitize them to the need to give careful study to unstressed syllables in their spelling. Figure 6-10 shows the results of a cooperative group word hunt for schwa vowels, using trade books. Note that additional unstressed syllable patterns are included in the supplemental word list section for this feature.

OTHER FEATURES FOR STUDY

◆

Plurals and Possessives

With *es* and *s*				Words: p. 252
add *s*	**add *es***			
consonant/e horns, cakes	sh/ch dishes, inches	ss/s guesses, gases	x boxes	
With consonant-y				
no change		**change y to i**		
add *s* writers, pieces	add *es* classes	add *es* flies, ladies		

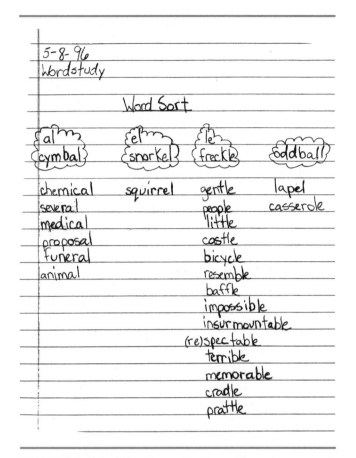

FIGURE 6–10. Word hunt findings: The schwa vowel.

After introducing students to the syllable juncture stage with a study of compound words, I often move on to *plurals*. Although plurals (words meaning more than one) are formed in different ways, there are generalizations that students can discover through their work with words that will help them avoid spelling difficulties. The three most useful are likely to be these:

1. The most common way to form a plural is to add *s* to the singular form of the noun (*cats* and *toys*).
2. Add *es* to words that end in *sh, ch, ss, s, x,* and in a very few cases *z* (*bushes, matches, guesses, buses, boxes,* and *quizzes*). When deciding between *s* and *es*, students can use sound as a clue to the correct ending. As they say the plural, if they hear a syllable *after* the base word or singular form of the word, there needs to be an *e* before the *s*, since every syllable has at least one vowel: *bush•es*, not *bushs*, and *tents*, not *tent•es*).
3. In words that end with *consonant-y*, the *y* is changed to an *i* before *es* is added (*cry/cries* and *baby/babies*). Plurals are formed with *vowel-y* words by simply adding *s* (*turkeys* and *valleys*).

Students may discover other generalizations about less frequently occurring plural forms. In some words with final *f*, the *f* is changed to a *v* before the *es* is added (*wife, half, leaf* → *wives, halves, leaves*). Plurals for nouns ending in *o* are sometimes formed with *s* and sometimes with *es*. Confusions are common with this type of plural form—*potatos* or *potatoes*? Although the more frequent pattern is *os*, there are numerous words with *oes*; encourage students to check the dictionary when making an *o*-ending word plural. For some words, the plural form is the same as the singular (*deer* and *sheep*); for others the base word itself is changed when the plural is made (*tooth/teeth* and *mouse/mice*). Marvin Terban's *Your Foot's on My Feet and Other Tricky Nouns* is an enjoyable book that highlights nearly a hundred irregular plurals.

Many students confuse *possessives*, nouns and pronouns that show ownership, with plurals (*The boys' caps were on the ground* versus *The boys walked down the road*). They erroneously include an apostrophe in a plural (*The boys' walked . . .*) and omit or misplace apostrophes in possessives (*The boys caps . . .* or *The boy's caps . . .*). The problem can usually be cleared up through writing workshop minilessons, which help students discover how possessives are formed and when to use them, and through reinforcement when students edit their writing pieces. Students are likely to notice the following:

1. For singular nouns and plural nouns that do not end in *s*, add apostrophe *s* (*girl/ girl's, house/house's,* and *children/children's*).
2. For plural nouns that end in *s*, just add the apostrophe (*cars/cars', babies/babies',* and *kittens/kittens'*).

Other generalizations are more subtle and may need to be pointed out. For example, in some words the possessive can be formed by either adding just an apostrophe or by adding *s* and the apostrophe. Most of these words are proper nouns (*Chris' book* or *Chris's book*), but some are singular nouns that end in *s* (*iris' petal* or *iris's petal* and *atlas' cover* or *atlas's cover*). Also, students will likely find it interesting to learn that an apostrophe is sometimes used to show the *plural* of numbers and letters (*1990's* and *ABC's*).

Prefixes and Suffixes

Prefixes and suffixes, also known as *affixes*, are units of meaning (morphemes) that are attached to a base word or root. In the word *rebuilding, re* is the prefix, *build* is the base word, and *ing* is the suffix. As students work with prefixes and suffixes, be sure they have opportunities to examine words that have a double consonant at the juncture of the base word and affix (*un_noticed, real_ly, thin_ness*). Words of this type encourage students to think about the base word and its affix and the fact that they are two distinct meaning units. *Mispell* is an error frequently made by students. Conscious thought that the word is comprised of a prefix, *mis* ("wrong"), and a base word, *spell,* and that the two are joined to create the word *misspell* can help students avoid this and other such errors. Exceptions, such as *relish* and *forest* below, are good to include for this same reason. These words appear to have prefixes, but in fact do not. *Re* and *fore* are merely the beginning letters of base words. Students who use sight alone to make their decisions will incorrectly categorize such words. Meaning needs to be taken into account.

Prefixes				Words: pp. 253–255
un unwrap	*re* rebuild	*dis* disarm		*?* relish
un untie, unnamed	*en* enlarge	*mis* misuse, misspell		*?* misty
re retrace	*in* indoor, inflame	*fore* forehead	*pre* precut	*?* forest

Suffixes				
ful earful	*less* careless	*ness* coolness	*ly* loudly, really	*?* apply, belly

Unlike suffixes such as *ed* and *ing* that begin with a vowel, those that start with a consonant rarely require *e*-drop or doubling. Rather than telling students this, you can help them discover the difference. Choose base words, such as those below, to which both types of suffixes can be added. Ask students to sort the words with the vowel-beginning suffix into *e-drop*, *double*, and *no change* categories. When finished, they can match the second set of words with the first (see below), and then discuss their observations. You may want to have students highlight the suffix in each word prior to the discussion in order to draw their attention to the remaining letters of the base word.

E-drop	(No change)	Double	(No change)		No change
braver	bravely	sadder	sadly	deeper	deeply
closer	closely	hotter	hotly	cheaper	cheaply
later	lately	flatter	flatly	shorter	shortly
wider	widely			harder	hardly

E-Drop, Double, and No Change with Suffixes		
no change + er/est smaller, cheapest	**e-drop + er/est** wider, closest	**double + er/est** flatter, saddest
no change + y grouchy	**e-drop + y** shaky	**double + y** yummy

The final suffix comparison is more difficult because it involves two-syllable base words. You may want to reserve it for later in the stage.

Spelling Changes with Suffixes—*y* to *i*			
y to i + est noisiest	**y to i + ful** beautiful	**y to i + ness** happiness	**y to i + ly** busily

Homographs

Homographs are words that are spelled alike but that have different pronunciations and different meanings—*read/read, bow/bow*. Polysyllabic homographs, like those discussed in this section, are a good way to introduce students to syllable stress (see feature L) because the differences in their pronunciation stem directly from stress variations—ADdress and adDRESS. The study of stress is important for both spelling and reading. Being able to identify which syllable is stressed and which is not aids students in learning to spell words. In reading, knowing how to shift the stress from one syllable to another helps students decode words they have heard before but are unable to identify in print.

Homographs		Words: p. 256
stress 1	**stress 2**	
address (residence)	address (to direct words to)	
desert (dry place)	desert (to go away from)	
object (a thing)	object (to oppose)	
present (gift)	present (to give to)	
convict (criminal)	convict (to prove guilty)	
minute (60 seconds)	minute (tiny)	

Homographs can also be used to focus students' attention on meaning connections related to stress placement. For example, in two-syllable homographs, nouns typically have a stress on the first syllable and verbs on the second; adjectives vary. To examine this concept with students, ask them to sort homographs into stress-related categories (stress 1 or 2), going with the pronunciation and meaning that first comes to mind. Share and discuss their results and observations.

More Homophones

Homophones of more than one syllable are studied at this stage. Although meaning is a central issue, students can also key their attention to spelling differences by categorizing their words according to where the spelling variation occurs—stressed syllable, unstressed syllable, or both. Card games like Concentration and Homophone Rummy can be used to reinforce understandings. For Homophone Rummy directions and a list of homophone and word play books, see "Other Features for Study" in Chapter 5.

Identifying Spelling Differences in Homophones			Words: p. 257
stressed 1		**stressed 2**	
morning mourning		review revue	
unstressed 1		**unstressed 2**	
accept except		bridal bridle	
unstressed 1	**unstressed 2**	**stressed & unstressed**	
affect effect	council counsel	cymbal symbol	

Final /k/ Sound Revisited

At the within word pattern stage, students examined words ending in *ck, ke,* and *k.* Two new patterns for the final /k/ sound occur in polysyllabic words: *c* and *que.* They provide an opportunity for students to take a second look at this feature during their syllable juncture experiences. The *c* spelling is by far the most common pattern in polysyllabic words. Many words of this type are adjective forms of base words (*angelic, graphic, allergic, atmospheric*). Although *que* is relatively uncommon, its unique spelling makes it interesting to study.

ck	*ke*	*k*	*c*		**Words:**
seasick	awake	remark	plastic		**p. 258**
ck	*ke*	*k*	*c*	*que*	
hammock	dislike	cornstalk	cubic	antique	

The inflectional *ed* and *ing* endings are sometimes added to certain of the *c* words. These present a special challenge worth investigating. In order to maintain the /k/ sound before the *e* or *i* that follows, the letter *k* must be added. Thus, it is not *picnicing,* or *panicing,* but *picnicking, panicking, frolicking,* and so on.

◆

CHAPTER 7

Derivational Constancy
Word Study

A small group of students complete a blind sort.

A student records words during a cooperative group word hunt.

Chapter at a Glance

◆

Students who reach this final stage of spelling development are proficient readers and writers. Many of the words they encounter in their reading are of lower frequency and of Greek and Latin origin. For example, a random selection of four consecutive pages from books enjoyed by skilled readers in the upper-elementary and middle-school grades produced the following Latin- and Greek-based words:

Redwall by Brian Jacques (1986)—fantasy, Chapter 1: cloisters, novice, enormous, Abbot, immediately, solemnly, expression, dignity, humility, experience, sedate, conversed, nonchalantly, successive, generation, magnificent, chronicle, impressive, admiration, courageous, orphaned, victorious, transformed, vocation, impoverished, ambitions, celebrate, benignly.

The Witch of Blackbird Pond by Elizabeth George Speare (1958)—historical fiction, Chapter 15: occasionally, demonstration, governor, opposite, commanding, cavalier, elegantly, defiance, reception, discipline, magnificence, procession, confidence, resignation, presence, sanctuary, astonishment, reverently, disappeared, afford, annexed, appointed, acknowledged.

Eleanor Roosevelt: A Life of Discovery (Freedman, 1993)—biography, Chapter 4: complexion, cordially, assassin's, reception, expedition, relative, admission, inadmissible, exuberant, strenuous, eligible, disappoint, attentive, confided, respectable, inexperienced, solemnity, suspected.

Clearly, a well-developed vocabulary is needed for students to comprehend such text. Strategic knowledge is also important. Context clues—other words in the sentence or paragraph—are one aid to word recognition and meaning that students should use. Structural analysis—identifying meaningful word parts (base word, root, prefixes, and suffixes)—is a second. At the derivational constancy stage, students become aware of another strategy for understanding and spelling words—the spelling–meaning connection.

The principle that words related in meaning tend to be related in spelling is a powerful one (Templeton, 1983). Sounds that are obscure and give no clue to spelling in one word are often obvious in a related form, as in *relative/relate* and *solemn/solemnity*. Students can clear up many spelling confusions by associating related words. Spelling/meaning connections also aid students' memory and understanding of new vocabulary. Consider the likely unfamiliar words *sedate* and *impoverished* from *Redwall*. Students who are familiar with *sedative*, *sedentary*, or *poverty* can use their knowledge of these words to grasp and remember the two previous words.

Because much of the focus at this stage is on derivationally related words, in the spelling feature discussions that follow, *pairs* of words are often presented. This makes it easier for you and students to detect the relationships. The first features addressed in this chapter are those that involve changes in consonant or vowel sounds (*haste/hasten, critic/criticize, invite/invitation*). Later feature studies extend students' understanding of previously explored features, such as suffixes and prefixes, and initiate an examination of Greek and Latin roots. As at other stages, be sensitive to your students' needs. Some groups of students may understand a feature after just a few sorts, other may need more.

SILENT AND SOUNDED CONSONANTS: FEATURE P

◆

silent	sounded	Words:
musc**l**e	musc**u**lar	p. 261

This feature looks at words that have a sounded consonant in one word and a silent one in another, as in *condemn/condemnation* and *benign/benignant*. Although the list of words for this feature is not extensive, "Silent and Sounded Consonants" provides an excellent starting point for study at this stage of spelling development. An awareness of the relative ease of spelling the "sounded" word compared to the "unsounded" encourages learners to consider derived forms when trying to spell words. Most students do not make such connections on their own.

CONSONANT CHANGES (ALTERNATIONS): FEATURE Q

◆

Consonant alternations usually involve a sound change within related words. Compare the sounds of *t* in *instruct* and *instruction* or *c* in *office* and *official*. Students who are aware of derivational constancies think about the meaning connections between related words when they try to spell difficult words. They know that sound is not a reliable clue (*discussion*, not DISCUSSION; *criticize*, not CRITISIZE). Although consonant alternations sometimes require spelling changes, these tend to be predictable and can be approached through a study of word families. Notice, for example, the consistency of the spelling changes in the following group of words—*assume/assumption, consume/consumption, resume/resumption*).

		/shən/		Words: pp. 262–266
t direct	*t + ion* direction	*ss* express	*ss + ion* expression	
t adopt	*t + ion* adoption	*c* magic	*c + ian* magician	**?** tempt, temptation
te educate	*e-drop + ion* education	*se* televise	*e-drop + ion* television	
de explode	*de-drop + sion* explosion	*d* extend	*d-drop + sion* extension	
Predictable Spelling Changes by Word Family				
t admit permit omit	*t-drop + ssion* admission permission omission	*be* describe prescribe inscribe	*be-drop + ption* description prescription inscription	
Other Alternations with c, ce, and t				
ce office	*e-drop + ial* official	*t* part	*t + ial* partial	**?** essence, essential
ce malice	*e-drop + ious* malicious	*c* public	*c + ize* publicize	

When you walk students through this feature, be sure to provide them with both forms of the word. One way to approach the exploration is to ask students to pair up the words, then have them check for sound or pattern consistencies that can be used to further subdivide the list. Once this is accomplished, discuss their findings and see if any generalizations can be made. For example, in Figure 7-1 students are likely to notice that even though there is a change in sound between the base word and its derived form, the spelling remains constant *object/objection* and *magic/magician*. They may also discover that the final syllable is pronounced /shən/ regardless of whether *ion* or *ian* is used, and that *ian* signals a person *(musician)*. You can reinforce their understanding of the latter by talking about other *ian* words, like *Egyptian, librarian, Indian*.

When students engage in word hunts with this feature (and others that involve related words), have them find one form of the word and then generate the other through discussion. This encourages group problem solving and leads to the clarification of ideas. I once observed a small group of fifth graders cooperating on a hunt of this type. After successfully finding the word *educate* and quickly making the match, *education*, they were

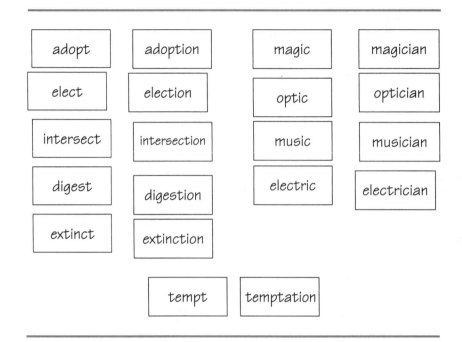

FIGURE 7–1. Discovering spelling-meaning connections in words with consonant alternations.

puzzling over a newly found word—*publication*. Although "publicate" had been suggested as the match, some group members rejected it. A lively discussion followed, and soon *publish* was established as the appropriate choice.

VOWEL CHANGES (ALTERNATIONS): FEATURE R

◆

Most vowel alternations entail a change in the sound of a vowel pattern from one related word to another, but no change in spelling. Vowels alter from long to short (*pl*e*ase/pl*e*as-ant*), long to schwa (*able/ability*), and schwa to short or short to schwa (*mobile/mobility* or *prohibit/prohibition*). (Alternations of the last type are grouped together in this book under the heading "short to schwa.") As at the syllable juncture stage, words with a schwa are the source of numerous spelling difficulties because sound is no help. For example, when writing a word like *definition*, students often wonder whether to use an *a, e, i, o,* or *u* in the second syllable. To gain a clue to the correct spelling, they need only think of a related word where the vowel sound is clear—*define*. Like consonant alternations, vowel alternations occasionally require spelling changes. However, these tend to involve families of words and are therefore predictable.

When students first begin to work with vowel alternations, be sure that they have access to both forms of the word. As they develop the habit of thinking of a related word,

Long to Short			
long *a* volc<u>a</u>no	**short *a*** volc<u>a</u>nic	**long *e*** athl<u>e</u>te	**short *e*** athl<u>e</u>tic
long *i* rev<u>i</u>se	**short *i*** rev<u>i</u>sion	**long *u*** prod<u>u</u>ce	**short *u*** prod<u>u</u>ction

Long to Schwa			
long *a* rel<u>a</u>te	***a* (schwa)** rel<u>a</u>tive	**long *i*** comb<u>i</u>ne	***i* (schwa)** comb<u>i</u>nation
long *o* opp<u>o</u>se	***o* (schwa)** opp<u>o</u>sition	**long *e*** com<u>e</u>dian	***e* (schwa)** com<u>e</u>dy

Short to Schwa			
short *a* emph<u>a</u>tic	***a* (schwa)** emph<u>a</u>sis	**short *e*** exc<u>e</u>l	***e* (schwa)** exc<u>e</u>llent
short *i* crit<u>i</u>c	***i* (schwa)** crit<u>i</u>cize	**short *o*** ec<u>o</u>logy	***o* (schwa)** ec<u>o</u>logical

Words: pp. 267–268

the partner words with their obvious spellings can be phased out. I sometimes introduce this feature with a dictation. I select six to eight words with alternations and dictate them to the students. Examples include *preparation*, *stability*, *comedy*, *combination*, *definition*, and *restoration*. Usually few, if any, of the students think that they have spelled all the words correctly. I go over the correct spellings with them, and we discuss the part of the word that gave them the most difficulty. Invariably, it is the schwa. In fact, even in a small group of students, you're likely to find that all five vowels were tried for some of the words. I then demonstrate the value of a related word by eliciting from them match-ups for the dictated words—*prepare/preparation*, and so on. These are written on the chalkboard, transparency, or word cards for their viewing. Students (and adults) are usually delighted to make this meaning connection and motivated to discover other word applications.

With Predictable Spelling Changes					
		y → i			
		classify	classification		
		certify	classification		
ai → a		***ai → e***		***ei → e***	
exclaim	exclamation	detain	detention	receive	reception
explain	explanation	retain	retention	deceive	deception

LATIN-DERIVED SUFFIXES: FEATURE S

◆

able and *ible*			Words: pp. 269–275
base + *able* afford affordable	**root + *ible*** aud- audible	**?** impecc- impeccable	
base + *able* prefer preferable	**e-drop + *able*** excite excitable	**?** notice noticeable change changeable	
e-drop + *able* measure measurable	**ate-drop + *able*** separate separable	**y to *i* + *able*** certify certifiable	

ant/ance/ancy and *ent/ence/ency*		
ant brilliant	*ance* brilliance	*ancy* brilliancy
ent emergent	*ence* emergence	*ency* emergency

ary, *ery*, and *ory*		
ary honorary	*ory* territory	*ary*, *ery*, *ory* salary, surgery, memory

ity		
base + *ity* **no change** original originality	**e-drop** extreme extremity	***ble → bil*** sensible sensibility

At the syllable juncture stage students learned to join basic suffixes (like *ly*, *ful*, and *er*) to base words and to understand how their addition affects the word meaning. Here, students expand their knowledge by exploring suffixes that often sound alike (*able/ible* and *ant/ent*). Sometimes there are principles at work, and an understanding of them can aid students' spelling. At other times, students simply need to realize that this is the part of the word that is likely to be confused during writing and will need their attention.

Consider *able* and *ible*, for example. Generally, when the suffix follows a base word, *able* is used—*reasonable*. If it follows a root that is not a full word, *ible* is used—*feasible* (see Figure 7-2). There are exceptions, but these are sometimes predictable. For example, roots sometimes require *able* in order to maintain a hard *c* sound: *amicable* and *impeccable*. With base words, a soft *c* or *g* is usually preserved by retaining the final *e* before adding *able* (*changeable* and *serviceable*), rather than by adding *ible*. The suffix also varies for words ending in *se* and *consonant-t*; it is best to check the dictionary for these.

The suffixes *ant/ent*, *ance/ence*, and *ancy/ency* can be particularly troublesome. It does help to realize that if you can spell one form of the word, you can spell the rest since

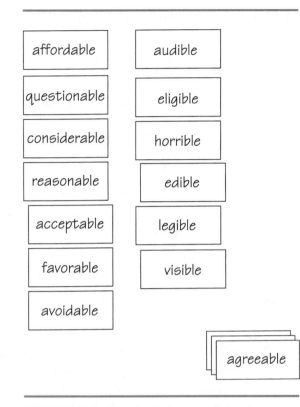

FIGURE 7-2. Categorizing words by pattern to discover consistencies in the use of *able* and *ible*.

the vowel remains constant (*relevant, relevance, relevancy*). Because of this consistency across forms, these suffixes are best studied as separate families—those with *ant/ance/ancy* as a group and those with *ent/ence/ency* as another—before they are compared.

When students address this feature in their studies, I like to share Cathi Hepworth's book, *Antics*. Although it is an alphabet book, more mature audiences best appreciate its humor. Each letter of the alphabet introduces a word with the letters *ant* in it. The letters do not represent suffixes in many of the words, but Cathi Hepworth's wonderful, detailed illustrations that depict the meanings of such words as *brilliant, deviant, hesitant, nonchalant,* and *observant* through ant-like characters are well worth a look. Students may enjoy creating their own illustrations for other *ant* (or *ent*) words.

Words ending in vowel-*ry* vary in difficulty. For some, the appropriate ending is relatively easy to determine because sound provides a hint (*monetary, necessary, customary,* and *allegory, category, dormitory*). Others are more challenging due to the schwa (*boundary, treachery, accessory*).

The suffix *ity* can also be problematic. Students frequently misrepresent it as *ety* or *aty*. Highlight the correct spelling by having them examine words with the suffix. The *ity* contrasts presented at left will help students learn how the suffix attaches to different words.

OTHER FEATURES FOR STUDY

◆

Doubling with Polysyllabic Base Words

With *ed* and *ing*			Words: p. 276
double propelled	**no change** explained existed limited	**?** *exhibited*	
double beginning	**no change** repeating collecting entering	**?** *inhabiting*	
With Other Suffixes			
double regrettable	**no change** appearance supporter honorable reference	**?** *regretful* *developed*	

At some point during the derivational constancy stage, students need to reexamine the doubling principle with a focus on polysyllabic base words. Base words of more than one syllable introduce a new player to the doubling scene—syllable stress. Words with a single vowel preceding a single final consonant still require doubling when the suffix starts with a vowel, but only if an additional condition is met. The final syllable of the base word must be stressed. So, for example, in *ocCURred, ocCURring, ocCURrence, reFERred,* and *reFERring,* doubling takes place, but in *REFerence* it does not. This is a valuable feature for students to study and one soon grasped with experience.

To heighten students' interest in learning how doubling works with polysyllabic words, begin this feature study by dictating several words that do and don't require doubling (be sure the stressed syllable varies). Go over the responses, but do not discuss the principles at work. Students will likely have numerous doubling-related errors. Then say something like "Doubling is a little more tricky when you're dealing with base words of two or more syllables. Today as you work with your words I want you to try to discover a way to tell when you should and should not double the final consonant." Have students explore their words through an open sort, or guide them through their investigation by asking them to start with a sound sort based on syllable stress. Students can self-check their word placements by reading aloud each group of words (see Figure 7-3). A misplaced word upsets the rhythm of an otherwise steady syllable beat. Next, suggest that students look for pattern consistencies in each column by focusing on the final syllable of the base word. Have them subdivide the stress categories to reflect these patterns (see Figure 7-4). Discuss the results and possible generalizations for when to add *ed* to polysyllabic words. If necessary, prompt students to consider both sound and pattern characteristics. The response of keen observers may be something like "Add *ed* to a word that has more than one syllable, when the final syllable ends in one consonant, has one vowel, and is stressed." As a follow-up, you may want to return to the initial set of dictated words and see if students understand their errors.

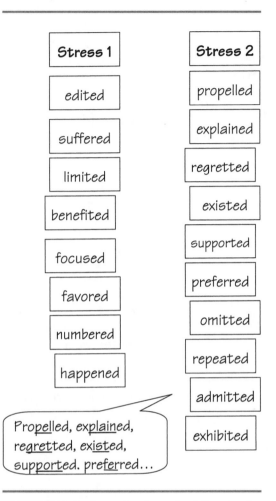

FIGURE 7–3. Learning how doubling works with polysyllabic base words—starting with sound (syllable stress).

When you select words for this feature, be sure that the "no change" category includes words with a first syllable stress (such as, *LIMited, ENtering, HONorable*) as well as words with a stress on the final syllable of the base that do not end in a single consonant or do not have just one vowel (such as *exISTed, colLECTing, supPORTer, exPLAINed, apPEARance*). The "?" words encourage students to think and assist them in drawing *accurate* conclusions about the principle at work. For example, the three-syllable base word in the sort in Figure 7-3 (*exhibited*) helps student recognize the *final* syllable as the one that must be stressed for doubling to occur, not the second. When students classify a word like *exhibited* or *developed* as an oddball, they are likely to generalize that doubling occurs when the second syllable of the base word is stressed. As you discuss their generalization, ask them if there is a way to refine it so that there are no exceptions.

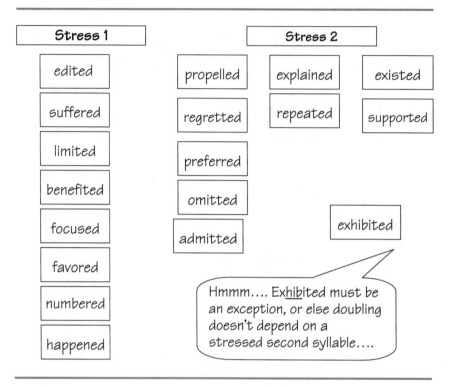

FIGURE 7–4. Learning how doubling works with polysyllabic base words–moving on to a focus on sound (syllable stress) and pattern.

You should note that base words that end in *el* can usually be written with either a doubled final consonant or without, regardless of the stress (*traveled* or *travelled* and *canceled* or *cancelled*).

More Homographs

The rime *ate*, which is very common in single-syllable words (*plate* and *date*), also occurs frequently in polysyllabic words (*dedicate, confiscate*). Many of these *ate* words are homographs, words that are spelled alike but have different pronunciations and different meanings, as in <u>separate</u> *the clean clothes from the dirty* and *they went their* <u>separate</u> *ways*. Unlike the homographs presented in Chapter 6, the *ate* family does not involve a shift in stress from one word to the other, just a change in vowel sound. In the verb form the *a* is long; in the adjective and noun forms it changes to a short *i*. To aid students' reading and writing of this type of word, share a couple of examples and then have students brainstorm or hunt for others.

Words:
p. 277

More Plurals

Words:
p. 278

Numerous Latin-based words form plurals in ways other than those discussed in Chapter 6. These words include *crisis/crises*, *bacterium/bacteria*, *persona/personae*, and *radius/radii*. Many of them relate to scientific terminology. Students at the derivational constancy stage are ready to learn such alternate plural forms and usually enjoy their novelty. Adding the customary *s* or *es* is often an option, as in *hippopotamus*, *hippopotami*, and *hippopotamuses*. Students may recall or come across other unusual plural forms in their reading, like *beau/beaux* and *chateau/chateaux* or *virtuoso/virtuosi* and *antipasto/antipasti*.

ASSIMILATED (ABSORBED) PREFIXES: FEATURE T

◆

Often, in words of Latin origin, the final letter of a prefix is *assimilated*, or absorbed, into the base or root that follows it, resulting in a double consonant—*in + literate = illiterate*. Unlike many of the syllable juncture doubling dilemmas, this type of issue is best resolved through meaning. For example, writers who know that *irresponsible* means "*not* responsible" realize that two *r*'s are needed to maintain the meaning connection. This spelling feature is the most difficult one assessed by the Developmental Spelling Analysis (Ganske, 1999). Indeed, students need considerable prior knowledge about affixation and word roots in order to explore the feature completely. Because meaning connections are more obvious between prefixes and base words, feature work should start with these and then move on to prefixes and roots—*im*mature ("not mature") versus *im*mense ("not measured").

Assimilation with Base Words		
Words: pp. 279–283

in "not"

in + base	*il* + *l*-base
in + correct = incorrect	*in* + legal = i*l*legal
in + numerable = innumerable	

im + *m*-base	*ir* + *r*-base
in + mortal = i*m*mortal	*in* + relevant = i*r*relevant

ad "to, toward"	*com* "with, together"	*sub* "under, lower"
ad	*com*	*sub*
adjoin	compassion	subconscious
account	co*l*league	su*f*fix
a*f*fix	connote	su*p*press
approve	correspond	surround

dis "opposite of, apart"	*ex* "out, from"	*ob* "toward, against"
dis	*ex*	*ob*
disadvantage	exterminate	obnoxious
dissatisfy	e*f*fuse	o*f*fend
di*f*fuse		o*p*position

A good place to begin exploration of this feature is with the prefix *in*, because it is prevalent in both assimilated and nonassimilated forms. Words of the latter type should include examples like *innumerable*, where a doubled consonant results even though there is no assimilation. Introduce the sort by asking students to examine their words for consistencies. They are likely to notice that some have a doubled consonant and some do not and that all of the words start with the letter *i*. Due to its disguise, they may not realize that the prefix *in* is present in all of the words. If they don't, suggest that they consider meaning to discover other similarities and differences. Ultimately, they should recognize the meaning connection ("not" in this case) and hypothesize that the spelling of the base word has influenced the spelling of the prefix. Point out that at one time the prefix was spelled *i-n* in all of the words. But because speech tended to blend the last letter of the prefix in some words with the beginning of the base, the spelling eventually changed to match the way people pronounced the word. Students may want to try saying a few of the words with assimilated prefixes as they were originally written to see how awkward it is—*inmeasureable* and *inlogical*—and to notice how the tongue has a natural tendency to want to merge the two sounds.

Before students examine assimilation with roots, they should have opportunities to learn about Greek and Latin roots. This integration will provide students with the necessary scaffolding to understand the meaning connection, and thus the assimilation, in words like *immense*. A working knowledge of prefixes, roots, and their assimilation enables students to unravel words that may otherwise seem a tangle of doubled consonants and helps them remember their spellings—*accommodate* = *ad* + *com* + *mod* + *ate* (two prefixes + the root + the verb ending. Recognition of such meaningful word parts also aids students in comprehending and recalling word meanings.

Assimilation with Roots			Words: pp. 279–283
	ad, com, in		
ad	**com**	**in**	
adhesive	companion	incubate	
addict	commemorate	innate	
accept	collision	illuminate	
affable	corruption	immerse	
apprehend	connection	irrigation	
	dis, ex, ob, sub		
dis	**ex**	**ob**	**sub**
disdain	excavate	obstruct	subjugate
disseminate	efficient	occasion	succinct
difference	eccentric	offensive	suffocate
		opportunity	suggestion

If the etymological, or derivational, information presented in dictionary entries is unfamiliar to students, this is a prime time to introduce it. Not only will it help them trace the assimilation of the prefix and base word or root; it will also provide them with root meanings. Word etymologies are presented in brackets immediately after the pronunciation in some dictionaries and at the end of the entry in others.

GREEK AND LATIN ROOTS

◆

Number-Related Prefixes			Words: pp. 284–297
mono monorail	**bi** biweekly	**tri** triangle	
penta pentagon	**octa** octagonal	**deca** decade	
uni unicycle	**quad(ri)** quadrangle	**cent(i)** centennial	

Study of Common Greek Roots (*cycl* and *auto*)

Continue study with other common Greek roots.

Study of Common Latin Roots (*aud* and *spect*)

Continue study with other common Latin roots.

Further Study of Prefixes

Study of Less Common Roots (*fer* and *miss/mit*)

Continue study with other less common roots.

Roots are meaningful parts of words to which affixes (prefixes and suffixes) are added. Roots and affixes are *morphemes*—namely, the smallest meaning units. Morphemes are either *free* or *bound*. Free morphemes are independent and can stand by themselves (*read, taste*). They are known as base words or *root words*. By contrast, bound morphemes are nonwords. Word roots and affixes are bound morphemes; they are dependent and cannot stand alone. Consider two examples. The word *tapes* has two morphemes—*tape*, which is free; and *s*, which is a bound morpheme used to indicate a plural. By contrast, although *inaudible* has no free morpheme, it does have three bound morphemes—the prefix *in*, which means "not"; the suffix *ible*, which means "able"; and the root *aud*, which comes from a Latin word meaning "to hear."

Many words in English have been borrowed from the Greek and Latin languages and share common roots. As a result, families of words abound. By organizing vocabulary study around these root families, students have opportunities to explore the meanings of roots and to extend their understanding to unfamiliar words through the use of analogy. For example, *spect* is a Latin root that means "look"; knowing this, makes it easy for students to deduce that all of the following words have something to do with looking: *spectator, spectacles, inspector, specter,* and *circumspect.* Furthermore, if they understand prefixes and suffixes, students can no doubt come close to figuring out the actual meaning of each word.

Upper-grade-level students typically encounter many new and highly complex words in their content studies. Students who can apply their knowledge of roots to the tasks of identifying words and building vocabulary have an edge up on those who cannot. I often use the "root analogy" strategy in my own reading and find it a relatively easy way to determine the meanings of unfamiliar words and to remember them. The more I learn about roots, the more I am impressed with what a valuable strategy this is. How regrettable that its use isn't as commonplace in upper-level classrooms as is the memorization of isolated word lists!

Number-related prefixes are a good prelude to the study of roots. Their meanings tend to be obvious, and by this time students are likely very familiar with the concept of a prefix as a meaning unit. These two conditions facilitate students' investigations of meaning relationships. I generally target two or three prefixes at a time (see above). After presenting students with some examples, I invite them to contribute their own exemplars to the prefix categories. This is followed by a discussion of their observations.

Word webs (Figure 7-5) can also be used to help students make connections among words with the same prefix or root. Students may be familiar with this strategy from the "webbing" or "clustering" often used during process writing. If so, little modeling will be needed. Beginning with a root or prefix, students brainstorm other words with the same word part and expand the web by writing down their word associations.

As you move to the study of roots from prefixes, focus on those of Greek origin first. In general, they have more evident meanings than do those of Latin origin. For example, compare *sphere*, *therm*, *graph*, *photo*, and *scope* to *cred*, *fid*, *jest*, *ject*, and *mem*. After deciding on two or three roots to examine, select several words that highlight each. Then use a think-aloud strategy to model the process of inferring the meaning of an unfamiliar

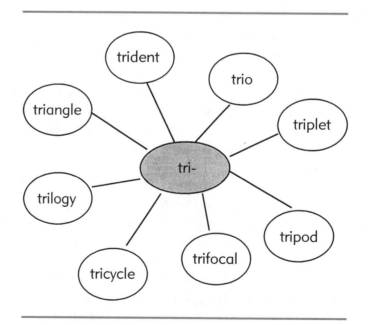

FIGURE 7–5. Word web for the prefix *tri*.

critimal: an animal that is picky, or critical. "The *critimal* did not like his food today."

spectivore: a slimy creature that eats glasses. It can travel on both land and sea. "The *spectivore* was last seen eating sunglasses on the sandy beach."

FIGURE 7-6. Create-a-word results by derivational constancy spellers.

word by using knowledge of the root in a known word. With repeated modeling, students will soon enjoy using this strategy to unlock the meanings of new words themselves. Even a very challenging word like *somnambulate* becomes comprehensible to older students who, in groups or individually, associate it with other words that have the same root(s). By relating the first part of the word to *insomnia*, which means "not sleeping," and the second to words like *amble, ambulance,* and *ambulate*, which have to do with "walking" or "moving about," students soon discover that *somnambulate* means "to sleepwalk."

Create-a-word is an enjoyable activity for students during their study of Greek and Latin roots. Using one or more of the roots being studied, students create a new word. They can create a dictionary entry for the word, including such information as pronunciation, part of speech, meaning, a sentence example, and even an illustration (Figure 7-6). The class collection of novel words can be compiled into a Dictionary of the Future.

After students have studied numerous roots, have them try making a family tree (see Figure 7-7). This is a challenging activity and is best done in cooperative groups with large-sized paper, such as that used for bulletin boards. Students begin with a word and build word families down and out from that word in the style of a traditional family tree. Venn diagrams can also be used for this sort of related word activity (see Figure 7-8).

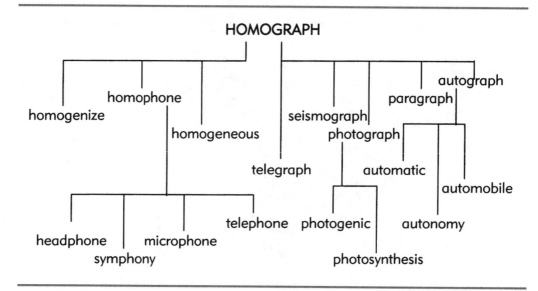

FIGURE 7-7. Root family tree for *homograph*.

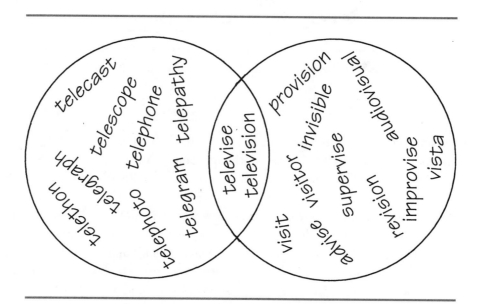

FIGURE 7-8. Venn diagram of words related to *televise*.

CHAPTER 8

◆

Questions and Answers

An activity like "fishing for letters" helps this kindergartner learn to recognize letters of the alphabet.

185

While reviewing questions that teachers and future teachers often ask me about word study, I discovered a few that either haven't been addressed in previous chapters or that warrant a more detailed discussion. Here they are:

What's the best way to organize the word sorts I make? This is a good question and one I failed to consider the first year I started creating word sorts for my students. Caught up in the children's enthusiasm and the advances they were making, I simply put a rubber band around old sets of word cards and stuck them in the back of a drawer—with no labels and no indication of what the completed sort looked like! I vowed to use a template the following year and to record the sorted columns on the back. I did just that and stored the originals by stage in a file folder. Over the years, I've made other refinements. Although these may not work best for you, they may spark additional ideas that will.

A template of the word cards and a copy of the words in sorted columns are musts for me. I generate both on the computer and clip them together to store in file folders. I use a separate folder for each spelling feature and identify the stage and feature on the tab. For example, sorts for the vowel–consonant–*e* feature at the within word pattern stage might be labeled "WWP—F," homophones at the same stage as "WWP—Homophones," and syllable juncture *e*-drop and doubling as "SJ—K." Some folders have only a couple of sorts in them; others have many. When I'm ready to address a particular feature, I pull out the appropriate folder and locate the sort I want to photocopy. I copy the sorted sheet as well, so that students can check their own work when they practice independently or with a buddy.

Although folders work well for me, they're not the only way to go. I know a middle-school teacher who keeps her sorts in a large three-ring binder. For easy access, she uses a plastic sleeve for each sort; the template is on one side and the sorted copy is on the other. When she is ready to address a particular feature, she removes the sleeve she wants and marks the spot for later refiling.

Saving sets of word or picture cards, especially if they have been run on card stock, is worthwhile. They are useful at centers, in game-playing, and for small group review. There are many convenient ways to store the cards. They can be placed in labeled manila envelopes or empty computer disk boxes. A three-ring notebook equipped with plastic sleeves subdivided for baseball cards is another possibility. Some teachers like to keep them in small plastic chests with drawers identified by feature (such chests are readily available where nails and other hardware are sold).

You make it sound like the sorts can be used from year to year. Can they? The likelihood is that you will have students with similar needs from year to year, unless you make a major grade-level change. When I moved from fifth grade to second, I found that numerous sorts could still be used with minor adaptations. *Adapt* is a key word, however. Even without a grade-level change, you should look over a previous year's sort before using it and consider which words may not be appropriate for the particular group of students about to work on the feature. Sorts generated on the computer are easily modified; even those that are handwritten can be altered with minimal effort. Just cut out a card from a blank template, write in the new word, and attach it to the old space with a piece of tape. You should expect to refine old sorts and add new ones, but you should not be starting from scratch every year.

So much information is new to me right now. How will I ever know enough to teach the kids? I'm not surprised if you feel there is much to learn about how words work. Knowledge about the structure of our language is not something we naturally pick up. Furthermore, it is often not included in teacher-training or recertification programs (Moats, 1995). However, you don't have to be a linguist to enhance students' understanding of words. You do need a fundamental grasp of how our orthographic system works at each stage of development *and you need to understand where your students are in their spelling development*. With these as starting points and this book as a guide, you can continue to increase your own knowledge while working with your students. Over the years, one of my most frequent (and honest) comments during word study has been "Gee, I'm not sure, but let's find out." Your interest and curiosity can provide a positive model for students' learning.

I like the idea of word study, but there are so many demands on my schedule already. How do I find the time to fit it in on a regular basis? Two words hold the answer—*priorities* and *organization*. If providing developmentally appropriate instruction in word study is important to you, you will find the time. The only day that requires a sizable block is the first day, when you introduce the feature. Twenty minutes is reasonable for a word walk, but you should definitely keep track of time and bring closure to the small group session after twenty minutes have elapsed. It's easy to lose sight of how long you've been engaged, because it's interesting to observe and hear what students have to say. Once you've walked them through their words a few times, you'll be more efficient in carrying out the process. For example, you'll know how much time you can allow for discussing word meanings, how you can keep things moving during the modeling, and how much time is needed for follow-up practice. If exploring the feature takes longer than expected, have students do the follow-up sort at their desks while you meet with the next small group. Be creative. Who says you need to introduce each group's new feature the same day? Some teachers stagger the schedule. Other activities require considerably less teacher time and can often be carried out independently or with a partner. Keep in mind that you're not just helping students advance their knowledge of words so they can spell more accurately; learning to spell also strengthens students' reading (Ehri, 1998; Treiman, 1998).

One of the best ways to maximize the time you do have is to be organized. It's amazing how many minutes slide into oblivion while students, or teacher, seek materials and deliberate on the next course of action. As discussed in Chapter 3, it helps to establish a routine. When students know where to find and put materials, understand what they will need when they meet as a small group or with a partner, and know the order for various activities, they can act more independently. That means fewer interruptions for you to answer logistical questions and more time to work with individuals or small groups. Also, let the class know that when you are working with a small group, you'd like them to save their questions until you're finished.

Another way to increase time for learning about words is by integrating word study with other aspects of the curriculum in the same way that reading and writing are. This also sets the tone that word-learning can occur any time and any place there are words—during music, science, or math, while reading food labels at lunch or billboards on the way home. Words can be appreciated, puzzled over, hunted, categorized, and even created.

What do you do about words that students want to learn or that are an important part of a thematic unit but that don't fit in with the features you're studying? Theme-based studies often give rise to words that students will use a lot over the course of the unit (*rainforest, canopy, emergent layer*). As an aid to spelling, post words of this type on a wall area, or have students include them in a personal word journal, so that they are readily available for copying during written activities.

Sometimes in their theme-based studies or process writing, students think of special words they want to learn to spell (for example, *tyrannosaurus* and *boomerang*). Their enthusiasm should not be dampened, but these self-chosen extra words should be limited to one or two a week; the primary emphasis for word study should be on spelling patterns. If students are not familiar with the "look, say, cover, write, check" self-study strategy, you will need to model it to help them learn their special words. It works like this:

1. Write down the word. **Look** carefully at it while you **say** it to try to recognize any known word parts. For example, for *tyrannosaurus*, a student might associate *ty* with *by*, see the words *ran* and *no*, and recognize the word *us* at the end. The main word part that this student needs to carefully attend to is *s-a-u-r*.
2. **Cover** the word up with a card, and think about how it looks as you say it.
3. **Write** the word from memory.
4. Uncover the word to **check** your spelling.
5. Repeat steps 2 through 4 until the spelling is correct.

To monitor students' ability to spell the extra words, simply have them add the words to the bottom of their word study quiz. Since the words are few in number, individual dictation will likely be unnecessary.

What do I do about high-frequency words? High-frequency words are those that occur most frequently in students' writing and in material they read. Many of these words actually fit patterns that students will be exploring through their word sorts, such as *had, like, went, which, play,* and even *there, their,* and *they're,* and can be included in these studies. Others, like *have, said, been, one, some,* and *they,* can also be included, but as oddball words. For example, *have* can be examined when the focus is on *aCe* words—it has the pattern but not the sound—and *they* when the *ay* pattern is the focus—it has an open *a* sound like *play* but is spelled with a different pattern. Other high-frequency words can be posted a few at a time (four or five) on a wall area or in a personal word journal with the expectation that students will use the correct spelling when writing these words. On a regular basis, perhaps once a month, the words are replaced with new ones. Students who continue to have trouble spelling a word can add it to their journals or notebooks so that they can still meet the expectation of correctly spelling it. Words like *once, friend,* and *because* are good candidates for this type of approach. Some teachers prefer to focus on 6 to 10 of these high-frequency words during the occasional shortened weeks that occur in the school calendar or when a change of pace is needed. Keep in mind that the learning of these words will primarily be a matter of memorization. Therefore, be sure students know how to study them (refer to the previous response).

What are some specific activities I can do with students who are not yet at the letter name stage? A few possibilities follow, but you should also refer to the resources mentioned in Chapter 1 in the discussion on emergent spelling.

- Create individual or class alphabet books after students have been introduced to several during read-aloud times. Pictures that start with a particular letter-sound can be drawn or cut from magazines and glued to separate letter sheets.
- Have the students make "rainbow" letters. Letters are formed with a favorite colored crayon, then traced over several times with other favored colors.
- Do letter sorts, where students group letters that have been printed in different fonts (**g**, **g**, **g**) by like kind. This helps children recognize the outstanding characteristics of each letter. A computer works well to generate letter cards, or letters can be cut from magazines and newspapers and glued to cards. (See "Initial and Final Consonants" in Chapter 4 for a discussion of letter contrasts to avoid.)
- Use magnetic letters or letter cards to match uppercase and lowercase letters.
- Make an alphabet collage of a favorite letter. Letters and pictures from magazines are cut and glued to the sheet. Students may add their own drawings as well. This one is fun to do in small groups.
- Read books with rhymes aloud, like *Is Your Mama a Llama?* (Guarino, 1989) or *Each Peach Pear Plum* (Ahlberg & Ahlberg, 1978), a rhyming book that features nursery rhyme characters, and let students complete the rhyming phrase. For example: "Cinderella on the stairs, I spy Three _____."
- Play rhyming games with songs like those by Raffi, available in book, tape, and CD format.
- Recall words from a read-aloud that start with a particular letter sound, like /m/ or /s/.
- Sort pictures or real objects by their beginning sound, like /b/ and /m/.
- Sort pictures or objects by concept, such as color, shape, city/country.
- Play the "yes/no" game (see Chapter 3).

- Give students opportunities to pretend-read favorite books.
- Model morning message writing.
- Give students time to draw and "write" in a journal. (Many teachers make these by stapling sheets of paper together and adding wallpaper covers.)
- Read aloud big books and model fingerpointing for concept of word development.

What do I do about students who have difficulty learning to spell? Most importantly, find out where they are in their spelling development so that you can appropriately target instruction for them. Typically, learning disabled students who have trouble with reading and writing also have trouble with spelling. However, research has shown that most of these students make the same types of spelling errors as other students *who are at their same stage of spelling development* and advance through the same developmental sequence (Abouzeid, 1992; Worthy & Invernizzi, 1990). As a result, it is *timely* instruction, rather than unique instruction, that is the primary issue. Unfortunately, students who struggle with spelling often experience an instructional fare that is grade-level based rather than student-centered and thus not within their zone of proximal development (Vygotsky, 1978) where learning is maximized.

Once you know the student's stage of spelling development, instruction should focus on features at that stage. It may be helpful to reduce the number of words used or to make other instructional adaptations, such as being more explicit in your teaching. During the word walk, be sure to point out the sound of each of the letter sequences under study, and as you model the sort draw students' attention to similarities and differences in the categories. Make it a common practice to start with a sound sort and move on to a pattern sort so that sound–pattern relationships are made clear. It is likely to take these students longer to progress through a stage, so be sure they have plenty of opportunities to practice the sorts and apply the features in their reading and writing, and keep reviewing concepts. The sorting contrasts presented in this book encourage review. Because known concepts serve as the basis for building new understandings, previously studied features are often revisited. This type of scaffolding helps students experience much-needed success and feel in charge of their learning.

My school uses a basal speller. What can I do to incorporate word study? Again, a good starting point is to assess where your students are in their spelling development. This will enable you to identify who is likely to be bored and who frustrated by grade-level materials. Instruction should be differentiated for these students, especially the latter. Simply reducing the number of words is not the answer; if the word elements being focused on are too difficult, instruction with that feature is not appropriate. Granted, students may be able to memorize the words, often with extraordinary effort, but to what extent has orthographic knowledge increased if the words are not retained a week later? Cross-grade-level use of books in the series is one possibility for providing more developmentally appropriate instruction (Morris, Blanton, Blanton, & Perney, 1995). However, this must be at least a schoolwide decision, as other grade levels will be affected.

Word study activities, like word hunts and blind sorts, can be substituted for spelling book activities that seem of questionable value. Also, the words may be written on cards so that a word walk can be used to introduce the feature(s); an exception or contrasting sound could even be added.

The same techniques discussed above could also be used to incorporate word study into a literature-based series, when use of the spelling and phonics components is expected.

How can I involve parents in word study? Communication is an excellent starting point. Parents can best be partners in their child's word-learning when they are informed. They need to have a basic idea of how children develop a knowledge of words and know where their child is along the developmental spelling continuum. They also need to know what will be taught during word study and understand how you will determine appropriate instruction. Finally, they need concrete suggestions for helping their child at home. Parents' night, conferences, and newsletters are all avenues for educating parents.

At parents' night, you can

- Briefly describe how spelling develops and explain that learners use their knowledge of letters and sounds when they read and write.
- Let parents know you will assess their children's word-learning needs by analyzing spellings from their writing and from a dictated list of words and that the results will be discussed during conferences.
- Demonstrate or, if time allows, have parents participate in a word walk (index cards with a piece of magnetic tape on the back make it possible to model a word sort on most chalkboards).

In advance of conferences, you may want to prepare a display card for each of the spelling stages, showing the types of misspellings children are likely to make at each stage (see Chapter 1 for examples). Place the cards at the conference table, arranged from easiest to most difficult. As you discuss a particular child's performance, you can use the cards as points of reference to help parents understand where their child is along the developmental spelling continuum. Point out words in the child's writing and inventory that demonstrate strengths and weaknesses, and minimize the use of technical jargon; you want to inform parents, not overwhelm them. Have in mind a course of action for furthering the child's spelling knowledge; parents will want to know how you plan to help their child.

Newsletters are an effective way to give parents suggestions for working with their child at home. Here are a few ways you can use them for word study:

- Provide directions for specific activities, like how to play Concentration with the word cards sent home or how to use a blind or written sort to practice sorting.
- Help parents understand that invented spellings give young learners an opportunity to exercise what they know about letters and sounds and enable them to express their ideas more clearly when they write. Describe the process of inventing words so parents can help their child to do this at home, and stress the importance of being able to read back what is written.
- Make parents aware of ways to foster language appreciation and word play—for example, talking about special words and phrases during a read-aloud, drawing

attention to unusual words heard in speech or noticed in the environment, and playing games like Boggle, Pictionary, or Scrabble. Encourage them to talk to their child about words learned in school.

Parents can make a real difference in their child's word-learning. Most welcome involvement and just need to know how they can help.

What about those of us who teach middle school? I'd like to do word study, but I teach several classes and have only a limited time with each. By middle school, many students have advanced to the derivational constancy spelling stage. As an entry into word study, teachers often engage the whole class in structured minilessons that explore the spelling–meaning connection or a particular word root. For instance, a teacher may write the root *vis* and the word *television* on the chalkboard or an overhead transparency. After drawing students' attention to the meaning connection between the two, the teacher asks students to contribute other examples. These are listed under *television,* and their meaning relationship to *vis* is discussed. Students then break into small groups and use dictionaries to find more examples. Later, when the whole group reconvenes, new discoveries are discussed and added to the list. At the end of the minilesson, students copy the words and root into a journal for future reference. *NTC's Dictionary of Latin and Greek Origins* (Moore & Moore, 1997) is a particularly useful resource for this activity. It contains an alphabetical listing of roots and includes a description of words that share the root, as well as words that look like they do but don't. This makes it easy to verify the correctness of student responses.

As soon as the whole-class activity is working smoothly, greater attention can be given to meeting diverse needs. Sometime during the class period, while students read or work independently on literature responses or process writing pieces, the teacher pulls aside small groups of students who need to work on spelling features at earlier stages and walks students through the sort. Word hunts and sorting practice are incorporated into the word study routine; however, scheduling frequently differs from the elementary school setting where there is more integration of subjects, less departmentalization, and therefore greater flexibility with time. Study of a particular feature may be planned for just two or three times a week but span a two-week period. To save class time, assignments are frequently done as homework. Student helpers keep track of who has completed the work on a class roster. Students also often check each other's assignments and partner-up for quiz-taking.

As at the elementary level, informal word-learning should also be encouraged and modeled. Middle-school students usually love learning the histories of words (see Figure 8-1 for resources other than those listed in Chapter 3) and being introduced to other forms of word play, like those that follow.

- *Acronyms:* words formed from the first letters of a phrase—*radar* = <u>ra</u>dio <u>d</u>etect<u>i</u>ng <u>a</u>nd <u>r</u>anging and AIDS = <u>A</u>cquired <u>I</u>mmune <u>D</u>eficiency <u>S</u>yndrome.
- *Anagrams:* words or phrases that are made from other words or phrases by rearranging the letters—*team* and *meat* or *dread* and *adder.*

📖 Resources for Exploring Word Histories

Almond, J. (1995). *Dictionary of word origins: A history of the words, expressions and cliches we use.* Secaucus, NJ: Carol. Another good resource.

Dickson, P. (1992). *Dickson's word treasury: A connoisseur's collection of old and new, weird and wonderful, useful and outlandish words.* New York: Wiley. Although this book does not contain word histories per se, its unusual list of words makes it a useful adjunct to this type of study. The author has been collecting words throughout his adult life, and this book includes "58 museum-style displays" of words from his growing collection. There are acronyms, antonyms, synonyms, junk words, travel words, phobias (315!)....

Levitt, P. M., Burger, D. A., & Guralnick, E. S. (1990). *The weighty word book.* Boulder, CO: Manuscripts Ltd. Students will be ready to write their own word stories after hearing some of these pun-filled short stories about big words, like *expedient.* There are 26 in all.

Room, A. (1994). *NTC's dictionary of word origins.* Lincolnwood, IL: National Textbook. This book is "a comprehensive reference to the true and false origins of English words."

Tuleja, T. (1991). *Marvelous monikers: The people behind more than 400 words and expressions.* New York: Crown. *Mother Goose, Dr. Pepper, Tootsie Roll, round robin, nerd, Frisbee, Barbie doll, sequoia,* and *cereal* are just a few of the eponyms in this collection.

Many of the word origin book authors indicate that they have used the *Oxford English Dictionary* in researching their word histories. This multivolume work is available on CD-ROM (1994), published by Oxford University Press.

FIGURE 8-1. Resources for exploring word histories.

- *Malapropisms*: similar sounding words that are confused—*disguise* and *despise, prodigy* and *progeny,* or *decrease* and *decease.*
- *Oxymora:* figures of speech that juxtapose contradictory words—*deafening silence* and *sweet sorrow.*
- *Palindromes:* words, phrases, and numbers that read the same frontward and backward—*madam* and *1991.*
- *Portmanteau words*: words made by combining parts of words and their meanings—*motor* + *hotel* = *motel,* or *smoke* + *fog* = *smog.*
- *Spoonerisms*: accidental mixing-up of the beginning sounds of two words—*a well-boiled icicle* for *a well-oiled bicycle,* and *a pew noodle* for *a new poodle.*

Students will enjoy finding other examples of these special words and creating their own. Books like *Too Hot to Hoot* by Marvin Terban (1985) or *So Many Dynamos!* (1994) and

Sit on a Potato Pan, Otis (1999) by Jon Agee are sure to inspire students to write their own palindromes. Spoonerisms and malapropisms can be incorporated into writing through a character's speech.

While students learn about spoonerisms and malapropisms, they can also explore *eponyms*, words named for people. The word *spoonerism* is named after Reverend Spooner of Oxford, who was famous for using words in this way, and *malapropism* is named after a character in a play, Mrs. Malaprop, who made numerous blunders of speech. Marvin Terban's *Guppies in Tuxedoes* tells the stories of over 100 eponyms. Numerous eponymous words have their origins in figures from the Greek myths. Students can discover meaning connections between words like Vulcan/*volcano*, Arachne/*arachnid*, Mars/*martial*, and Epicurus/*epicure*.

Eponym investigations can lead to studies of the origin and meaning of students' own names. Many first names are included in the dictionary, complete with their etymologies (*Sarah*—Hebrew, "princess," or *Philip*—Greek, "fond of horses"). A resource, such as the *Concise Dictionary of First Names* (Hanks, 1997), can also be of help, as can conversations with parents. Last names have various origins. Some pertain to where the family resided (*French, Fields, Wood*), some refer to an occupation the family once had (*Cooper, Carpenter, Taylor, Archer, Smith*), and others developed from a family relationship (*Johnson* = "son of John"). Talking to family members or consulting a foreign language dictionary is helpful for last name searches, because many have origins in other languages (*Rivers* = English, but *Rios* = Spanish). The introduction of other languages during name searches may provide the impetus for discovering words that have come to us from other languages. Food-related terms are a good starting point—Spanish (*taco, tortilla, enchilada,*), German (*sauerkraut, pumpernickle*), French (*buffet, gourmet, croissant*), Italian (*cappuccino, spaghetti, macaroni*), Chinese (*chow mein*), and Japanese (*sushi*).

A FINAL WORD

◆

In order to become skilled readers and writers, learners need many opportunities to read and write for pleasure and meaningful purposes. They also need a firm understanding of the sound, pattern, and meaning relationships of English orthography, acquired through explorations of words and word play. These word journeys should be appropriately timed to maximize students' learning, but they should also foster a love of words and their use that will prompt students to continue their literacy learning. Over the years, my own word journeys have given me a real appreciation for our language. Words are amazing; they enable us to communicate, to think, and to enjoy. I can't imagine a world without them.

Chapter 1

Emergent	LN	WW	SJ	DC
k	jrep	tite	complante	invisable
t	mod	brigde	doted	confesion
lt	shad	gril	mottel	compesition
	yat	maik	disterb	iliterate
	lad	cowch	soler	hasen

Chapter 2

LN	WW	SJ	DC
1. 2	1. 0	1. 1	1. 2
2. 1	2. 0	2. 2	2. 2
3. 0	3. 1	3. 2	3. 2
4. 2	4. 2	4. 2	4. 1
5. 2	5. 0	5. 2	5. 2
6. 1	6. 0	6. 2	6. 2
7. 0	7. 2	7. 2	7. 1
8. 0	8. 2	8. 0	8. 2
9. 2	9. 0	9. 0	9. 2
10. 2	10. 2	10. 2	10. 2
11. 2	11. 2	11. 2	11. 0
12. 2	12. 2	12. 2	12. 0
13. 2	13. 0	13. 0	13. 2
14. 0	14. 0	14. 2	14. 0
15. 0	15. 2	15. 2	15. 2
16. 0	16. 0	16. 2	16. 2
17. 0	17. 2	17. 1	17. 1
18. 2	18. 0	18. 0	18. 1
19. 2	19. 2	19. 1	19. 2
20. 0	20. 0	20. 2	20. 2
21. 2	21. 2	21. 0	21. 2
22. 1	22. 2	22. 2	22. 1
23. 1	23. 2	23. 2	23. 0
24. 1	24. 1	24. 0	24. 2
25. 0	25. 0	25. 0	25. 2

Stage Score

LN	WW	SJ	DC
11	12	15	16

Features

LN	WW	SJ	DC
A 5	F 5	K 3	P 5
B 3	G 3	L 4	Q 5
C 2	H 2	M 4	R 4
D 3	I 2	N 4	S 4
E 3	J 2	O 3	T 3

FIGURE 8–2. Answers to Chapter 1 and Chapter 2 activities.

APPENDIX 1

◆ ◆ ◆

Supplemental Word Lists

Appendix at a Glance

Letter Name

INITIAL AND FINAL CONSONANTS

b		c	d		f	g
bad	club	cab	dad	wed	fad	gap
bag	crab	can	dam	clod	fan	gas
bat	crib	cap	den	glad	fat	get
bed	drab	cat	did	grid	fed	got
beg	glob	cob	dig	plod	fib	gum
bet	grab	cop	dim	sled	fig	gun
bib	grub	cub	dip	slid	fin	gang
bid	scab	cup	dog	thud	fit	gift
big	slab	cut	dot		fix	
bit	slob	camp	dud		fog	bag
bob	stab	cash	dug		fox	beg
box	stub	cast	damp		fun	big
bud		cost	dash		fast	bug
bun			deck		felt	dig
bus			dent		film	dog
but			desk		fish	fig
band			dish		fist	fog
bang			dock			hog
bank			dunk			hug
bath			dust			jog
belt						leg
bend			bad			log
best			bed			mug
bump			bid			peg
			bud			pig
bib			cod			rag
bob			cud			rug
cab			dad			tag
cob			did			tug
cub			dud			wag
dab			fad			wig
fib			fed			brag
gab			had			drag
gob			hid			flag
hub			kid			frog
jab			lad			plug
job			led			slug
lab			lid			
mob			mad			
rib			mud			
rob			nod			
rub			pad			
sob			pod			
sub			red			
tab			rid			
tub			rod			
web			sad			
blob			sod			

(cont.)

INITIAL AND FINAL CONSONANTS (*cont.*)

h	j	k	l	m		n
had	jab	keg	lap	mad	slam	nap
ham	jam	kid	led	man	slim	net
has	jet	kit	leg	map	stem	nip
hat	jig	kept	let	mat	swam	nod
hem	job	king	lid	men	swim	not
hen	jog		lip	met	them	nun
him	jug		lit	mix	trim	nut
hip	junk		log	mob		nest
his	just		lot	mom		next
hit			lug	mop		
hog			lamp	mud		bin
hop			land	mug		bun
hot			last	mask		can
hug			lend	mast		den
hum			lift	math		fan
hut			limp	melt		fin
hand			link	mend		fun
hang			lint	milk		gun
held			list	mink		hen
help			long	mint		man
hint			lost	mist		men
honk			lump	moth		on
hump			lung	much		pan
hung				must		pen
hunt						pin
hush				bum		ran
				dam		run
				dim		sun
				gum		tan
				ham		ten
				hem		van
				him		win
				hum		bran
				jam		chin
				mom		clan
				mum		grin
				ram		plan
				rim		skin
				sum		spin
				yam		than
				chum		then
				clam		thin
				drum		twin
				glum		when
				gram		
				grim		
				plum		
				skim		

(*cont.*)

INITIAL AND FINAL CONSONANTS (*cont.*)

p		r	s	t		v/w/y/z
pad	clip	rag	sad	tab	set	van
pan	crop	ran	sag	tag	sit	vent
pat	drip	rap	sap	tan	tot	vest
peg	drop	rat	sat	tap	wet	vet
pen	flap	red	set	tax	yet	
pet	flip	rib	sit	ten	brat	wag
pig	flop	rid	six	tin	chat	wax
pin	grip	rig	sip	tip	flat	web
pit	plop	rim	sob	top	shot	wet
pod	prop	rip	sod	tub	shut	wig
pop	ship	rob	sub	tug	skit	win
pot	shop	rod	sum	tank	slit	won
pup	skip	rot	sun	tent	slot	wow
pant	slap	rub	sand	test	spit	went
past	slip	run	sang	tusk	spot	west
path	snap	rut	sank		that	wind
pest	snip	raft	send	bat	trot	wing
pink	step	ramp	sent	bet		wink
pond	stop	rang	sift	bit		wish
pump	trap	rash	silk	but		with
	trip	rent	sing	cat		
	whip	rest	sink	cot		
cap		rich	soft	cut		yak
cop		ring	song	dot		yam
cup		risk	such	fat		yes
dip		romp	sung	fit		yet
gap		rump	sunk	get		yank
hip		rung		got		yelp
hop		rush		gut		
lap		rust	bus	hat		zap
lip			gas	hit		zip
map			yes	hut		zest
mop				jet		
nap				kit		
pop				let		
pup				lit		
rap				lot		
rip				mat		
sap				met		
sip				net		
tap				not		
tip				nut		
top				pat		
zap				pet		
zip				pit		
chap				pot		
chip				rat		
chop				rot		
clap				rut		
				sat		

INITIAL CONSONANT BLENDS AND DIGRAPHS

l-blends		*r*-blends		*s*-blends		Digraphs
bl	plus	**br**	grant	**sc**	stamp	**ch**
blab	plank	brag	grasp	scab	stand	chap
blob	plant	brat	grump	scan	sting	chat
blank	plump	brim	grunt	scat	stink	chin
blast		brand		scum	stomp	chip
blend	**sl**	bring		scalp	stump	chop
blink	slab	brush	**pr**	scamp	stung	chum
	slam		prod		stunt	chant
cl	slap	**cr**	prom	**sk**		chest
clam	sled	crab	prop	skid	**sw**	chimp
clap	slid	crib	print	skim	swam	chomp
clip	slim	crop	prong	skin	swim	chunk
clod	slip	craft		skip	swept	
clog	slit	cramp	**tr**	skit	swift	**sh**
club	slop	crank	trap	skunk	swing	shed
clamp	slot	crash	trim		swish	ship
clang	slug	crest	trip	**sl***	swung	shop
clash	slang	crisp	trot			shot
clasp	slant	crush	tramp	**sm**		shut
cling	slept	crust	trash	smog		shaft
cloth	sling		trend	smug		shelf
clump	slump	**dr**	trunk	smash		shift
		drag	trust			
fl		drip		**sn**		**th**
flag		drop		snag		than
flap		drug		snap		that
flat		drum		snip		them
flip		draft		snug		then
flop		drank				this
flash		drift		**sp**		
flesh		drunk		span		thank
fling				sped		thin
flint		**fr**		spin		thing
flush		frog		spit		think
		from		spot		thud
gl		fresh		spun		thump
glad		front		spank		
glob		frost		spend		**wh**
glum				spent		wham
gland		**gr**		spunk		when
		grab				whip
pl		gram		**st**		which
plan		grid		stem		
plod		grim		step		
plop		grin		stop		
plot		grip		stub		
plug		grit				
plum		grand		*See *l*-blends.*		

WORD FAMILIES ENDING IN A SINGLE CONSONANT

a		*e*	*i*		*o*	*u*
ab	**an**	**ed**	**id**	zip	**ob**	**ub**
cab	can	bed	bid	chip	bob	cub
dab	fan	fed	did	clip	cob	rub
jab	man	led	hid	drip	job	tub
nab	pan	red	kid	flip	mob	club
lab	ran	wed	lid	grip	rob	grub
tab	tan	sled	skid	ship	sob	stub
crab	van		slid	skip	blob	
grab	plan			slip	snob	**ug**
scab	than	**eg**	**ig**	snip		bug
stab		beg	big	trip	**og**	dug
	ap	keg	dig	whip	bog	hug
ad	cap	leg	fig		dog	jug
bad	lap	peg	pig	**it**	fog	mug
dad	map		rig	bit	hog	rug
fad	nap	**en**	wig	fit	jog	tug
had	rap	den	twig	hit	log	drug
lad	sap	hen		kit	frog	plug
mad	tap	men	**im**	lit		snug
pad	zap	pen	dim	pit	**op**	
sad	chap	ten	him	sit	hop	**um**
glad	clap	then	skim	skit	mop	bum
	flap	when	slim	slit	pop	gum
ag	slap		swim	spit	top	hum
bag	snap	**et**	trim		chop	drum
lag	trap	bet			crop	plum
nag		get	**in**		drop	slum
rag	**at**	jet	bin		flop	
sag	bat	let	fin		shop	**un**
tag	cat	met	pin		slop	bun
wag	fat	net	tin		stop	fun
brag	hat	pet	win			gun
drag	mat	set	chin		**ot**	run
flag	pat	wet	grin		cot	spun
snag	rat	yet	shin		dot	sun
	sat	fret	skin		got	
am	brat		spin		hot	**ut**
am	chat		thin		jot	but
dam	flat		twin		lot	cut
ham	that				not	hut
jam			**ip**		pot	nut
ram			dip		rot	rut
yam			hip		blot	shut
clam			lip		shot	
cram			rip		slot	**up**
slam			sip		spot	cup
swam			tip		trot	pup

SHORT VOWELS

a			e		i	
am	and	path	bed	melt	bid	brisk
as	ant	plan	beg	mend	big	chimp
at	ask	plank	bet	next	bin	chin
bad	band	plant	den	nest	bit	chip
bag	bang	rang	fed	pelt	did	cling
bat	bank	raft	get	pest	dig	clip
cab	bath	sand	hem	rent	dim	crib
can	blank	sang	hen	rest	dip	crisp
cap	brag	sank	jet	self	fig	dish
cat	brand	shaft	led	send	fin	drift
dad	camp	slam	leg	sent	fit	drink
dam	cash	slap	let	shed	fix	drip
fan	chap	smash	men	shelf	hid	film
fat	chat	snap	met	sled	him	fish
had	clam	spank	net	slept	hip	fist
ham	clang	stab	peg	sped	his	fling
has	clank	stamp	pen	spent	hit	flip
hat	clap	stand	pet	stem	if	gift
jab	crab	swam	red	step	in	grin
jam	cramp	tank	set	swept	is	grip
lab	crank	task	ten	tend	it	hint
lad	crash	than	web	tent	jig	inch
lap	damp	that	wed	test	kid	king
mad	dash	tramp	wet	them	lid	lift
man	draft	trap	yes	then	lip	limp
map	drag	wham	yet	went	lit	link
mat	fang		belt	wept	mix	list
pad	fast		bend	west	nip	milk
pal	flag		bent	when	pig	mink
pan	flap		best		pin	mint
pat	flash		chest		pit	mist
rag	flat		crept		rib	ping
ram	glad		crest		rid	pink
ran	grab		desk		rig	print
rap	gram		elf		rim	rich
rat	grand		end		rip	ring
sad	grasp		felt		sip	risk
sag	hand		fled		sit	shift
sat	hang		flesh		six	shin
tag	lamp		fresh		tin	ship
tan	land		held		tip	sift
tax	last		help		wig	sing
van	mask		jest		win	sink
wag	mast		kept		zip	skid
wax	math		left		blink	skim
yam	pant		lend		brim	skin
yap	past		lent		bring	skip

(cont.)

SHORT VOWELS (*cont.*)

i	o	u	
slid	bob	bud	hump
slim	box	bug	hunk
sling	cob	bun	hunt
slit	dot	bus	hush
spin	fox	but	jump
spit	got	cub	junk
sting	hop	cud	just
stink	hot	cup	lump
swift	job	cut	lung
swim	jog	dug	lush
swish	lot	fun	much
thin	mob	gum	mush
thing	mom	gun	must
this	mop	hug	plug
tilt	nod	hum	plum
trim	not	hut	plump
trip	pop	jut	plunk
twig	pot	lug	plus
twin	pox	mud	pump
twist	rob	mug	rung
whip	rot	nut	rush
which	sob	pup	rust
whiz	sod	rub	shut
wind	top	rug	skunk
wing	blob	run	slum
wink	blot	rut	slump
wish	chop	sum	slung
with	crop	sun	slush
	drop	tub	smug
	flop	tug	snug
	fond	up	spun
	plod	us	stub
	plop	blush	stump
	plot	brush	stun
	pond	bump	stung
	prod	bunk	such
	prop	club	sung
	romp	clump	sunk
	shop	clung	thud
	shot	crush	thump
	slop	drug	trust
	slot	drum	tuft
	spot	dump	tusk
	stomp	dusk	
	stop	dust	
	trot	grunt	
		gust	

WORD FAMILIES ENDING IN TWO CONSONANTS

a		e	i		o/u	u

ack
back
jack
pack
rack
sack
tack
black
crack
stack
track

all
all
ball
call
fall
hall
mall
tall
wall
small
stall

amp
camp
damp
lamp
ramp
champ
clamp
cramp
stamp
tramp

and
and
band
hand
land
sand
brand
grand
stand

ang
bang
fang

gang
hang
rang
sang
clang

ank
bank
sank
tank
yank
blank
crank
drank
plank
thank

ant
ant
pant
chant
grant
plant
slant

ash
cash
dash
mash
rash
crash
flash
smash
trash

ast
cast
fast
last
mast
past

eck
deck
neck
peck
check
fleck
speck

ell
bell
fell
jell
sell
tell
well
shell
smell
spell
swell

end
bend
end
lend
mend
send
tend
blend
spend
trend

est
best
nest
pest
rest
test
vest
west
zest
chest
crest

ick
lick
kick
pick
sick
tick
wick
brick
chick
click
flick
stick
thick
trick

iff
cliff
sniff
stiff
whiff

ill
bill
dill
fill
hill
kill
pill
will
chill
drill
grill
skill
spill
still

ing
king
ring
sing
wing
bring
cling
fling
sling
sting
swing
thing

ink
ink
link
mink
pink
rink
sink
wink
blink
drink
slink
stink
think

ish
dish
fish
wish
swish

ist
fist
list
mist
twist

ock
dock
lock
rock
sock
block
clock
flock
shock
smock
stock

ond
bond
fond
pond
blond

ong
gong
long
song
tong
prong

uck
buck
duck
luck
puck
suck
yuck
cluck
pluck
stuck
truck

uff
buff
cuff
huff
muff
puff
bluff
fluff
gruff
stuff

ump
bump
dump
hump
jump
lump
pump
rump
clump
grump
plump
slump
stump
thump

unk
bunk
dunk
hunk
junk
sunk
chunk
drunk
skunk

ush
gush
hush
rush
blush
brush
crush
flush
slush

ust
bust
dust
just
must
rust
crust
trust

FINAL CONSONANT BLENDS AND DIGRAPHS

f-blends/ *l*-blends	Preconsonantal nasals			*s*-blends	Digraphs	
ft	**mp**	junk	grant	**sk**	**ch**	clash
craft	bump	link	grunt	ask	much	crash
draft	camp	mink	plant	desk	rich	crush
drift	damp	pink	print	disk	such	flash
gift	dump	rank	slant	dusk	which	flesh
left	hump	rink	spent	husk		flush
lift	jump	sank	stunt	mask	**ng**	fresh
raft	lamp	sink		risk	bang	slush
shaft	limp	sunk		task	fang	smash
shift	lump	tank		tusk	gang	swish
sift	pump	wink			gong	trash
soft	ramp	yank		**st**	hang	
swift	rump	blank		best	hung	**th**
theft	plump	blink		bust	king	bath
	slump	chunk		cast	long	math
lf	stamp	clink		cost	lung	path
elf	stomp	clank		dust	rang	with
golf	stump	crank		fast	ring	cloth
gulf	thump	drank		fist	rung	
self	tramp	drink		just	sang	
shelf		drunk		last	sing	
	nd	plank		list	song	
lk	and	prank		lost	sung	
elk	band	spank		mast	wing	
milk	bend	stink		mist	bring	
	end	thank		must	clang	
lp	fond	think		nest	cling	
help	hand	trunk		past	prong	
yelp	land			pest	slang	
	lend	**nt**		rest	sling	
lt	mend	ant		rust	swing	
belt	pond	bent		test	thing	
felt	sand	bunt		vest		
kilt	send	dent		west	**sh**	
melt	tend	hunt		blast	cash	
tilt	wind	lint		chest	dash	
wilt	blend	pant		crest	dish	
	brand	punt		crust	fish	
	grand	rent		trust	hush	
	spend	runt		twist	mash	
	stand	sent			mesh	
		tent			rash	
	nk	vent			rush	
	bank	went			sash	
	bunk	blunt			wish	
	dunk	chant			blush	
	honk	flint			brush	

Within Word Pattern

LONG VOWELS VC*e*

aCe		eCe	iCe		oCe	uCe
age	lane	these	bike	slice	bone	/yo͞o/
ape	late	eve	bite	slide	broke	cube
ate	made	theme	chime	smile	choke	cute
bake	make		crime	spice	chose	fume
base	male		dime	spike	close	fuse
blame	mane		dive	spine	code	huge
blaze	mate		drive	spite	cone	mule
brake	pace		fife	stride	dome	muse
cage	page		file	strike	doze	mute
cake	pale		fine	stripe	drove	use
came	place		five	thrive	froze	
cane	plane		glide	tide	globe	/o͞o/
cape	plate		guide	time	hole	brute
case	quake		hide	tribe	home	crude
cave	race		hike	twice	hope	dude
chase	rage		hive	vine	hose	duke
crane	rake		kite	while	joke	dune
crate	rate		knife	whine	lone	flute
date	safe		lice	white	mole	June
daze	sake		life	wide	nose	lute
drake	sale		like	wife	note	nude
drape	same		lime	wipe	owe	plume
face	save		line	wise	phone	prune
fade	scale		live*	write	poke	rude
fake	shade		mice		pose	rule
fame	shake		mile		quote	spruce
fate	shape		mine		robe	tube
flake	slate		mite		rode	tune
flame	slave		nice		role	
frame	space		nine		rope	
game	stage		pile		rose	
gape	stake		pine		slope	
gate	stale		pipe		smoke	
gave	state		price		spoke	
gaze	take		pride		stole	
grace	tale		prime		stone	
grade	tame		prize		stove	
grape	tape		quite		stroke	
grave	trace		rice		those	
graze	trade		ride		throne	
hate	vane		ripe		vote	
haste	vase		rise		whole	
haze	wade		scribe		woke	
jade	wake		shine		wove	
lace	wave		side		wrote	
lake	whale		site		yoke	
lame			size		zone	

*Also pronounced /ĭ/.

R-CONTROLLED VOWEL PATTERNS

a		e	i	o		u
ar	**are**	**er**	**ir**	**or**	**ore**	**ur**
arch	bare	clerk	birch	born	bore	blur
arm	blare	fern	bird	cord	chore	blurt
art	care	germ	birth	cork	core	burn
bar	dare	her	chirp	corn	more	burp
barb	fare	jerk	dirt	for	ore	burr
barge	flare	nerve	fir	force	pore	burst
bark	glare	perch	firm	ford	score	church
car	hare	stern	first	forge	shore	churn
card	mare	swerve	girl	fork	snore	curb
cart	rare	term	shirt	form	sore	curl
carve	scare	verse	sir	fort	spore	curve
charm	share		skirt	forth	store	fur
chart	snare	**ear**	squirm	gorge	swore	hurl
dark	spare	earl	squirt	horn	tore	hurt
dart	square	earn	stir	horse	wore	lurch
far	stare	earth	swirl	lord		lurk
harm		heard	third	nor	**oar**	nurse
hard	**air**	learn	thirst	north	boar	purr
harp	air	pearl	twirl	or	board	purse
jar	chair	search	whir	pork	oar	spur
large	flair	yearn	whirl	porch	roar	spurt
lark	hair			port	soar	surf
mar	lair	**beard**	**ire**	scorch		surge
march	pair	clear	fire	scorn		turf
park	stair	dear	hire	short		turn
part		ear	sire	sort		
scar		fear	spire	sport		**ure**
scarf		gear	tire	stork		/yo͞or/
shark		hear	wire	storm		cure
sharp		near		sworn		pure
smart		rear		thorn		
snarl		spear		torch		/o͞or/
spark		tear		torn		lure
star		year		worn		sure
start						
starve		**eer**				
tar		cheer				
tart		deer				
yard		jeer				
yarn		peer				
		queer				
		sneer				
		steer				

Note: The final e in words like *barge, starve, nurse,* and *force* is not part of the vowel pattern; it serves the preceding consonant. Final e follows v except in the case of proper nouns like *Kiev* or *Yugoslav* and gives a soft sound to the letters *g, c,* and *s.*

OTHER COMMON LONG VOWEL PATTERNS

Long *a*			Long *e*		
ai	*ay*	*ei*	*e*	*ee*	
aid	bay	eight	be	bee	sheet
aim	day	eighth	he	beef	sleek
bail	gay	freight	me	beep	sleep
bait	gray	neigh	she	beet	sleet
braid	hay	reign	(the)	bleed	sleeve
brain	jay	rein	we	cheek	speech
chain	lay	seine		cheese	speed
claim	may	skein		creek	steel
drain	pay	sleigh		creep	steep
fail	play	veil		deed	street
faint	pray	vein		deep	sweep
faith	ray	weigh		eel	sweet
frail	say	weight		fee	teeth
gain	slay			feed	thee
grain	spray			feel	three
hail	stay			feet	tree
jail	stray			flee	wee
laid	sway			fleet	weed
maid	tray			free	week
mail	way			glee	weep
main				greed	wheel
nail				green	
paid				greet	
pail				heel	
pain				jeep	
paint				keen	
plain				keep	
praise				knee	
quaint				kneel	
rail				meet	
rain				need	
sail				peel	
saint				peep	
snail				preen	
sprain				queen	
stain				reed	
straight				reef	
strain				reel	
strait				screen	
tail				see	
trail				seed	
train				seek	
vain				seem	
wail				seen	
waist				seep	
wait				sheep	

(cont.)

OTHER COMMON LONG VOWEL PATTERNS (*cont.*)

Long *e*			Long *i*		
ea		**ie**	**igh**	**y**	**iCC**
beach	sea	brief	bright	by	bind
bead	seal	chief	fight	cry	blind
beak	seam	field	flight	dry	child
beam	seat	fiend	fright	fly	climb
bean	sneak	grief	high	fry	find
beast	speak	grieve	knight	guy	grind
beat	squeak	liege	light	my	hind
breathe	squeal	niece	might	pry	kind
cheat	steal	piece	night	shy	mind
clean	steam	priest	right	sky	rind
cream	stream	shield	sigh	sly	sign
deal	tea	shriek	sight	spry	wild
dream	teach	siege	slight	spy	wind***
each	team	thief	thigh	try	
ease	treat	yield	tight	why	
east	weak				
eat	weave				
feast	wheat				
flea					
heal	**short e**				
heap	bread				
heat	breast				
knead	breath				
lead*	dead				
leaf	deaf				
leak	death				
lean	dread				
leash	head				
least	health				
leave	lead**				
meal	meant				
mean	read**				
meat	realm				
neat	spread				
pea	stealth				
peace	sweat				
peach	thread				
peak	threat				
plea	tread				
real	wealth				
reach					
read*					

*Also pronounced /ĕ/.
**Also pronounced /ē/.
***Also pronounced /ĭ/.

(*cont.*)

OTHER COMMON LONG VOWEL PATTERNS (*cont.*)

Long o				Long u		
oa	*oe/o*	*oCC*	*ow*	*ew**	*ue*	*ui*
boast	doe	bold	blow	blew	blue	bruise
boat	foe	bolt	blown	brew	clue	cruise
cloak	hoe	both	bow	chew	cue	fruit
coach	toe	cold	bowl	crew	due	juice
coal	woe	colt	crow	dew	flue	suit
coast		comb	flow	drew	glue	
coat	go	fold	flown	few	hue	
coax	ho	folk	glow	flew	sue	
croak	no	ghost	grow	grew	true	
float	so	gold	growth	knew		
foam		hold	know	mew		
goal		host	known	new		
goat		jolt	low	screw		
groan		mold	mow	shrew		
load		most	own	shrewd		
loaf		old	show	stew		
loan		poll	shown	threw		
moan		post	slow	yew		
moat		roll	snow			
oak		scold	sow			
oat		sold	stow			
oath		stroll	throw			
poach		told	thrown			
roach		volt	tow			
road						
roam						
roast						
soak						
soap						
throat						
toad						
toast						
whoa						

*The ew pattern is also included with "Abstract Vowels."

COMPLEX CONSONANT PATTERNS

Digraphs	Triple-letter blends					
qu	*scr*	*shr*	*spl/spr*	*squ*	*str*	*thr*
quack	scram	shrank	splash	squad	straight	thrash
quail	scrap	shred	splay	squall	strain	thread
quaint	scrape	shrew	splice	square	strait	threat
quake	scratch	shrewd	splint	squash	strand	three
quart	scrawl	shriek	split	squat	strange	thresh
quartz	scream	shrill	splotch	squaw	strap	threw
queen	screech	shrimp	splurge	squawk	straw	thrift
queer	screen	shrink		squeak	stray	thrill
quench	screw	shrine	sprain	squeal	streak	thrive
quest	scribe	shroud	sprang	squeeze	stream	throat
quick	scrimp	shrub	sprawl	squelch	street	throb
quill	script	shrug	spray	squid	strength	throng
quilt	scroll	shrunk	spread	squint	stress	throne
quince	scrub		spree	squire	stretch	through
quirk	scruff		sprig	squirm	strew	throw
quiet	scrunch		spring	squirt	strict	thrown
quit			sprint		stride	thrush
quite			sprite		strife	thrust
quiz			sprout		strike	
quoits			spruce		string	
quote			sprung		strip	
					stripe	
					strive	
					strode	
					stroll	
					stroke	
					strong	
					struck	
					strum	
					strung	
					strut	

(cont.)

COMPLEX CONSONANT PATTERNS (*cont.*)

Sound-alike final consonant patterns

ck		ke	k		ch	tch
back	speck	bake	beak	bark	beach	batch
black	stack	bike	break	clerk	beech	blotch
block	stick	brake	cheek	cork	coach	botch
brick	stock	broke	cloak	dark	couch	catch
buck	struck	cake	creek	fork	peach	clutch
check	stuck	choke	croak	jerk	poach	crotch
chick	suck	drake	leak	park	pouch	crutch
click	tack	duke	oak	pork	reach	ditch
clock	thick	fake	peak	shark	roach	fetch
cluck	tick	flake	seek	spark	teach	hatch
cock	track	hike	sleek	stork		hitch
crack	trick	joke	sneak		belch	hutch
deck	truck	lake	soak		bench	latch
dock	tuck	like	speak		birch	match
duck	whack	make	squeak		branch	notch
fleck	wick	poke	steak		bunch	patch
flick	wreck	quake	weak		church	pitch
flock		rake	week		cinch	scratch
frock		sake			crunch	sketch
jack		shake	book		drench	snatch
kick		smoke	brook		finch	stitch
knock		spoke	chalk		gulch	switch
lack		stake	cook		hunch	thatch
lick		strike	crook		launch	twitch
lock		stroke	hook		lunch	witch
luck		take	shook		march	
mock		wake	squawk		mulch	
neck		woke	stalk		munch	
pack		yoke	took		perch	
peck					pinch	
pick			ask		porch	
pluck			bank		punch	
prick			blank		ranch	
quack			blink		scorch	
quick			desk		scrunch	
rack			drink		search	
rock			junk		starch	
sack			link		torch	
shack			mask		trench	
shock			milk		wrench	
sick			sank			
slack			sink			
slick			skunk			
smack			stink			
smock			tank			
snack			wink			
sock						

(cont.)

COMPLEX CONSONANT PATTERNS (*cont.*)

More sound-alikes		Soft consonants		Silent consonants	
ge	**dge**	**g***	**c**	**gn/kn**	**mb/wr**
age	badge	gee	bounce	**gn**	**mb**
cage	bridge	gel	chance	gnarl	bomb
gauge	budge	gem	choice	gnash	climb
gouge	dodge	genes	dance	gnat	comb
huge	dredge	germ	dice	gnaw	crumb
page	edge	gist	face	gnome	dumb
rage	fledge	gym	fence	gnu	jamb
sage	fudge		fierce		lamb
siege	grudge		force	**kn**	limb
stage	hedge		glance	knack	numb
stooge	judge		ice	knave	plumb
	ledge		juice	knead	thumb
binge	lodge		lace	knee	tomb
bulge	midge		mice	kneel	womb
change	nudge		nice	knelt	
charge	pledge		niece	knew	**wr**
cringe	ridge		once	knife	wrap
forge	sledge		peace	knight	wrath
fringe	smudge		piece	knit	wreath
gorge	trudge		place	knob	wreck
hinge	wedge		pounce	knock	wren
large			prance	knoll	wrench
lounge			price	knot	wring
lunge			race	know	wrist
merge			rice	known	write
plunge			sauce		wrong
range			since		wrote
singe			slice		wrung
sponge			space		wry
surge			spice		
urge			spruce		
verge			trace		
			twice		
			voice		
			cease		
			cell		
			cent		
			cinch		
			cite		
			cyst		

*See also *ge/dge* lists.

ABSTRACT VOWELS

/o͞o/		/o͝o/	/oi/	
ew/ou*	oo	oo/ou	oy	oi
blew	bloom	book	boy	boil
brew	boom	brook	coy	broil
chew	boost	cook	joy	coil
crew	boot	crook	soy	coin
dew	broom	foot	toy	foil
drew	cool	good		hoist
few	coop	hood		join
flew	food	hoof		joint
grew	fool	hook		loin
knew	gloom	look		moist
mew	goof	shook		oil
new	groom	soot		point
screw	hoot	stood		soil
shrew	loom	took		spoil
shrewd	loop	wood		toil
skew	moo	wool		void
stew	mood			
threw	moon	could		
yew	noon	should		
	pool	would		
croup	proof			
ghoul	roof			
group	room			
route*	roost			
soup	root			
through	school			
you	scoop			
youth	scoot			
	shoot			
	smooth			
	snoop			
	soon			
	spool			
	spoon			
	stool			
	swoop			
	too			
	tool			
	toot			
	troop			
	whoop			
	zoo			
	zoom			

*This pattern could be studied with long *u*.
**Also pronounced /ou/.

(cont.)

ABSTRACT VOWELS (*cont.*)

/ou/		/ô/			/ä/ /ör/
ou	*ow*	*au*	*aw*	*al*	*wa*
bound	brow	caught	bawl	all	swab
cloud	brown	cause	caw	bald	swamp
couch	clown	fault	claw	balk	swan
count	cow	fraud	crawl	ball	swap
crouch	crowd	gauze	dawn	call	swat
doubt	crown	haul	draw	chalk	swatch
foul	down	haunch	drawl	fall	swath
found	drown	haunt	drawn	false	wad
grouch	fowl	launch	fawn	hall	waft
ground	frown	sauce	gnaw	halt	walk
hound	gown	taught	hawk	mall	wall
loud	how	vault	jaw	malt	waltz
mound	howl		law	salt	wand
mount	growl		lawn	scald	want
mouth	now		paw	small	wash
ouch	ow		pawn	stalk	wasp
out	owl		raw	stall	watch
pouch	plow		saw	talk	watt
pound	pow		shawl	tall	
proud	prowl		slaw	walk	dwarf
round	scowl		sprawl	wall	swarm
scout	sow		squawk	waltz	war
shout	town		straw		ward
snout	vow		thaw		warm
sound	wow		yawn		warn
south					warp
spout					wart
sprout					
stout					

SOUNDS FOR THE *ED* INFLECTIONAL ENDING

/ĭd/		/d/		/t/	
acted	batted	aimed	grabbed	asked	dropped
boasted	dotted	bloomed	grinned	blinked	shopped
bounded	patted	boiled	hugged	bumped	skipped
drifted		buzzed	planned	cracked	stopped
dusted	stated	cheered		chirped	stripped
ended	traded	claimed	cared	coached	trapped
floated		cleaned	closed	crushed	
folded		crowed	dared	dashed	baked
lasted		filled	raised	dressed	chased
lifted		flowed	smiled	fished	hoped
loaded		groaned		fussed	
handed		joined	tried	heaped	
melted		mailed		jerked	
needed		rained		jumped	
painted		roamed		missed	
parted		rolled		mixed	
planted		sailed		passed	
rented		screamed		peeped	
roasted		seemed		picked	
shifted		showed		pushed	
squirted		snowed		reached	
started		squealed		rushed	
treated		squirmed		splashed	
trusted		trailed		stamped	
twisted		trained		walked	
waited		turned		winked	
wanted		yelled		worked	

Note: The examples with e-drop and doubling changes that are included in the three short columns above are appropriate for sorting activities with this feature, but students should not be expected to correctly apply the e-drop and doubling principles in their spelling.

HOMOPHONES

a			*e*		
ant	made	sail	be	genes	rest
aunt	maid	sale	bee	jeans	wrest
air	mail	slay	beach	heal	scene
heir	male	sleigh	beech	heel	seen
aid	main	stake	beat	hear	sea
aide	Maine	steak	beet	here	see
	mane				
ate		stair	berth	heard	seam
eight	maize	stare	birth	herd	seem
	maze				
brake		straight	bread	knead	shear
break	mall	strait	bred	need	sheer
	maul				
bare		tacks	cell	lead	steal
bear	pail	tax	sell	led	steel
	pale				
bail		tail	cent	leak	suite
bale	pain	tale	scent	leek	sweet
	pane		sent		
base		their		meat	tea
bass	pair	there	cheap	meet	tee
	pare	they're	cheep		
days	pear			peace	tear
daze		vail	creak	piece	tier
	pause	vale	creek		
fair	paws			peak	we
fare		vain	dear	peek	wee
	plain	vane	deer		
flair	plane	vein		peal	weak
flare			earn	peel	week
	pray	waist	urn		
gait	prey	waste		peer	weave
gate			eaves	pier	we've
	rain	wait	eves		
grate	reign	weight		per	we'd
great	rein		feat	purr	weed
		ware	feet		
hair	rap	wear		read	(sense)*
hare	wrap	where	flea	red	(since)
			flee		
hall	raise	way		real	(than)
haul	rays	weigh	freeze	reel	(then)
			frieze		
hay	sac				
hey	sack				

*Not true homophones but often confused.

(cont.)

HOMOPHONES (*cont.*)

i		o			u	
aisle	lie	beau	hole	soar	blew	plum
I'll	lye	bow	whole	sore	blue	plumb
isle						
	might	boar	hour	throne	brews	root
eye	mite	bore	our	thrown	bruise	route
I						
	right	bough	knot	toe	bundt	rough
been	write	bow	not	tow	bunt	ruff
bin						
	ring	brows	know	warn	chews	scull
buy	wring	browse	no	worn	choose	skull
by						
bye	stile	chord	loan	your	chute	some
	style	cord	lone	you're	shoot	sum
cite						
sight	tic	close	moan		coop	son
site	tick	clothes	mown		coupe	sun
die	thyme	coarse	morn		crews	tern
dye	time	course	mourn		cruise	turn
fir	which	core	oh		dew	threw
fur	witch	corps	owe		do	through
					due	
gilt	vice	doe	pole			to
guilt	vise	dough	poll		ewe	too
					yew	two
him		flour	pore		you	
hymn		flower	pour			
					flew	troop
hi		for	road		flu	troupe
high		fore	rode		flue	
		four				who's
in			role		gnu	whose
inn		forth	roll		knew	wood
		fourth			new	would
its			rose			
it's		foul	rows		loot	yoke
		fowl			lute	yolk
knight			rote			
night		groan	wrote		one	
		grown			won	
knit			sew			
nit		hoarse	so			
		horse	sow			

CONTRACTIONS

am	is, has	us
I'm	here's	let's
	he's	
are	how's	**will**
they're	it's	I'll
we're	she's	it'll
you're	that's	he'll
	there's	she'll
had, would	what's	that'll
he'd	where's	they'll
I'd	who's	we'll
she'd		you'll
they'd	**not**	
there'd	aren't	
we'd	can't	
who'd	couldn't	
you'd	doesn't	
	don't	
have	hadn't	
I've	hasn't	
could've	haven't	
should've	isn't	
they've	shouldn't	
we've	wasn't	
would've	weren't	
you've	wouldn't	

◆

Syllable Juncture

◆

COMPOUND WORDS

By word family

Two syllables

aircraft	catnip	foothills	inland	rainfall
airline	cattail	foothold	inside	rainstorm
airmail	**class**mate	footnote	into	**rail**road
airplane	classroom	footprint	**land**fall	railway
airport	**corn**cob	footstep	landfill	**road**block
airtight	cornfield	footstool	landlord	roadside
airwaves	cornhusk	**grape**fruit	landmark	roadway
backbone	cornmeal	grapevine	landslide	roadwork
background	cornstalk	**hair**brush	**life**boat	**run**down
backstop	cornstarch	haircut	lifeguard	runoff
backyard	popcorn	hairdo	lifelike	runway
bareback	**court**house	hairpin	lifelong	**sea**coast
barefoot	courtroom	hairstyle	lifetime	seafood
baseball	courtyard	**hand**cuff	**light**house	seaman
baseboard	**door**bell	handmade	lightweight	seaport
bathrobe	doorknob	handshake	daylight	seasick
bathroom	doorman	handsome	flashlight	seashore
bathtub	doormat	handspring	sunlight	seaside
birdbath	doorstep	**head**ache	**mail**box	seaweed
bedbug	doorstop	headband	mailman	**snow**ball
bedroll	doorway	headdress	**news**cast	snowdrift
bedroom	**down**cast	headfirst	newsprint	snowflake
bedspread	downfall	headlight	newsstand	snowman
bedtime	downhill	headline	**night**fall	snowplow
birthday	downpour	headphone	nightgown	snowshoe
birthmark	downstairs	headway	nightmare	snowstorm
birthplace	downstream	**high**lands	nighttime	**south**east
birthstone	downtown	highlight	**north**east	southwest
blackberry	**egg**plant	highway	northwest	**stair**case
blackbird	eggshell	**home**land	**out**burst	stairway
blacksmith	**eye**ball	homemade	outcast	stairwell
blacktop	eyebrow	homeroom	outcome	**tooth**brush
bookcase	eyelid	homesick	outcry	toothpaste
bookend	eyesight	homestretch	outdoors	toothpick
bookmark	eyestrain	homework	outfield	**up**date
bookshelf	**farm**house	**horse**back	outfit	uphold
bookworm	farmland	horsefly	outline	upright
cookbook	farmyard	horseman	outside	uproar
scrapbook	**fire**arm	horseshoe	**play**ground	upset
textbook	firefly	**house**boat	playhouse	upstairs
campfire	fireman	household	playmate	upstream
campground	fireplace	housewife	playpen	**wind**burn
campsite	fireproof	housework	playroom	windmill
catbird	fireworks	housetop	**rain**bow	windpipe
catfish	**foot**ball	**in**come	raincoat	windshield
catnap	footbridge	indoor	raindrop	windstorm

(cont.)

COMPOUND WORDS (*cont.*)

By word family		Other compounds	
Two syllables	**Three syllables**	**Two syllables**	**Three syllables**
withdraw	**any**body	beehive	afternoon
withhold	anyone	breakfast	basketball
within	anything	broadcast	bookkeeper
without	anytime	broomstick	businessman
withstand	anywhere	cannot	candlestick
	buttercup	chairman	cheerleader
	butterfly	coastline	cheeseburger
	buttermilk	cowboy	hamburger
	butternut	daylight	coffeepot
	butterscotch	driftwood	commonplace
	for**ever**	driveway	fingerprint
	however	drugstore	flowerpot
	whenever	earthquake	furthermore
	whoever	farewell	gingerbread
	everybody	flagpole	heavyweight
	everyone	flashlight	however
	everything	framework	masterpiece
	everywhere	goldfish	mountainside
	grandchildren	halfway	nevertheless
	granddaughter	hillside	otherwise
	grandfather	lookout	policeman
	grandmother	mainland	quarterback
	grandparents	network	rattlesnake
	grandson	notebook	salesperson
	overall	offspring	skyscraper
	overboard	paintbrush	storekeeper
	overcast	pancake	summertime
	overcoat	peanut	thanksgiving
	overcome	proofread	townspeople
	overflow	rowboat	typewriter
	overhead	sailboat	
	overlook	scarecrow	
	overview	sidewalk	
	undergo	smallpox	
	underground	spaceship	
	undergrowth	springtime	
	underline	stagecoach	
	underlying	starfish	
	undermine	steamboat	
	understand	suitcase	
	underwater	throughout	
	watercolor	warehouse	
	waterfall	weekend	
	watermelon	widespread	
	waterproof	wildlife	
	waterway	worthwhile	

HYPHENATED COMPOUND WORDS

age-old
all-stars
bare-handed
baby-sit
best-seller
blast-off
bleary-eyed
break-in
broken-down
built-in
cave-in
cease-fire
chin-ups
chock-full
clean-cut
color-blind
cover-up
cross-country
cross-examine
cross-eyed
cure-all
cut-rate
daughter-in-law
do-it-yourself
dog-eat-dog
double-breasted
double-cross
down-to-earth
drip-dry
empty-handed
eye-opener
fair-minded
father-in-law
first-class
follow-up
forget-me-not
forty-five
free-for-all
freeze-dried
fuddy-duddy
full-time
go-getter
good-bye
good-for-nothing
grown-ups
hair-raising
hands-on
hard-hearted
hard-core

head-on
heavy-duty
helter-skelter
high-strung
hocus-pocus
ice-skating
ill-advised
in-depth
jack-o'-lantern
king-sized
know-how
left-handed
letter-perfect
lift-off
light-headed
long-distance
long-winded
make-believe
man-made
merry-go-round
middle-aged
mix-up
mother-in-law
mother-of-pearl
narrow-minded
nerve-racking
nitty-gritty
old-fashioned
old-timer
one-sided
one-way
open-ended
open-minded
out-of-bounds
part-time
pigeon-toed
play-offs
polka-dotted
push-button
push-ups
red-handed
right-handed
rip-off
run-of-the-mill
run-down
runners-up
self-cleaning
self-control
self-defense

short-term
show-off
sight-seeing
sit-ups
so-so
step-by-step
time-out
tip-top
tongue-tied
topsy-turvy
trade-off
tug-of-war
tune-up
two-way
up-to-date
vice-president
walk-in
walkie-talkie
warm-blooded
weather-proofed
well-defined
well-done
well-known
well-to-do
wishy-washy
yo-yo

DOUBLING AND *E*-DROP WITH *ED* AND *ING*

No change

CVCC	CVVC (CVV)
ask: asked asking	aim: aimed aiming
back: backed backing	bail: bailed bailing
blend: blended blending	bowl: bowled bowling
call: called calling	braid: braided braiding
catch: (caught) catching	chain: chained chaining
comb: combed combing	cheer: cheered cheering
climb: climbed climbing	chew: chewed chewing
cross: crossed crossing	claim: claimed claiming
draft: drafted drafting	clean: cleaned cleaning
dress: dressed dressing	coach: coached coaching
drift: drifted drifting	creak: creaked creaking
fish: fished fishing	drain: drained draining
farm: farmed farming	eat: (ate) eating
fill: filled filling	fail: failed failing
guard: guarded guarding	fool: fooled fooling
guess: guessed guessing	keep: (kept) keeping
hand: handed handing	gain: gained gaining
hiss: hissed hissing	groan: groaned groaning
hunt: hunted hunting	heal: healed healing
jump: jumped jumping	lean: leaned leaning
land: landed landing	load: loaded loading
lift: lifted lifting	loan: loaned loaning
limp: limped limping	mail: mailed mailing
march: marched marching	meet: (met) meeting
mark: marked marking	need: needed needing
melt: melted melting	peep: peeped peeping
miss: missed missing	play: played playing
munch: munched munching	point: pointed pointing
nest: nested nesting	preen: preened preening
puff: puffed puffing	pout: pouted pouting
pull: pulled pulling	rain: rained raining
punt: punted punting	roar: roared roaring
push: pushed pushing	sail: sailed sailing
rock: rocked rocking	scoop: scooped scooping
slump: slumped slumping	scream: screamed screaming
smell: smelled smelling	seal: sealed sealing
spill: spilled spilling	shout: shouted shouting
sprint: sprinted sprinting	sneak: sneaked sneaking
stamp: stamped stamping	snow: snowed snowing
start: started starting	speak: (spoke) speaking
talk: talked talking	speed: speeded (or sped) speeding
twist: twisted twisting	spoil: spoiled spoiling
want: wanted wanting	spray: sprayed spraying
wash: washed washing	trail: trailed trailing
watch: watched watching	train: trained training
wreck: wrecked wrecking	wait: waited waiting

(cont.)

DOUBLING AND *E*-DROP WITH *ED* AND *ING* (*cont.*)

Double	e-drop
CVC	**CVCe**
bat: batted batting	bake: baked baking
beg: begged begging	blame: blamed blaming
blur: blurred blurring	care: cared caring
can: canned canning	chase: chased chasing
chip: chipped chipping	chime: chimed chiming
chop: chopped chopping	dare: dared daring
clip: clipped clipping	drive: (drove) driving
dip: dipped dipping	file: filed filing
drag: dragged dragging	flame: flamed flaming
drip: dripped dripping	fume: fumed fuming
drop: dropped dropping	grade: graded grading
fan: fanned fanning	hope: hoped hoping
fit: fitted (or fit) fitting	ice: iced icing
hop: hopped hopping	like: liked liking
hug: hugged hugging	line: lined lining
jog: jogged jogging	make: (made) making
knit: knitted knitting	mine: mined mining
knot: knotted knotting	name: named naming
mop: mopped mopping	note: noted noting
net: netted netting	owe: owed owing
pad: padded padding	pile: piled piling
pet: petted petting	pipe: piped piping
pin: pinned pinning	place: placed placing
plan: planned planning	price: priced pricing
plug: plugged plugging	race: raced racing
pop: popped popping	ride: (rode) riding
quit: quitted (or quit) quitting	save: saved saving
rob: robbed robbing	score: scored scoring
rub: rubbed rubbing	shade: shaded shading
scar: scarred scarring	shake: (shook) shaking
ship: shipped shipping	share: shared sharing
shop: shopped shopping	skate: skated skating
slip: slipped slipping	shape: shaped shaping
snap: snapped snapping	slope: sloped sloping
sob: sobbed sobbing	smile: smiled smiling
star: starred starring	stare: stared staring
step: stepped stepping	store: stored storing
stir: stirred stirring	strike: (struck) striking
stop: stopped stopping	take: (took) taking
tap: tapped tapping	tame: tamed taming
thin: thinned thinning	trade: traded trading
tip: tipped tipping	tune: tuned tuning
trap: trapped trapping	use: used using
trip: tripped tripping	vote: voted voting
tug: tugged tugging	wave: waved waving
win: (won) winning	write: (wrote) writing

OTHER SYLLABLE JUNCTURE DOUBLING

First syllable stress					
VCCV			**Doublet**		**VCV (open)**
absent	injure	sandwich	apple	narrow	able
after	insect	scarlet	attic	offer	acorn
album	instant	seldom	ballot	office	agent
argue	kerchief	sentence	battle	passage	baby
artist	kingdom	servant	better	pattern	bacon
athlete	lantern	shelter	blizzard	pebble	basic
basket	lobster	signal	blossom	pillow	beaver
biscuit	lumber	sister	bottle	planning	bison
border	market	Sunday	button	puddle	bugle
cactus	master	temper	cabbage	puppet	china
canyon	merchant	texture	carry	puzzle	climate
capture	midget	thunder	cattle	rabbit	clover
carpet	mischief	trumpet	channel	scribble	cocoa
center	monster	turkey	classic	shallow	cozy
census	morning	twenty	coffee	simmer	crater
chapter	mushroom	umpire	comment	skinny	crisis
children	mustard	under	copper	slipper	duty
chimney	napkin	urgent	cottage	soccer	eager
chipmunk	nonsense	velvet	dipper	spatter	even
comfort	normal	victim	dizzy	spelling	evil
compass	nostril	walnut	effort	stopping	famous
concert	number	walrus	errand	sudden	favor
constant	orbit	welcome	fellow	supper	feature
contact	orchard	whimper	flutter	tennis	female
contest	order	window	foggy	traffic	fever
costume	orphan	winter	follow	trapper	final
custom	panther	wonder	funny	trolley	flavor
dentist	pardon		gallon	tunnel	focus
distant	pencil		getting	valley	freedom
district	perfect		glasses	village	frequent
dolphin	person		gossip	wallet	Friday
elbow	picnic		hammock	wedding	future
emblem	picture		happen	wiggle	glider
engine	pilgrim		happy	willow	human
enter	plastic		hello	worry	humid
expert	portrait		hollow	wrapper	item
fabric	powder		huddle	written	ivy
furnish	pretzel		hugging	yellow	labor
further	problem		inning	yucca	ladies
garden	public		kitten		lazy
ginger	publish		ladder		legal
harvest	pumpkin		lesson		local
helmet	purchase		letter		major
hundred	ransom		mammal		meter
husband	reptile		message		migrate
index	rescue		muffin		moment

(cont.)

OTHER SYLLABLE JUNCTURE DOUBLING (*cont.*)

First syllable stress			Second syllable stress		
VCV open	**VCV closed**		**VCCV**	**Doublet***	**VCV open**
music	atom	never	absorb	afford	amount
navy	balance	novel	admire	balloon	around
notice	cabin	olive	admit	bassoon	because
photo	camel	oven	although	dessert	before
pilot	cavern	palace	cartoon	pollute	believe
pirate	chili	panel	complete	possess	beside
pony	civil	panic	compose	raccoon	beyond
private	clever	parent	conclude		cement
profile	closet	planet	confess		debate
program	comet	polish	confuse		decide
pupil	comic	prison	contain		declare
radar	credit	profit	control		demand
reason	decade	promise	discuss		deny
recent	digit	punish	disguise		elect
ripen	dozen	radish	disturb		event
robot	driven	rapid	employ		hotel
rodent	edit	refuge	enjoy		obey
rotate	famine	robin	entire		police
ruby	figure	salad	exchange		polite
rumor	finish	savage	excite		prepare
sequel	frigid	second	explain		pretend
shiny	govern	shiver	express		prevent
silent	gravel	shovel	forbid		proceed
siren	habit	sliver	forget		propel
soda	heaven	solid	ignore		recite
sofa	honest	spinach	improve		relief
solar	honey	stomach	include		remain
solo	honor	talent	indeed		repair
species	image	taxi	inspect		resist
spicy	jacket	tenant	instead		resume
spiral	legend	timid	invite		return
spoken	lemon	topic	observe		reveal
student	level	travel	percent		reward
super	lever	value	perform		secure
treason	lily	vanish	perfume		select
tulip	limit	visit	perhaps		severe
tuna	linen	vivid	sincere		superb
unit	lizard	volume	surprise		unite
vacant	manage	wagon	until		
widen	menace	weather			**VCV closed**
zebra	menu	wizard			exact
	mimic				exist
	model				giraffe
	modern				
	money				

*Most words of this type have *assimilated prefixes* (a<u>cc</u>ept) and are listed at the DC stage.

LONG AND SHORT VOWEL PATTERNS IN THE STRESSED SYLLABLE

Short *a*	Long *a*			
a	*aCe*	*ai*	*ay*	*open a*
accent	amaze (2)	acquaint (2)	astray (2)	agent
adapt (2)	awake (2)	afraid (2)	betray (2)	April
alas (2)	baseball	await (2)	crayfish	basil
ambush	basement	campaign	crayon	basin
attach (2)	behave (2)	complain (2)	daydream	basic
attic	bracelet	contain (2)	daylight	basis
background	cascade (2)	dainty	decay	cradle
ballot	create (2)	drainage	dismay	crater
bandage	debate (2)	exclaim (2)	grayish	data
campfire	disgrace (2)	explain (2)	hooray (2)	fable
cannon	embrace (2)	failure	layer	fatal
canvas	engage (2)	mailbox	maybe	glacier
cattle	engrave (2)	mainland	mayor	hatred
daddy	erase (2)	painter	okay (2)	labor
enchant (2)	escape (2)	railroad	payment	ladle
exact (2)	estate (2)	rainbow	player	lazy
expand (2)	exchange (2)	raincoat	playmate	nation
falcon	graceful	raisin	portray (2)	navy
flashlight	grapefruit	refrain (2)	prayer	patient
gallop	mistake (2)	remain (2)	sayings	rabies
halfway	parade (2)	sailor	today (2)	radar
lantern	pavement	strainer		raven
hammer	persuade (2)	sustain (2)		sacred
massive	safety	tailor		savor
matter	skateboard	trainer		shaky
package	spacecraft	traitor		skater
patent	statement	waiter		vapor
pattern				
perhaps (2)				
rancher				
rapid				
sample				
satin				
scamper				
scatter				
shadow				
tablet				
talons				
tragic				
transfer				
translate				
unpack (2)				

Note: Words included in this feature have a first-syllable stress unless otherwise indicated—for example, *enchant (2)*.

(cont.)

LONG AND SHORT VOWEL PATTERNS IN THE STRESSED SYLLABLE (*cont.*)

Short e		Long e		
e	ea	ee	ea	ie
address (2)	ahead (2)	agree (2)	appeal (2)	achieve (2)
arrest (2)	breakfast	asleep (2)	beaver	apiece (2)
ascend (2)	deafen	baleen (2)	cheaply	belief (2)
attend (2)	dreadful	between (2)	conceal (2)	believe (2)
beggar	feather	breezy	creature	besiege (2)
blender	healthy	canteen (2)	defeat (2)	debrief (2)
center	heaven	cheetah	disease (2)	diesel
collect (2)	heavy	degree (2)	eager	relief (2)
confess (2)	instead (2)	esteem (2)	easel	relieve (2)
condense (2)	leather	exceed (2)	easy	reprieve (2)
connect (2)	meadow	freedom	ideal (2)	retrieve (2)
defend (2)	measure	freeway	increase (2)	
depend (2)	pheasant	gleeful	leakage	
depress (2)	pleasant	greenish	meanwhile	
descend (2)	ready	greeting	mislead (2)	
distress (2)	steady	indeed (2)	ordeal (2)	
edit	steadfast	kneecap	peanut	
effect (2)	sweatshirt	proceed (2)	reason	
effort	treadmill	redeem (2)	release (2)	
elect (2)	treasure	seedling	repeal (2)	
engine	weapon	sleeping	repeat (2)	
envy	weather	speedway	reveal (2)	
event (2)		steeply	treason	
exit		steeple	weasel	
expect (2)		succeed (2)		
extend (2)		sweeper		
extra		sweeten		
freshly		tureen (2)		
intend (2)		tweezers		
neglect (2)		wheelchair		
never		unseen (2)		
percent				
pretend (2)				
prevent (2)				
profess (2)				
protect (2)				
refresh (2)				
request (2)				
respect (2)				
revenge (2)				
select (2)				
suggest (2)				
unless (2)				

(*cont.*)

LONG AND SHORT VOWEL PATTERNS IN THE STRESSED SYLLABLE (*cont.*)

Long e			Short i	
open e	eCe	ei	i	y
being	compete (2)	caffeine (2)	admit (2)	abyss (2)
cedar	complete (2)	ceiling	assist (2)	crystal
decent	concede (2)	conceive (2)	brittle	cymbal
depot	convene (2)	deceive (2)	chimney	cynic
detour	delete (2)	either	crimson	gymnast
even	deplete (2)	leisure	district	gypsy
evil	discrete (2)	neither	enlist (2)	mystery
female	extreme (2)	perceive (2)	equip (2)	physics
femur	impede (2)	receipt (2)	exist (2)	pygmy
fever	precede (2)	receive (2)	extinct (2)	rhythm
legal	recede (2)	seizure	figure	symbol
meter	secede (2)		index	symptom
prefix	serene (2)		injure	system
preview	stampede (2)		illness	
recent	supreme (2)		image	
regal	trapeze (2)		insect	
sequence			instant	
species			instill (2)	
tepee			kidnap	
veto			kitchen	
zebra			liquid	
			listen	
			midget	
			middle	
			mixture	
			nickname	
			picket	
			pillow	
			princess	
			ribbon	
			shrivel	
			silver	
			simmer	
			sister	
			sixty	
			sizzle	
			splinter	
			stingy	
			timid	
			tissue	
			until (2)	
			village	
			whisper	
			window	
			winner	
			wisdom	

(*cont.*)

LONG AND SHORT VOWEL PATTERNS IN THE STRESSED SYLLABLE (*cont.*)

Long *i*

iCe	igh	iCC	y	open i
advice (2)	brightness	align (2)	apply (2)	biker
advise (2)	delight (2)	assign (2)	bypass	bison
alive (2)	fighter	behind	cycle	bridle
arrive (2)	highlight	binder	cyclist	cider
awhile (2)	highness	bindings	cyclone	climax
confide (2)	highway	blindfold	cypress	diner
confine (2)	lighten	childhood	defy (2)	dining
beside (2)	lighthouse	childish	dryer	diver
decide (2)	lightning	climber	flyer	icy
decline (2)	mighty	design (2)	flyspeck	iris
despite (2)	nightmare	findings	gyro	item
device (2)	nighttime	hindsight	hybrid	lichen
devise (2)	sightsee	kindness	hydrant	minus
dislike (2)	tighten	remind (2)	hygiene	miser
divide (2)	tonight (2)	resign (2)	hyphen	pirate
driveway		rewind (2)	imply (2)	pliers
excite (2)		wildcat	July (2)	rhino
finely		wildlife	nylon	rifle
iceberg		unkind (2)	python	rival
ignite (2)			rely (2)	sinus
invite (2)			reply (2)	slimy
lively			rhyme	spider
ninety			skylark	tiger
oblige (2)			skyline	timer
polite (2)			spyglass	title
precise (2)			stylish	tripod
provide (2)			supply (2)	triumph
recite (2)			thyroid	virus
recline (2)			typhoid	visor
refine (2)			typist	writer
revive (2)			tyrant	
revise (2)				
sidekick				
sidewalk				
surprise (2)				
survive (2)				
widely				
widespread				

(cont.)

LONG AND SHORT VOWEL PATTERNS IN THE STRESSED SYLLABLE (*cont.*)

Short o	Long o			
o	oCe	oa	oCC	ow
adopt (2)	abode (2)	afloat (2)	almost (2)	aglow (2)
beyond (2)	alone (2)	approach (2)	behold (2)	below (2)
body	arose (2)	boathouse	coldness	bestow (2)
bonfire	awoke (2)	coaching	enroll (2)	whole
bother	boneless	coastal	folder	bowling
bottle	coleslaw	coaster	folklore	crowbar
bronco	compose (2)	coastline	foretold (2)	disown (2)
chocolate	decode (2)	coattail	goldfinch	glowworm
chopstick	devote (2)	goalie	hostess	lower
cobweb	dispose (2)	loafer	molding	owner
comma	enclose (2)	roadblock	molten	rowboat
comment	erode (2)	roadway	polka	rowers
congress	explode (2)	soapy	pollster	showdown
conquer	expose (2)	toadstool	postage	snowball
constant	homeless	toaster	postcard	snowfall
copper	homemade	unload (2)	poster	snowflake
cotton	homesick		postmark	snowman
doctor	homestead		revolt (2)	snowshoe
forgot (2)	homework		smolder	snowstorm
hobby	hopeful		soldier	
hockey	lonely		stroller	
hollow	lonesome		tollbooth	
honest	notebook		uphold (2)	
lobby	postpone (2)		withhold(2)	
lobster	promote (2)		voltage	
modern	propose (2)			
monster	remote (2)			
nonsense	rosebush			
nostril	stovepipe			
novel	suppose (2)			
pocket				
popcorn				
posture				
problem				
profit				
promise				
province				
respond (2)				
robber				
rotten				
scholar				
sloppy				
sonnet				
spotlight				
topic				
yonder				

(*cont.*)

LONG AND SHORT VOWEL PATTERNS IN THE STRESSED SYLLABLE (*cont.*)

Long o	Short u	Long u	
open o	u	uCe	open u*
bony	begun (2)	abuse (2)	bugle
chosen	bubble	acute (2)	futile
cobra	bundle	amuse (2)	future
donate	buzzer	compute (2)	humid
focus	chuckle	conclude (2)	human
frozen	clumsy	confuse (2)	humor
gopher	cluster	consume (2)	music
grocer	custom	dilute (2)	pupil
locate	disgust (2)	dispute (2)	ruby
local	distrust (2)	exclude (2)	ruling
moment	dungeon	excuse (2)	rumor
motor	erupt (2)	include (2)	student
nomad	fumble	jukebox	sumac
notice	funny	lukewarm	super
notion	grumpy	misuse (2)	truly
ocean	hundred	perfume (2)	tuba
odor	hungry	pollute (2)	tulip
pony	husband	presume (2)	tumor
potion	instruct (2)	protrude (2)	tuna
program	jungle	reduce (2)	tunic
pronoun	muffin	resume (2)	tutor
protein	mustang	salute (2)	
rodent	mustard	tubeless	
rotate	number	yuletide	
smoky	public		
social	publish		
soda	pumpkin		
sofa	punish		
solo	puppy		
spoken	result (2)		
total	rubber		
trophy	rugged		
	rustle		
	snuggle		
	study		
	thunder		
	trumpet		
	tunnel		
	ugly		
	uncle		
	under		

*See also ew under "Abstract Vowels."

R-CONTROLLED VOWEL PATTERNS IN THE STRESSED SYLLABLE

a

ar		are	air	ar/er
afar (2)	marble	aware (2)	aircraft	baron
ajar (2)	margin	bareback	airlines	barracks
alarm (2)	market	barefoot	airmail	barrel
apart (2)	marshal	barely	airplane	barren
barber	martyr	beware (2)	airport	carat
bargain	parchment	carefree	airwaves	carol
barley	parkway	careful	affair (2)	carriage
barnyard	parsley	compare (2)	chairman	carrot
barter	parsnip	declare (2)	dairy	carry
carbon	partner	prepare (2)	despair (2)	larynx
carcass	parcel	rarely	fairground	marriage
cardboard	pardon	rarest	fairway	marrow
cargo	parka	spareribs	fairy	narrate
carpet	parlor	warehouse	hairbrush	narrow
carport	partial		haircut	parent
carton	partridge		hairpin	parish
cartridge	party		prairie	parrot
cartwheel	sarcasm		repair (2)	sparrow
charcoal	scarlet		staircase	tariff
charter	sharpen		stairway	vary
darkness	sparkle			scarab
farmhouse	starchy			
farther	stardom			berry
garbage	starfish			cherish
garden	starlings			cherry
gargle	starlight			cherub
gargoyle	startle			derrick
garland	tartness			herald
garlic	tardy			heron
garment	target			herring
garnet	tarnish			merit
garnish	varnish			merry
guardrail	yardage			peril
guitar (2)	yardstick			perish
harbor				serrate
hardly				sheriff
hardwood				sterile
harmful				terrace
harness				terror
harpist				alert (2)
harvest				certain
jargon				clergy
larva				derby

Note: Words included in this feature have a first-syllable stress unless otherwise noted—for example, *guitar (2)*.

(cont.)

R-CONTROLLED VOWEL PATTERNS IN THE STRESSED SYLLABLE (*cont.*)

e

er	ear	ear	eer	ere
emerge (2)	bleary	appear (2)	career (2)	adhere (2)
exert (2)	early	beardless	cheerful	austere (2)
gerbil	earthen	clearing	deerskin	cashmere (2)
herbal	earthquake	dearest	jeering	hereby
herdsman	earthworm	dreary	leery	merely
hermit	learner	fearful	peering	revere (2)
jerky	pearly	earache	sheerest	severe (2)
jersey	rehearse (2)	gearshift	steerage	sincere (2)
kerchief	relearn (2)	nearby	veneer (2)	
kernel	research (2)	nearly		
merger	searchlight	rearward		
merchant	unearned	teardrop		
mercy	yearning	tearful		
mermaid		smeary		
nervous		spearhead		
perky		spearmint		
perfect		unclear (2)		
perjure		weary		
person		yearling		
prefer (2)		yearly		
reserve (2)		yearbook		
reverse (2)				
serfdom				
sermon				
serpent				
service				
sternly				
thermal				
thermos				
verbal				
verdict				
version				
versus				

(cont.)

R-CONTROLLED VOWEL PATTERNS IN THE STRESSED SYLLABLE (*cont.*)

i		o		
ir	*ire*	*or*		*ore*
astir (2)	acquire (2)	abhor (2)	normal	adore (2)
birdbath	admire (2)	adorn (2)	northeast	ashore (2)
birdhouse	afire (2)	border	northwest	before (2)
birdseed	aspire (2)	borrow	porthole	boredom
birthday	attire (2)	choral	porpoise	deplore (2)
birthmark	desire (2)	chorus	porridge	explore (2)
birthstone	entire (2)	coral	portion	galore (2)
chirping	expire (2)	cordial	portrait	horehound
circle	direful	corkboard	scorching	ignore (2)
circuit	firearm	corkscrew	shortage	restore (2)
circus	firefly	corncob	shortcake	scoreless
confirm (2)	fireman	corner	snorkel	shorebird
dirty	fireplace	cornfield	sorghum	shoreline
firmly	fireproof	cornhusk	sorrel	storefront
flirting	inquire (2)	cornmeal	sorrow	storehouse
girlfriend	inspire (2)	cornstalk	sorry	storeroom
girdle	perspire (2)	cornstarch	sportsmen	
irksome	rehire (2)	dormant	stormy	
shirttail	require (2)	dormer	story	
sirloin	retire (2)	floral	torchlight	
skirmish	tiresome	florist	torment	
swirling	wiretap	forage	torrent	
thirsty		forceful	tortoise	
twirler		forest	torture	
virtue		forfeit		
whirlpool		forging		
whirlwind		forklift		
		formal		
		former		
		fortnight		
		fortress		
		fortune		
		forty		
		forward		
		glory		
		hornet		
		horrid		
		horror		
		horseback		
		lorry		
		moral		
		morning		
		morsel		
		mortal		
		mortgage		

(cont.)

R-CONTROLLED VOWEL PATTERNS IN THE STRESSED SYLLABLE (*cont.*)

o		u		
oar	**our**	**ur**		**ure**
aboard (2)	courthouse	burden	surgeon	assure (2)
boarding	courtship	burglar	surplus	brochure (2)
boardroom	courtyard	burlap	surrey	endure (2)
boardwalk	foursome	burly	Thursday	impure (2)
coarsely	fourteen	burro	turban	manure (2)
hoarding	mournful	bursting	turkey	mature (2)
hoarsely	mourning	curbstone	turmoil	obscure (2)
hoarseness	pouring	curdle	turnip	procure (2)
	sources	curfew	turnstile	purebred
	yourself	curler	turquoise	secure (2)
		curly	turret	surefire
		currant	turtle	surely
		current		unsure (2)
		curry		
		cursive		
		cursor		
		curtain		
		curtsy		
		curvy		
		during		
		flurry		
		furnace		
		furnish		
		furrow		
		further		
		gurgle		
		hurdle		
		hurry		
		juror		
		jury		
		murder		
		murky		
		murmur		
		nurture		
		plural		
		purchase		
		purple		
		purpose		
		purring		
		rural		
		scurry		
		sturdy		
		surcharge		
		surface		
		surfboard		

(cont.)

ABSTRACT VOWELS IN THE STRESSED SYLLABLE

/ōō/	/ŏŏ/	/oi/	/ou/		/ô/
oo/ew	**oo**	**oy/oi**	**ou**	**ow**	**au/aw**
aloof (2)	bookcase	ahoy (2)	bounty	allow (2)	applaud (2)
balloon (2)	bookshelf	annoy (2)	council	bowsprit	August
bassoon (2)	bookworm	boycott	counsel	brownie	author
baboon (2)	cookbook	destroy (2)	counter	chowder	because (2)
cartoon (2)	cookout	employ (2)	county	coward	daughter
cocoon (2)	football	enjoy (2)	devour (2)	cowhand	exhaust
doodle	foothill	joyful	doubtful	dowdy	faucet
harpoon (2)	footprints	loyal	foundry	dowel	gaudy
kazoo (2)	footage	oyster	fountain	downfall	haughty
lagoon (2)	mistook (2)	royal	mountain	dowry	haunches
maroon (2)	rookie	soybean	mousetrap	drowsy	jaundice
monsoon (2)	sooty	voyage	mouthwash	endow (2)	laundry
moody	woodchuck		profound (2)	flower	naughty
noodle	woodland	appoint (2)	scoundrel	powder	pauper
poodle	woodwind	avoid (2)		power	saucer
raccoon (2)		doily		powwow	saunter
rooster		exploit (2)		prowler	sausage
shampoo (2)		loincloth		rowdy	sauna
tatoo (2)		loiter		shower	slaughter
toothache		moisture		towel	
		poison		tower	awkward
anew		rejoice (2)		townsmen	awful
askew		toilet		trowel	awning
cashew				vowel	brawny
chewy					dawdle
crewmen					flawless
dewdrop					gawky
dewlap					guffaw (2)
jewel					lawsuit
pewter					macaw (2)
sewage					pawnshop
skewer					rawhide
steward					sawmill
					tawny

UNSTRESSED SYLLABLE VOWEL PATTERNS

/'n/ /ən/

ain/an	en		in	on
bargain	**noun**	**adjective**	**noun**	**noun**
captain	aspen	barren	basin	apron
certain	chicken	golden	bobbin	arson
chaplain	children	molten	cabin	bacon
chieftain	garden	often	coffin	baron
curtain	heaven	olden	cousin	beacon
fountain	kitten	open*	dolphin	bison
mountain	linen	rotten	goblin	button
villain	mitten	silken	margin	caldron
	oxen	spoken*	muffin	cannon
noun	raven	sullen	muslin	carton
airman	siren	sunken	penguin	colon
human	warden	swollen	puffin	cotton
organ	women	wooden	pumpkin	dragon
orphan			raisin	falcon
seaman	**verb**		resin	felon
slogan	blacken		robin	gallon
sultan	brighten		satin	glutton
tartan	broaden		toxin	heron
titan	broken*		urchin	iron
turban	chosen		vermin	lemon
urban	darken			lesson
yeoman	deafen			mason
	flatten			melon
	freshen			mutton
	frighten			pardon
	given			patron
	lengthen			person
	listen			poison
	open*			prison
	sharpen			reason
	shorten			ribbon
	soften			salmon
	spoken*			season
	strengthen			sermon
	sweeten			squadron
	thicken			summon
	weaken			talon
	widen			treason
				wagon
				weapon

Note: Words included in this feature have an unstressed second syllable, unless otherwise indicated—for example, *select (1)*.
*Denotes verb or adjective.

(cont.)

UNSTRESSED SYLLABLE VOWEL PATTERNS *(cont.)*

/'l/ /əl/

al	il/ile	el	le	
adjective	anvil	angel	able	hustle
bridal	April	barrel	amble	idle
central	basil	bagel	angle	juggle
crystal*	civil	bushel	ankle	jungle
dental	council	camel	apple	kettle
equal	evil	cancel	babble	knuckle
fatal	fossil	channel	battle	little
final	gerbil	chapel	beagle	mantle
focal	lentil	counsel	beetle	maple
formal	nostril	diesel	bottle	middle
global	pencil	easel	bramble	mumble
legal	peril	flannel	brittle	needle
local	pupil	funnel	bridle	nestle
loyal	stencil	gavel	bubble	noodle
mental	tonsil	gravel	buckle	noble
metal*	tranquil	hazel	bundle	paddle
nasal	vigil	jewel	bugle	pebble
naval		kennel	cackle	people
neutral	docile	kernel	candle	pickle
normal	facile	label	castle	poodle
oval	fertile	level	cattle	purple
plural*	fragile	model	cable	puzzle
postal	futile	morsel	chuckle	riddle
rival*	hostile	mussel	circle	rifle
royal	missile	nickel	cradle	saddle
rural	mobile	novel	cripple	sample
spiral*	sterile	panel	crumble	scribble
tidal		parcel	cuddle	settle
total*		quarrel	cycle	single
vital		ravel	dawdle	sniffle
vocal		sequel	dimple	sprinkle
		shovel	doodle	staple
noun		shrivel	double	steeple
journal		snorkel	drizzle	struggle
mammal		squirrel	eagle	stumble
medal		swivel	fable	tackle
opal		tassel	fiddle	thistle
pedal		tinsel	freckle	tickle
petal		towel	fumble	title
rascal		travel	gamble	triple
sandal		tunnel	gargle	trouble
scandal		vessel	gentle	twinkle
signal		vowel	giggle	turtle
vandal		weasel	grumble	waffle
		yodel	handle	whistle
			hurdle	wrinkle

*Denotes noun or adjective.

(cont.)

UNSTRESSED SYLLABLE VOWEL PATTERNS (*cont.*)

/ər/

ar	er		or	
noun:	**noun:**	fiber	**noun:**	motor
agentive	**agentive**	filter (v)	**agentive**	parlor
beggar	barber	freezer	actor	razor
burglar	dreamer	ledger	author	rumor
	founder	lever	doctor	scissors
noun:	grocer	liter	donor	tractor
concrete	jogger	litter (v)	juror	tremor
altar	miser	lumber (v)	mayor	vapor
briar	peddler	luster	neighbor	visor
cellar	planner	manner	sailor	equator (3)
cedar	plumber	poster	sculptor	meteor (3)
cheddar	printer	scooter	senior	
collar	racer	shower (v)	sponsor	
cougar	ranger	timber	tailor	
dollar	reader	toaster	traitor	
grammar	seller	trouser	tutor	
hangar	skater	tweezers	vendor	
molar	shopper	warbler	director (3)	
mortar	soldier	cylinder (3)	editor (3)	
nectar	speaker	disaster (3)	emperor (3)	
pillar	trooper	reminder (3)	governor (3)	
scholar	usher		surveyor (3)	
sugar	voter	**adjective:**	visitor (3)	
tartar	beginner (3)	**comparison**		
calendar (3)	composer (3)	bigger	**noun:**	
	consumer (3)	blacker	**abstract**	
	employer (3)	briefer	favor	
adjective	manager (3)	cheaper	fervor	
lunar	officer (3)	cleaner	honor	
polar	rescuer (3)	coarser	horror	
solar		farther	humor	
stellar		fiercer	rigor	
circular (3)	**noun (verb):**	flatter	splendor	
muscular (3)	**concrete**	frailer	terror	
peculiar (3)	banner	gentler		
singular (3)	blister (v)	lighter	**noun:**	
	border (v)	quicker	**concrete**	
	boulder	simpler	anchor	
	cancer	younger	arbor	
	cider	busier (3)	armor	
	clover	earlier (3)	color	
	cluster (v)	heavier (3)	cursor	
	coaster		error	
	crater		harbor	
	fender		mirror	

(*cont.*)

UNSTRESSED SYLLABLE VOWEL PATTERNS (*cont.*)

More /ər/ spellings		/ət/		Schwa /ə/
ure	*cher/sher*	*et*	*it*	*a, e, i, o, u*
/chər/	**/chər/**	banquet	audit	**a**
capture	archer	basket	bandit	alarm (1)
creature	bleacher	blanket	credit	baton (1)
culture	butcher	bonnet	digit	canal (1)
denture	catcher	bucket	edit	career (1)
feature	marcher	budget	exit	carouse (1)
fixture	pitcher	carpet	habit	fatigue (1)
fracture	poacher	closet	hermit	lapel (1)
gesture	preacher	comet	limit	marine (1)
juncture	rancher	couplet	merit	maroon (1)
lecture	richer	cricket	orbit	parole (1)
mixture	searcher	egret	profit	patrol (1)
moisture	stretcher	faucet	rabbit	tuna
nature	teacher	ferret	spirit	
pasture	trencher	fidget	summit	**e**
picture	voucher	gadget	unit	agent
posture		hatchet	visit	believe (1)
puncture	**/shər/**	helmet	vomit	cement (1)
rupture	crusher	hornet		neglect (1)
sculpture	flasher	jacket		select (1)
structure	fresher	locket		severe (1)
texture	usher	magnet		velour (1)
torture	washer	mallet		veneer (1)
vulture		midget		
		musket		**i**
/shər/		nugget		divide (1)
censure		omelet		divine (1)
fissure		pamphlet		divorce (1)
pressure		picket		gossip
		planet		pizzazz (1)
/jər/		poet		
conjure		puppet		**o**
injure		racket		atom
		scarlet		cocoon (1)
/yər/		secret		confide (1)
failure		skillet		gallop
figure		sonnet		polite (1)
tenure		tablet		pollute (1)
		target		propose (1)
/zhər/		thicket		provoke (1)
closure		toilet		
leisure		trivet		**u**
measure		trumpet		chorus
pleasure		turret		focus
seizure		velvet		supply (1)
treasure		wallet		upon (1)

(*cont.*)

UNSTRESSED SYLLABLE VOWEL PATTERNS (*cont.*)

		Reduced final stress /ē/		
/ĭj/	**/ĭs/**	**ey***	**ie**	**y**
age	**ace**	alley	birdie	angry
bandage	furnace	barley	bootie	beauty
cabbage	grimace	chimney	cookie	berry
carriage	menace	covey	eerie	body
cottage	necklace	curtsey	genie	bossy
courage	palace	donkey	goalie	buggy
damage	preface	galley	movie	bury
dosage	surface	hockey	pinkie	candy
drainage	terrace	honey	prairie	carry
garbage		jersey	rookie	crazy
homage	**ice**	jockey	specie	cherry
hostage	bodice	journey	sweetie	clergy
image	cornice	kidney	zombie	clumsy
language	crevice	medley		county
luggage	justice	money		daily
manage	lattice	monkey		dairy
marriage	malice	parsley		daisy
message	novice	pulley		dingy
mortgage	notice	trolley		dizzy
package	office	turkey		drowsy
passage	practice	valley		early
plumage	service	volley		easy
postage	solstice			empty
rummage				envy
sausage	**uce**			forty
savage	lettuce			gaudy
scrimmage				gravy
sewage	**ise**			guilty
shortage	anise			heavy
storage	porpoise			hungry
suffrage	promise			lily
usage	tortoise			pastry
village	treatise			pity
voyage				puny
wreckage	**is**			quarry
	axis			ruby
edge	basis			sorry
knowledge	crisis			stingy
selvedge	iris			sturdy
	tennis			tidy
idge	trellis			treaty
cartridge				trophy
partridge				vary
porridge				very
				weary
				worry

*Final ey tends to follow *k*, *l*, and *n*.

PLURALS

Add s		Add es		Change y to i
apples	hotels	**sh**	**x**	armies
badges	labels	ashes	boxes	babies
bases	medals	bushes	indexes	berries
bridges	mittens	brushes	foxes	bodies
canoes	parents	crashes	lynxes	booties
chances	results	dishes	sixes	bounties
changes	robots	leashes	taxes	buddies
eagles	rulers	pushes		buggies
features	screams	sashes		bullies
horses	shadows			bunnies
judges	sirens	**ch**		cities
movies	spools	arches		copies
nurses	streets	batches		counties
paces	topics	beaches		cries
parades	trains	bunches		dairies
pebbles	trousers	finches		daisies
pieces	tulips	flashes		diaries
puzzles	wagons	hitches		fairies
riddles	writers	inches		ferries
sleeves		latches		flies
sneezes		leeches		flurries
species		lunches		fries
spices		notches		guppies
sponges		peaches		jellies
squares		riches		juries
statues		roaches		ladies
stooges				levies
voices		**s**		lilies
		atlases		nineties
acorns		bonuses		parties
actors		gases		pastries
adults		irises		pennies
agents				ponies
alleys		**ss**		posies
angles		bosses		quarries
bagels		classes		rubies
basics		crosses		skies
braids		guesses		spies
cabins		kisses		supplies
cakes		losses		trophies
coins		masses		
cousins		passes		
crayons		tosses		
dragons				
exams				
fields				
flowers				
horns				

PREFIXES AND SUFFIXES

Prefixes

dis "opposite of"	*en* "to put into, make"	*fore* "before, in front of"	*in* "in, or into"	*mis* "wrong[ly]"	*pre* "before"
disable	enable	forearm	inboard	misbehave	precook
disagree	enact	forecast	income	miscount	precut
disappear	encamp	foreclose	indent	misdeal	predate
disarm	encase	forefather	indoor	misfire	predawn
disbelieve	encode	foreground	infield	misfit	preexisting
discharge	encrust	forehand	inflame	misgivings	prefix
disclose	endanger	forehead	ingrown	misguide	pregame
discolor	endear	foreleg	inlaid	mishandle	preheat
discomfort	enfold	foreman	inland	misinform	prejudge
discover	enforce	foremost	inmate	misjudge	premature
disfavor	engulf	forenoon	input	mislay	premix
disfigure	enlarge	forepaw	inseam	mislead	premolar
dishonest	enjoy	forerunner	inset	mismanage	prepackage
disinfect	enjoin	foresail	inside	mismatch	prepay
dislike	enlist	foresee	insight	misplace	preschool
disloyal	enrage	foreshadow	intake	misprint	preset
disobey	enrich	foreshorten		misread	preshrunk
disorder	enroll	foresight		misspell	presoak
disregard	enslave	foretell		mistake	preteen
disrespect	ensnare	forethought		mistreat	pretest
distaste	entomb	forewarn		mistrust	preview
distrust	entrust	foreword		misuse	

Note: Words with suffixes are grouped according to any changes made to the base word when the ending was added (i.e., no change, e-drop, double, or change y to i).

(cont.)

PREFIXES AND SUFFIXES (*cont.*)

Prefixes		Suffixes		
re "again"	*un* "not opposite of"	*er/est* "comparatives/ superlatives"		*ful* "full of/having"
react	unable	blacker blackest	fatter fattest	armful
readjust	unafraid	bolder boldest	flatter flattest	boastful
rebound	unalike	brighter brightest	grimmer grimmest	careful
rebuild	unarmed	cheaper cheapest	hotter hottest	cheerful
recall	unaware	cleaner cleanest	madder maddest	colorful
recapture	unbeaten	clearer clearest	redder reddest	doubtful
recharge	unbroken	colder coldest	sadder saddest	dreadful
reclaim	unbuckle	darker darkest	slimmer slimmest	earful
reconstruct	unbutton	dearer dearest	tanner tannest	fearful
recopy	uncertain	fairer fairest	thinner thinnest	forgetful
recount	unclean	firmer firmest	wetter wettest	graceful
recycle	unclear	fuller fullest		harmful
redirect	uncommon	harder hardest	angrier angriest	hopeful
reelect	uncooked	lighter lightest	bonier boniest	lawful
reenact	uncover	louder loudest	bossier bossiest	mournful
refill	undone	meaner meanest	bumpier bumpiest	mouthful
refinish	unequal	nearer nearest	busier busiest	peaceful
refocus	uneven	odder oddest	cloudier cloudiest	playful
reform	unfair	plainer plainest	creamier creamiest	powerful
refresh	unfold	quicker quickest	crispier crispiest	restful
regain	unfreeze	quieter quietest	daintier daintiest	respectful
relearn	unhappy	rougher roughest	dirtier dirtiest	rightful
relocate	unhook	smaller smallest	drier driest	spoonful
remind	unkind	stiffer stiffest	easier easiest	stressful
remodel	unleash	sweeter sweetest	fancier fanciest	tasteful
renew	unlike	tougher toughest	foggier foggiest	thoughtful
reorder	unlock	warmer warmest	fuzzier fuzziest	truthful
repay	unnamed		happier happiest	useful
rephrase	unnoticed	bluer bluest	icier iciest	wasteful
reprint	unpack	braver bravest	itchier itchiest	wishful
rerun	unpaid	closer closest	juicier juiciest	wonderful
research	unreal	coarser coarsest	lazier laziest	youthful
reshape	unripe	fiercer fiercest	luckier luckiest	
restore	unscramble	finer finest	merrier merriest	beautiful
retake	unselfish	larger largest	naughtier naughtiest	bountiful
retrace	unstable	littler littlest	noisier noisiest	dutiful
return	unsteady	looser loosest	prettier prettiest	fanciful
review	untangle	nicer nicest	saltier saltiest	merciful
rewrite	untie	riper ripest	sillier silliest	pitiful
	unwrap	safer safest	skinnier skinniest	plentiful
		scarcer scarcest	wackier wackiest	
		bigger biggest		
		dimmer dimmest		

(*cont.*)

PREFIXES AND SUFFIXES (*cont.*)

Suffixes

less (without)	*ly* (like/in a manner)		*ness* (state of being)	*y* (having)
ageless	abruptly	spryly	awareness	bumpy
armless	avidly	strangely	bareness	catchy
beardless	badly		closeness	chilly
bottomless	barely	angrily	coolness	cloudy
breathless	blindly	bodily	darkness	creepy
careless	bravely	busily	dullness	crispy
ceaseless	certainly	cheerily	firmness	curly
cloudless	chiefly	daintily	fondness	dirty
defenseless	closely	easily	goodness	dressy
effortless	coarsely	gloomily	moistness	dusty
endless	constantly	greedily	openness	filthy
faultless	costly	happily	ripeness	frosty
formless	cowardly	hastily	sickness	gloomy
friendless	crudely	heavily	sharpness	grouchy
fruitless	cruelly	hungrily	stiffness	needy
helpless	deadly		stillness	rainy
homeless	deeply		thinness	rusty
jobless	directly		vastness	sandy
lawless	distinctly		weakness	soapy
limitless	eagerly			snowy
meaningless	entirely		bagginess	speedy
odorless	equally		business	stormy
painless	falsely		dizziness	sugary
powerless	finally		eeriness	sweaty
priceless	frequently		emptiness	thirsty
reckless	friendly		fuzziness	toasty
regardless	gladly		happiness	windy
scoreless	hourly		haziness	worthy
seamless	kindly		laziness	
sleeveless	lately		nosiness	breezy
speechless	legally		readiness	bubbly
spotless	likely		scariness	easy
tasteless	loudly		silliness	greasy
thankless	loyally		ugliness	injury
timeless	nicely		weariness	noisy
wordless	nightly			
	proudly			chatty
merciless	quietly			choppy
penniless	really			floppy
pitiless	rudely			gritty
	sadly			scabby
	safely			skinny
	shortly			starry
	shyly			
	smoothly			

HOMOGRAPHS: STRESS AND PARTS OF SPEECH

Noun first syllable	Verb second syllable	Adjective first or second syllable
	absent'	ab'sent
ab'stract	abstract'	
ad'dress	address'	
af'fect	affect'	
af'fix	affix'	
al'ly	ally'	
an'nex	annex'	august'
Au'gust		
com'bat	combat'	compact' or com'pact
com'pact	compact'	complex' or com'plex
com'plex		
con'duct	conduct'	
con'flict	conflict'	
con'serve	conserve'	
con'sole	console'	
con'sort	consort'	
con'struct	construct'	content'
con'tent	content'	
con'test	contest'	
con'tract	contract'	
con'vert	convert'	
con'vict	convict'	
des'ert	desert'	
en'trance	entrance'	ex'port
ex'port	export'	
ex'tract	extract'	
im'print	imprint'	
in'cline	incline'	
in'crease	increase'	
in'sert	insert'	minute'
min'ute		
ob'ject	object'	per'fect
	perfect'	
pres'ent	present'	
proj'ect	project'	
pro'test	protest'	
reb'el	rebel'	rec'ord
rec'ord	record'	
sub'ject	subject'	
sus'pect	suspect'	
trans'port	transport'	

POLYSYLLABIC HOMOPHONES

With two syllables

Spelling variation in the stressed syllable

allowed	aural	ceiling	colonel	morning	review	holy
aloud	oral	sealing	kernel	mourning	revue	wholly
ascent	bearing	censor	incite	parish	vary	
assent	Bering	sensor	insight	perish	very	

Spelling variation in the unstressed syllable

accept	bases	Chile	epic*	hostel	miner	patience
except	basis	chili	epoch	hostile	minor	patients
		chilly				
affect	bridal		feudal	idle	muscle	presence
effect	bridle	council	futile	idol	mussel	presents
		counsel		idyll		
altar	canvas		desert		manner	taper
alter	canvass	currant	dessert	lessen	manor	tapir
		current		lesson		
baron	(carat		gamble		naval	
barren	karat)	dual	gambol	mantel	navel	
	caret	duel		mantle		
basal	carrot		hangar		palate	
basil			hanger		palette	
					pallet	

Spelling variations in both syllables

ante	bazaar	beadle	cellar	medal	pedal	roomer
auntie	bizarre	beetle	seller	meddle	peddle	rumor
				metal	petal	
awful	borough	berry	cymbal			
offal	burrow	bury	symbol	peeking	profit	
				piquing	prophet	

With three syllables

addition	cereal	principal
edition	serial	principle
capital	complement	stationary
capitol	compliment	stationery

*The unaccented syllables of these two words do not have identical vowel sounds. One has a short *i*, and the other has a schwa sound. For all practical purposes, however, they can be considered homophones.

FINAL /K/ REVISITED

c		que	ke	k	ck
aerobic	organic	antique	breaststroke	aardvark	attack
angelic	Pacific	baroque	clambake	artwork	bedeck
aquatic	panic	bisque	cupcake	benchmark	bullock
archaic	picnic	boutique	earthquake	berserk	burdock
Arctic	poetic	brusque	evoke	cornstalk	carsick
arsenic	public	clique	forsake	crosswalk	cassock
atomic	relic	critique	keepsake	earmark	cowlick
attic	rubric	mystique	mistake	embark	derrick
basic	rustic	oblique	namesake	hallmark	fetlock
ceramic	scenic	opaque	pancake	homework	gimmick
chaotic	septic	physique	provoke	landmark	haddock
chronic	shellac	pique	slowpoke	network	hammock
civic	static	plaque	turnpike		hassock
classic	sumac	torque			hemlock
clinic	tactic	unique			henpeck
colic	tonic				hillock
comic	topic				homesick
cosmic	toxic				hummock
critic	tragic				mattock
cubic	tropic				oarlock
cynic	tunic				paddock
drastic	zodiac				padlock
dynamic					potluck
elastic					ransack
ethnic					rollick
exotic					seasick
fabric					
fanatic					
frantic					
frolic					
garlic					
generic					
graphic					
havoc					
hectic					
heroic					
italic					
lilac					
logic					
lunatic					
magic					
melodic					
metric					
mimic					
mosaic					
music					
nomadic					
olympic					

◆
Derivational Constancy
◆

SILENT VERSUS SOUNDED CONSONANTS

Silent	Sounded
assig_n	assig_nation
autum_n	autum_nal
benig_n	benig_nant
bom_b	bom_bard
colum_n	colum_nar, colum_nist
condem_n	condem_nation
crum_b	crum_ble
de_bt	de_bit
desig_n	desig_nate, desig_nation
dou_bt	du_bious
fas_ten	fas_t
has_ten	has_te
_heir	in_herit
hym_n	hym_nal
malig_n	malig_nant, malig_nancy
mois_ten	mois_t
_mnemonic	a_mnesia
mus_cle	mus_cular
of_ten	of_t
paradig_m	paradig_matic
pro_hibition	pro_hibit
resig_n	resig_nation
sig_n	sig_nal
sof_ten	sof_t
solem_n	solem_nity
ve_hicle	ve_hicular
wres_tle	wres_t

CONSONANT ALTERNATIONS WITH /SHƏN/

With pronunciation changes

/t/ to /sh/ ct + ion		nt, pt, rt, st + ion	
abstract	abstraction	adopt	adoption
affect	affection	assert	assertion
attract	attraction	congest	congestion
collect	collection	contort	contortion
conduct	conduction	corrupt	corruption
connect	connection	desert	desertion
construct	construction	distort	distortion
contract	contraction	digest	digestion
contradict	contradiction	disrupt	disruption
convict	conviction	erupt	eruption
correct	correction	except	exception
detect	detection	exempt	exemption
direct	direction	exert	exertion
distract	distraction	exhaust	exhaustion
eject	ejection	extort	extortion
elect	election	insert	insertion
evict	eviction	intercept	interception
extinct	extinction	interrupt	interruption
extract	extraction	invent	invention
infect	infection	prevent	prevention
inject	injection	suggest	suggestion
inspect	inspection		
instruct	instruction	**but**	
intersect	intersection		
object	objection	**add** *ation*	
obstruct	obstruction	adapt	adaptation
perfect	perfection	affect	affectation
predict	prediction	confront	confrontation
project	projection	document	documentation
protect	protection	import	importation
react	reaction	indent	indentation
reflect	reflection	infest	infestation
reject	rejection	lament	lamentation
restrict	restriction	pigment	pigmentation
retract	retraction	plant	plantation
select	selection	present	presentation
subtract	subtraction	protest	protestation
transact	transaction	tempt	temptation

(*cont.*)

CONSONANT ALTERNATIONS WITH /SHƏN/ (*cont.*)

With pronunciation changes

/s/ to /sh/ ss + ion		/k/ to /sh/ c + ian	
access	accession	clinic	clinician
aggress	aggression	cosmetic	cosmetician
compress	compression	diagnostic	diagnostician
confess	confession	electric	electrician
decompress	decompression	logic	logician
depress	depression	magic	magician
discuss	discussion	mathematics	mathematician
dispossess	dispossession	music	musician
digress	digression	optic	optician
express	expression	pediatric	pediatrician
impress	impression	physic	physician
obsess	obsession	politic	politician
oppress	oppression	statistic	statistician
possess	possession	tactic	tactician
process	procession		
profess	profession		
progress	progression		
recess	recession		
regress	regression		
repossess	repossession		
repress	repression		
suppress	suppression		

(*cont.*)

CONSONANT ALTERNATIONS WITH /SHƏN/ (*cont.*)

With pronunciation and spelling changes

/t/ to /sh/ e-drop + *ion*		/s/ or /z/ to /sh/ or /zh/ e-drop + *ion*	
abbreviate	abbreviation	averse	aversion
accumulate	accumulation	confuse	confusion
animate	animation	convulse	convulsion
anticipate	anticipation	diffuse	diffusion
appreciate	appreciation	disperse	dispersion
associate	association	fuse	fusion
calculate	calculation	immerse	immersion
celebrate	celebration	incise	incision
circulate	circulation	perverse	perversion
communicate	communication	precise	precision
complete	completion	pretense	pretension
concentrate	concentration	profuse	profusion
cooperate	cooperation	repulse	repulsion
create	creation	revise	revision
cultivate	cultivation	submerse	submersion
decorate	decoration	supervise	supervision
dedicate	dedication	televise	television
demonstrate	demonstration	tense	tension
devote	devotion	transfuse	transfusion
dictate	dictation		
donate	donation		
educate	education		
estimate	estimation		
evaporate	evaporation		
exaggerate	exaggeration		
frustrate	frustration		
graduate	graduation		
hesitate	hesitation		
hibernate	hibernation		
illustrate	illustration		
imitate	imitation		
irrigate	irrigation		
isolate	isolation		
locate	location		
migrate	migration		
navigate	navigation		
nominate	nomination		
operate	operation		
participate	participation		
pollute	pollution		
promote	promotion		
regulate	regulation		
separate	separation		
translate	translation		
vibrate	vibration		

(cont.)

CONSONANT ALTERNATIONS WITH /SHƏN/ (*cont.*)

With pronunciation and spelling changes

/d/ to /sh/ or /zh/ d(e)-drop + *sion*		Predictable changes by word family	
abrade	abrasion	admit	admission
allude	allusion	commit	commission
apprehend	apprehension	emit	emission
ascend	ascension	omit	omission
collide	collision	permit	permission
comprehend	comprehension	remit	remission
conclude	conclusion	submit	submission
condescend	condescension	transmit	transmission
corrode	corrosion		
decide	decision	ascribe	ascription
delude	delusion	describe	description
deride	derision	inscribe	inscription
divide	division	prescribe	prescription
elude	elusion	subscribe	subscription
erode	erosion	transcribe	transcription
evade	evasion		
exclude	exclusion	assume	assumption
expand	expansion	consume	consumption
explode	explosion	presume	presumption
extend	extension	resume	resumption
include	inclusion		
intrude	intrusion	concede	concession
invade	invasion	recede	recession
occlude	occlusion	secede	secession
persuade	persuasion		
preclude	preclusion	conceive	conception
pretend	pretension	deceive	deception
protrude	protrusion	perceive	perception
provide	provision	receive	reception
seclude	seclusion		
suspend	suspension	convert	conversion
		divert	diversion
		extrovert	extroversion
		introvert	introversion
		invert	inversion
		pervert	perversion
		revert	reversion
		subvert	subversion
		deduce	deduction
		induce	induction
		introduce	introduction
		produce	production
		reduce	reduction

OTHER CONSONANT ALTERNATIONS

With pronunciation changes		With pronunciation and spelling changes*	
/k/ to /s/ c + *ity* (or *ize*)		**/s/ to /sh/** e-drop + *ial* (or *tial*)	
authentic	authenticity	artifice	artificial
critic	criticize	commerce	commercial
domestic	domesticity	face	facial
eccentric	eccentricity	finance	financial
elastic	elasticity, elasticize	office	official
electric	electricity	prejudice	prejudicial
ethnic	ethnicity	province	provincial
italic	italicize	race	racial
plastic	plasticity	sacrifice	sacrificial
public	publicity, publicize		
romantic	romanticize	circumstance	circumstantial
specific	specificity	consequence	consequential
toxic	toxicity	essence	essential
		experience	experiential
/t/ to /sh/ t + *ial*		inference	inferential
		influence	influential
		palace	palatial
confident	confidential	preference	preferential
consequent	consequential	residence	residential
exponent	exponential	sequence	sequential
part	partial	space	spatial
potent	potential	substance	substantial
president	presidential		
provident	providential	**/s/ to /sh/** e-drop + *ious*	
resident	residential		
tangent	tangential	auspice	auspicious
torrent	torrential	avarice	avaricious
		caprice	capricious
		grace	gracious
		malice	malicious
		office	officious
		space	spacious

*For further examples of consonant alternations with pronunciation and spelling changes see *ant/ance* and *ent/ence* under "Latin-Derived Suffixes" (for example, *abundant/abundance* and *competent/competence*).

The issue of when to use *cial* and when *tial* seems confusing on the surface. Related words of both types end with *ce*. However, a knowledge of related words can still be of help in spelling some of the words (for example, *ence* words require *tial*). A look at the Latin ancestry of the others reveals the logic behind their seemingly arbitrary endings. For example, *palace* < *palatium* becomes *palatial*, and *office* < *officium* becomes *official*.

VOWEL ALTERNATIONS

Long to short		Long to schwa	
a		*a*	
cave	cavity	able	ability
flame	flammable	anticipate	anticipatory
grave	gravity	associate	associative
humane	humanity	declare	declaration
inflame	inflammable	degrade	degradation
nation	national	famous	infamous
nature	natural	indicate	indicative
profane	profanity	inflame	inflammation
deprave	depravity	major	majority
volcano	volcanic	narrate	narrative
e		native	nativity
anesthesia	anesthetic	prepare	preparation
athlete	athletic	relate	relative
convene	convention	sage	sagacity
diabetes	diabetic	stable	stability
discrete	discretion	*e*	
dream	dreamt	comedian	comedy
extreme	extremity	compete	competition
meter	metric	gene	genetic
please	pleasant	remedial	remedy
serene	serenity	*i*	
i		admire	admiration
crime	criminal	combine	combination
decide	decision	compile	compilation
divide	division	define	definition
divine	divinity	deprive	deprivation
ignite	ignition	derive	derivation
parasite	parasitic	divide	dividend
prescribe	prescription	final	finality
provide	provision	incline	inclination
revise	revision	inspire	inspiration
televise	television	invite	invitation
wise	wisdom	perspire	perspiration
o		preside	president
cone	conic	recite	recitation
microscope	microscopic	reside	resident
telescope	telescopic	*o*	
u		adore	adoration
assume	assumption	compose	composition
consume	consumption	dispose	disposition
construe	construction	explore	exploration
induce	induction	expose	exposition
introduce	introduction	harmonious	harmony
produce	production	ignore	ignorant
		impose	imposition

(cont.)

VOWEL ALTERNATIONS (*cont.*)

Long to schwa	Short to schwa

o

oppose	opposition
pose	position
propose	proposition
restore	restoration
social	society
suppose	supposition

With predictable spelling changes

exclaim	exclamation
explain	explanation
proclaim	proclamation
reclaim	reclamation
abstain	abstention
detain	detention
retain	retention
conceive	conception
deceive	deception
perceive	perception
receive	reception
apply	application
certify	certification
clarify	clarification
classify	classification
gratify	gratification
identify	identification
imply	implication
justify	justification
magnify	magnification
modify	modification
multiply	multiplication
notify	notification
personify	personification
purify	purification
qualify	qualification
simplify	simplification
specify	specification
unify	unification
verify	verification

a

abnormality	abnormal
academic	academy
academy	academic
actuality	actual
emphatic	emphasis
fatality	fatal
hospitality	hospital
legality	legal
locality	local
malice	malicious
metallic	metal
nationality	national
originality	original
personality	personal
systematic	systematize
totality	total
vitality	vital

e

academic	academy
celebrate	celebrity
celebrity	celebrate
democrat	democracy
excel	excellent
perfection	perfect
systemic	system

i

contribute	contribution
critic	criticize
distribute	distribution
docility	docile
habit	habitat
mobility	mobile
political	politics
prohibit	prohibition

o

chronic	chronology
democracy	democrat
ecology	ecological
economy	economics
economics	economy
editorial	editor
geometry	geometric
hypocrisy	hypocrite
inform	information
majority	major
periodic	period

LATIN-DERIVED SUFFIXES

able		*ible*	
Base word		**Root**	
accept	acceptable	*aud*	audible
account	accountable	*compat*	compatible
adapt	adaptable	*cred*	credible
adjust	adjustable	*cruc*	crucible
afford	affordable	*dirig*	dirigible
agree	agreeable	*ed*	edible
allow	allowable	*elig*	eligible
approach	approachable	*feas*	feasible
avoid	avoidable	*gull*	gullible
break	breakable	*horr*	horrible
comfort	comfortable	*incorrig*	incorrigible
commend	commendable	*indel*	indelible
consider	considerable	*invinc*	invincible
credit	creditable	*irasc*	irascible
depend	dependable	*leg*	legible
detest	detestable	*mand*	mandible
distinguish	distinguishable	*neglig*	negligible
expand	expandable	*ostens*	ostensible
fashion	fashionable	*plaus*	plausible
favor	favorable	*poss*	possible
laugh	laughable	*tang*	tangible
maneuver	maneuverable	*terr*	terrible
pay	payable	*vis*	visible
perish	perishable		
prefer	preferable	**but**	
predict	predictable	*amic*	amicable
profit	profitable	*impecc*	impeccable
punish	punishable	*implac*	implacable
question	questionable		
read	readable	**Predictable changes**	
reason	reasonable		
refill	refillable	access	accessible
remark	remarkable	compress	compressible
respect	respectable	express	expressible
season	seasonable	impress	impressible
transfer	transferable	repress	repressible
transport	transportable	suppress	suppressible
but		admit	admissible
		permit	permissible
combust	combustible	remit	remissible
contempt	contemptible	transmit	transmissible
corrupt	corruptible		
deduct	deductible	apprehend	apprehensible
digest	digestible	comprehend	comprehensible
distract	distractible	reprehend	reprehensible
resist	resistible		

(cont.)

LATIN-DERIVED SUFFIXES (*cont.*)

able

With *e*-drop		With *ate*-drop and change *y* to *i*	
achieve	achievable	abominate	abominable
admire	admirable	appreciate	appreciable
adore	adorable	calculate	calculable
advise	advisable	communicate	communicable
assume	assumable	cultivate	cultivable
attribute	attributable	demonstrate	demonstrable
believe	believable	educate	educable
blame	blamable	estimate	estimable
breathe	breathable	irritate	irritable
compare	comparable	navigate	navigable
conceive	conceivable	negotiate	negotiable
consume	consumable	operate	operable
debate	debatable	penetrate	penetrable
deplore	deplorable	separate	separable
describe	describable	tolerate	tolerable
desire	desirable	vegetate	vegetable
dispose	disposable	venerate	venerable
endure	endurable		
excite	excitable	certify	certifiable
excuse	excusable	classify	classifiable
like	likable	deny	deniable
love	lovable	envy	enviable
measure	measurable	identify	identifiable
note	notable	justify	justifiable
observe	observable	modify	modifiable
oppose	opposable	pity	pitiable
pleasure	pleasurable	ply	pliable
recognize	recognizable	quantify	quantifiable
recycle	recyclable	rectify	rectifiable
remove	removable	rely	reliable
reuse	reusable	remedy	remediable
size	sizable	vary	variable
value	valuable		

But		And	
pronounce	pronounceable	bridge	bridgeable
enforce	enforceable	change	changeable
notice	noticeable	damage	damageable
peace	peaceable	exchange	exchangeable
replace	replaceable	knowledge	knowledgeable
service	serviceable	manage	manageable
trace	traceable	marriage	marriageable
		recharge	rechargeable
		salvage	salvageable

(*cont.*)

LATIN-DERIVED SUFFIXES (*cont.*)

ant	ance	ancy
abundant	abundance	
arrogant	arrogance	
assistant	assistance	
attendant	attendance	
blatant		blatancy
brilliant	brilliance	brilliancy
buoyant		buoyancy
clairvoyant	clairvoyance	
cognizant	cognizance	
complaisant	complaisance	
compliant	compliance	
constant		constancy
defiant	defiance	
discrepant		discrepancy
dissonant	dissonance	
distant	distance	
dominant	dominance	
dormant		dormancy
elegant	elegance	
extravagant	extravagance	extravagancy
exuberant	exuberance	
flamboyant	flamboyance	flamboyancy
fragrant	fragrance	
hesitant	hesitance	hesitancy
ignorant	ignorance	
important	importance	
infant		infancy
instant	instance	
malignant	malignance	malignancy
nonchalant	nonchalance	
observant	observance	
occupant		occupancy
petulant	petulance	petulancy
piquant		piquancy
poignant		poignancy
pregnant		pregnancy
radiant	radiance	
redundant		redundancy
relevant	relevance	relevancy
reliant	reliance	
reluctant	reluctance	
resistant	resistance	
resonant	resonance	
significant	significance	
tolerant	tolerance	
vacant		vacancy
vigilant	vigilance	

(*cont.*)

LATIN-DERIVED SUFFIXES (*cont.*)

ent	ence	ency
absent	absence	
absorbent		absorbency
adherent	adherence	
adolescent	adolescence	
affluent	affluence	
agent		agency
benevolent	benevolence	
coherent	coherence	coherency
coincident	coincidence	
competent	competence	competency
complacent	complacence	complacency
congruent	congruence	congruency
consistent		consistency
constituent		constituency
contingent		contingency
convalescent	convalescence	
convenient	convenience	
correspondent	correspondence	
decadent	decadence	decadency
decent		decency
deficient		deficiency
delinquent		delinquency
dependent	dependence	dependency
despondent	despondence	despondency
deterrent	deterrence	
different	difference	
diffident	diffidence	
diligent	diligence	
dissident	dissidence	
effervescent	effervescence	
efficient		efficiency
eloquent	eloquence	
emergent	emergence	emergency
eminent	eminence	eminency
equivalent	equivalence	equivalency
evident	evidence	
excellent	excellence	excellency
expedient	expedience	expediency
florescent	florescence	
fluent		fluency
frequent		frequency
impatient	impatience	
impertinent	impertinence	
impudent	impudence	
incident	incidence	
independent	independence	
indulgent	indulgence	
innocent	innocence	

(*cont.*)

LATIN-DERIVED SUFFIXES (*cont.*)

ent	ence	ency
insistent	insistence	
intelligent	intelligence	
iridescent	iridescence	
lenient	lenience	leniency
magnificent	magnificence	
malevolent	malevolence	
negligent	negligence	
obedient	obedience	
omnipotent	omnipotence	
patient	patience	
permanent	permanence	permanency
persistent	persistence	persistency
phosphorescent	phosphorescence	
potent		potency
precedent	precedence	
present	presence	
president		presidency
prevalent	prevalence	
proficient		proficiency
prominent	prominence	
prudent	prudence	
referent	reference	
reminiscent	reminiscence	
repellent		repellency
resident	residence	residency
resilient	resilience	resiliency
reticent	reticence	
sufficient		sufficiency
translucent	translucence	translucency
transparent		transparency
turbulent	turbulence	
urgent		urgency
vehement	vehemence	
violent	violence	

(*cont.*)

LATIN-DERIVED SUFFIXES (*cont.*)

/âr' ē/		/ə rē/		/ôr'ē/
ary	*ery*	*ary/ery*	*ory*	*ory*
adversary	cemetery	anniversary	accessory	allegory
apiary	confectionery	auxiliary	compulsory	auditory
apothecary	imaginery	boundary	contradictory	category
arbitrary	stationery	burglary	cursory	circulatory
binary		complimentary	directory	conservatory
canary		diary	history	derogatory
commentary		documentary	introductory	dormitory
contemporary		elementary	memory	explanatory
customary		exemplary	pillory	inventory
dignitary		glossary	satisfactory	laboratory
estuary		granary	savory	mandatory
extraordinary		infirmary	sensory	migratory
fragmentary		parliamentary	theory	observatory
hereditary		rotary	victory	respiratory
honorary		rudimentary		territory
imaginary		salary		
involuntary		summary		
itinerary		supplementary		
judiciary				
legendary		artery		
library		bribery		
literary		celery		
mercenary		discovery		
military		drapery		
missionary		drudgery		
momentary		embroidery		
monetary		forgery		
necessary		gallery		
obituary		grocery		
preliminary		machinery		
primary		misery		
revolutionary		mystery		
sanctuary		nursery		
sanitary		periphery		
secretary		scenery		
solitary		sorcery		
stationary		surgery		
temporary		treachery		
tributary		upholstery		
vocabulary				
voluntary				

(cont.)

LATIN-DERIVED SUFFIXES (*cont.*)

ity

With base word		With e-drop	With ble → bil
abnormality	prosperity	activity	ability
absurdity	publicity	adversity	acceptability
acidity	rapidity	agility	accessibility
actuality	reality	antiquity	accountability
authenticity	regularity	austerity	adaptability
authority	rigidity	captivity	affability
brutality	seniority	community	availability
causality	similarity	continuity	capability
civility	solemnity	creativity	credibility
complexity	solidity	density	disability
conformity	specificity	diversity	eligibility
cordiality	stupidity	divinity	impossibility
domesticity	superiority	extremity	inevitability
eccentricity	technicality	femininity	irritability
elasticity	timidity	festivity	legibility
electricity	totality	futility	liability
equality	toxicity	gravity	nobility
eventuality	uniformity	hostility	predictability
familiarity	universality	immaturity	reliability
fatality	validity	immensity	reproducibility
formality	vitality	impurity	responsibility
frugality		insanity	sensibility
hospitality		insecurity	stability
humidity		intensity	visibility
inferiority		maturity	
legality		objectivity	
majority		opportunity	
mentality		purity	
minority		scarcity	
morality		sensitivity	
neutrality		security	
originality		senility	
peculiarity		serenity	
perplexity		severity	
personality		sincerity	
popularity		university	
principality		versatility	

DOUBLING ISSUES WITH POLYSYLLABIC BASE WORDS

Doubling*

abhor	abhorred, abhorring abhorrent, abhorrence
acquit	acquitted, acquitting acquittal
admit	admitted, admitting admittance
allot	allotted, allotting
begin	beginning, beginner
commit	committed, committing
compel	compelled, compelling
concur	concurred, concurring concurrence
confer	conferred, conferring
control	controlled, controlling controller
defer	deferred, deferring
embed	embedded, embedding
emit	emitted, emitting
equip	equipped, equipping
excel	excelled, excelling, *but* ex'cellent
expel	expelled, expelling
forbid	forbidding, forbidden
forget	forgetting
incur	incurred, incurring
infer	inferred, inferring
occur	occurred, occurring, occurrence
omit	omitted, omitted,
patrol	patrolled, patrolling
permit	permitted, permitting
prefer	preferred, preferring
propel	propelled, propelling, propeller
rebel	rebelled, rebelling rebellion
refer	referred, referring, referral
regret	regretted, regretting regrettable
repel	repelled, repelling, repellent
submit	submitted, submitting
transfer	transferred, transferring
transmit	transmitted, transmitting

No doubling**

Final consonant is preceded by two vowels

appear	appeared, appearing, appearance
complain	complained, complaining complainer
detour	detoured, detouring
explain	explained, explaining
repeat	repeated, repeating

Word ends with two consonants

attend	attended, attending
collect	collected, collecting
conduct	conducted, conducting
exist	existed, existing
insert	inserted, inserting
prevent	prevented, preventing
support	supported, supporting supporter, supportable

Suffix begins with a consonant

commit	commitment
defer	deferment
equip	equipment
regret	regretful

Accent is not on the last syllable of the base word

ben'efit	benefited, benefiting
car'ol	caroled, caroling, caroler
consid'er	considered, considering
cred'it	credited, crediting
devel'op	developed, developing
ed'it	edited, editing, editor
en'ter	entered, entering
exhib'it	exhibited, exhibiting
ex'it	exited, exiting
inhab'it	inhabited, inhabiting
lim'it	limited, limiting
sev'er	severed, severing
suf'fer	suffered, suffering

*Double if the suffix begins with a vowel and the syllable before the suffix (1) has one vowel, (2) ends with one consonant, and (3) is stressed. Stress sometimes shifts away from the last syllable in a related word: refer'/ ref'erence.

**For more examples of words that do not require doubling, scan the lists for "Other Syllable Juncture Doubling."

MORE HOMOGRAPHS

Verb /āt/	Noun /ĭt/	Adjective /ĭt/
advocate	advocate	
affiliate	affiliate	
aggregate	aggregate	aggregate
alternate	alternate	alternate
animate		animate
approximate		approximate
articulate		articulate
associate	associate	associate
certificate	certificate	
confederate	confederate	confederate
consummate		consummate
coordinate	coordinate	coordinate
delegate	delegate	
desolate		desolate
duplicate		duplicate
elaborate		elaborate
estimate	estimate	
graduate	graduate	graduate
inebriate	inebriate	inebriate
initiate	initiate	initiate
intimate	intimate	intimate
laminate		laminate
postulate	postulate	
predicate	predicate	predicate
separate	separate	separate
sophisticate	sophisticate	
subordinate	subordinate	subordinate
syndicate	syndicate	

Note: In verb forms, the vowel in the final syllable is always pronounced with a long *a*. The usual pronunciation for noun and/or adjective forms is indicated; in some cases long *a* is also acceptable. Unlike homographs presented at the syllable juncture stage, in the words above the stress does not change.

MORE PLURALS

sis → ses

analysis analyses
antithesis antitheses
basis bases
crisis crises
diagnosis diagnoses
ellipsis ellipses
emphasis emphases
hypothesis hypotheses
metamorphosis
   metamorphoses
nemesis nemeses
neurosis neuroses
oasis oases
parenthesis parentheses
prognosis prognoses
psychosis psychoses
synopsis synopses
synthesis syntheses
thesis theses

a → ae (also add s)

alga algae
alumna alumnae
antenna antennae
   antennas
formula formulae formulas
larva larvae larvas
minutia minutiae
nebula nebulae nebulas
nova novae novas
persona personae
   personas
pupa pupae pupas
vertebra vertebrae
   vertebras

um → a (also add s)

addendum addenda
arboretum arboreta
   arboretums
atrium atria atriums
bacterium bacteria
candelabrum candelabra
   candelabrums
cilium cilia
compendium compendia
   compendiums
consortium consortia
curriculum curricula
   curriculums
datum data
emporium emporia
   emporiums
flagellum flagella
honorarium honoraria
   honorariums
medium media mediums
memorandum memoranda
   memorandums
millennium millennia
   milleniums
moratorium moratoria
   moratoriums
referendum referenda
   referendums
solarium solaria solariums
stratum strata stratums
symposium symposia
   symposiums

us → i (also add es)

alumnus alumni
bronchus bronchi
cactus cacti
cirrus cirri
colossus colossi colossuses
cumulus cumuli
eucalyptus eucalypti
   eucalyptuses
focus foci focuses
fungus fungi funguses
hippopotamus
   hippopotami
   hippopotamuses
locus loci
narcissus narcissi
   narcissuses
nautilus nautili nautiluses
nimbus nimbi nimbuses
nucleus nuclei nucleuses
octopus octopi octopuses
radius radii radiuses
rhombus rhombi
   rhombuses
sarcophagus sarcophagi
   sarcophaguses
stimulus stimuli
stylus styli styluses
syllabus syllabi syllabuses
terminus termini
   terminuses
thesaurus thesauri
   thesauruses

ASSIMILATED (ABSORBED) PREFIXES

With base words	With roots

ad "to, toward"

adjoin: [ad + join]*
acclaim: [ad + claim]
account: [ad + count]
affirm: [ad + firm]
affix: [ad + fix]
allure: [ad + lure]
annotation: [ad + notation]
approve: [ad + prove]
assign: [ad + sign]
assorted: [ad + sorted]
assure: [ad + sure]
attempt: [ad + tempt]

(ad assimilates to ac before c and q; af before f, ag before g; al before l; an before n; ap before p; ar before r; as before s; at before t; and a before sc, sp, and st)

accelerate: [ad + celerare, hasten toward]
alliance: [ad + ligare, bind to]
addend*
addict*
adhesive*
adjacent*
abbreviate
accept
access
accessory
accident
accommodate
accomplish
accrue
accumulate
accurate
accuse
acquiesce
acquire
acquisition
affable
affect
affiance
affiliate
affinity
afflict
affluence
affricate
aggravate
aggregate
aggression
allegation
alleviate
alliance
alliteration
allow

allude
ally
annex
annihilate
announce
annul
apparatus
appeal
appear
appendix
appertain
appetite
applause
application
appreciate
apprehend
apprentice
approach
appropriate
approximate
arraign
arrogance
assault
assemble
assent
assertion
assess
asset
assiduous
assimilate
assist
associate
assuage
assume
assumption
attain
attempt
attendance

attention
attrition

Note: An asterisk is used to indicate words in which the prefix is simply joined to the base or root. No assimilation occurs; however, doubling may still result (for example, *dissatisfy*). Sometimes the final letter of a prefix does change, but to a letter other than that with which the base or root begins. For example, the prefix *ad* becomes *ac* before words and roots that begin with *q* (*acquit*). Similarly, the prefix *com* becomes *con* in words like *condescend* and *consign* and *co* before many words and roots that begin with vowels, *w*, or *h* (for example, *coexist*, *cohabit*). With the exception of the asterisked examples, words included in this section are limited to those with an assimilation that results in a doubled consonant.

(cont.)

ASSIMILATED (ABSORBED) PREFIXES (*cont.*)

With base words	With roots

com "with, together"

compatriot: [*com* + patriot]*
commingle: [*com* + mingle]*
commission: [*com* + mission]*
collapse: [*com* + lapse]
collateral: [*com* + lateral]
colleague: [*com* + league]
collocate: [*com* + locate]
connotation: [*com* + notation]
correlation: [*com* + relation]
correspond: [*com* + respond]

(*com* assimilates to *col* before *l*; *cor* before *r*; *con* before *c, d, g, j, n, q, s, t,* and *v*; and *co* before all vowels, *h,* and *w*)

collaborate: [*com* + *laborare*, work with]
connect: [*com* + *nectere*, fasten together]
commensurate*
combine*
companion*
compare*
collate
collect
collide
collision
colloquial
colloquy
collusion
correct
corrupt
corruption

dis "opposite of, not, apart"

disadvantage: [*dis* + advantage]*
dissatisfied: [*dis* + satisfied]*
diffraction: [*dis* + fraction]
diffuse: [*dis* + fuse]
diffusion : [*dis* + fusion]

(*dis* assimilates to *dif* before *f* and becomes *di* before *b, d, g, l, m, n, r,* and *v.*)

differ: [*dis* + *ferre*, bring or carry apart]
diffidence: [*dis* + *fidere*, opposite of trusting]
disseminate*
discern*
disdain*
difference
different
differentiate
difficulty

(*cont.*)

ASSIMILATED (ABSORBED) PREFIXES (*cont.*)

With base words	With roots

ex "out, from"

exchange: [ex + change]*
excommunicate: [ex + communicate]*
exterminate: [ex + terminate]*
eccentric: [ex + centric]
efface: [ex + face]
efflorescent: [ex + florescent]
effuse: [ex + fuse]

(ex assimilates to *ef* before *f*; *e* before *b, d, g, h, l, m, n, r,* and *v*; and often *ec* before *c* or *s*. In many words of French origin the *ex* appears as *es*—for example, *escape.*)

effervescence: [ex + *fervescere*, begin to boil out]
effusion: [ex + *fundere*, pour out]
excavate*
excerpt*
expansion*
eccentric
eccentricity
ecclesiastic
effect
efficacious
efficiency
effectual
effigy
effluvium
effrontery
effulgent

in "in, not, toward, together"

inaccurate: [*in* + accurate]*
inefficient: [*in* + efficient]*
innumerable: [*in* + numerable]*
inoperative: [*in* + operative]*
insecure: [*in* + secure]*
intemperate: [*in* + temperate]*
illegal: [*in* + legal]
illegible: [*in* + legible]
illimitable: [*in* + limitable]
illiterate: [*in* + literate]
illicit: [*in* + licit]
illogical: [*in* + logical]
immaterial: [*in* + material]
immature: [*in* + mature]
immeasurable: [*in* + measurable]
immemorial: [*in* + memorial]
immigrate: [*in* + migrate]
immobile: [*in* + mobile]
immoderate: [*in* + moderate]
immodest: [*in* + modest]
immoral: [*in* + moral]
immortal: [*in* + mortal]
immovable: [*in* + movable]
irradiate: [*in* + radiate]
irrational: [*in* + rational]
irreconcilable: [*in* + reconcilable]

immense: [*in* + *mensus*, not measured]
irrigate: [*in* + *rigare*, water in]
innate*
incubate*
intact*
illuminate
illusion
illustrate
immaculate
immerse
imminent
immune
immunity
immunization
immure
irrigation

(cont.)

ASSIMILATED (ABSORBED) PREFIXES *(cont.)*

With base words	With roots

in "in, not, toward, together"

irrefutable: [*in* + refutable]
irregular: [*in* + regular]
irrelevant: [*in* + relevant]
irreparable: [*in* + reparable]
irreplaceable: [*in* + replaceable]
irreproachable: [*in* + reproachable]
irresistible: [*in* + resistible]
irresolute: [*in* + resolute]
irresponsible: [*in* + responsible]
irretrievable: [*in* + retrievable]
irreversible: [*in* + reversible]
irrevocable: [*in* + revocable]

(*in* assimilates to *il* before *l*; *ir* before
r; and *im* before *b*, *m*, and *p*)

ob "to, toward, against"

oblong: [*ob* + long]*
offend: [*ob* + fend]
oppose: [*ob* + pose]
opposition: [*ob* + position]
oppress: [*ob* + press]

(*ob* assimilates to *oc* before *c*, *of*,
before *f*, and *op* before *p*; it becomes
o before *m*)

occlude: [*ob* + *claudere*, shut
   against]
offend: [*ob* + *fendere*, hit or thrust
   toward]
oblige*
obstruct*
occasion
occlusion
occupancy
occupation
occupy
occur
occurrence
offensive
offer
offering
opponent
opportune
opportunity
opposite
opprobrium

(cont.)

ASSIMILATED (ABSORBED) PREFIXES (*cont.*)

With base words	With roots

sub "under, lower"

With base words	With roots
subbasement: [*sub* + basement]*	su__ff__er: [*sub* + *ferre*, bear under]
subcommittee: [*sub* + committee]*	su__pp__ort: [*sub* + *portare*, carry under]
subdivision: [*sub* + division]*	subjugate*
subheading: [*sub* + heading]*	subpoena*
submarine: [*sub* + marine]*	subsequent*
su__ff__ix: [*sub* + fix]	succeed
su__ff__use: [*sub* + fuse]	success
su__pp__lant: [*sub* + plant]	succinct
su__pp__liant: [*sub* + pliant]	succor
su__pp__ortable: [*sub* + portable]	succumb
su__pp__ose: [*sub* + pose]	suffice
su__pp__osition [*sub* + position]	sufficient
su__pp__ress: [*sub* + press]	suffocate
su__rr__eal: [*sub* + real]	suffuse
su__rr__ender: [*sub* + render]	suggest
su__rr__ound: [*sub* + round]	suggestion
	supplement
(*sub* assimilates to *suc* before *c*; *suf*	supplicant
before *f*; *sug* before *g*; *sum* before *m*;	supply
sup before *p*; *sur* before *r*; and it	surreptitious
often changes to *sus* before *c*, *p*, and	surrogate
t—for example, *susceptible* and	
suspect)	

MORE USEFUL PREFIXES

anti "against"
antibiotic
anticlimactic
antidote
antifreeze
antihistamine
antipathy
antipodes
antiseptic
antithesis
antitoxin
antitrust
antiwar

auto "self"
autobiography
autocrat
autograph
automatic
automaton
automobile
autonomy
autopsy

cat, cata "down"
cataclysm
catacomb
catalepsy
catalogue
catapult
cataract
catarrh
catastrophe
catatonic

circum "around"
circumambulate
circumference
circumfuse
circumlocution
circumnavigate
circumpolar
circumscribe
circumspect
circumstance
circumvent

inter "between, among"
interact
intercede
interchange
intercollegiate
interdependence
interface
interfere
interject
interlace
interlock
interlocutor
interloper
intermediary
intermission

intra "within"
intramural
intrastate
intravenous

mal, male "bad, evil"
maladjusted
malady
malaria
malcontent
malediction
malefactor
malevolent
malfeasance
malfunction
malign
malinger
malnutrition
malpractice

peri "around, near"
pericardium
perigee
perihelion
perimeter
period
periodontal

peripatetic
periphery
periscope

post "after"
posterior
posterity
posthumous
postimpressionism
postmeridian
postpone
postscript

pro "before, forward"
proboscis
proceed
proclaim
proclivity
procrastinate
procreate
prodigy
produce
profane
profess
proficient
profile
profound
program
progress
prohibit
project
promote
promulgate
pronounce
propel
propensity
prophet
propitious
proponent
proportion
proscenium
prospect
protect
protract
proverb
provide

super "higher, greater"
superabundance
supercilious
superficial
superimpose
superintendent
supermarket
supernatural
superman
supernumerary
superpower
supersede
supersensitive
supersonic
superstition
supervision

trans "over, across"
transatlantic
transcend
transcribe
transfer
transfigure
transfuse
transgress
transit
translate
translucent
transmigration
transmit
transparent
transpire
transplant
transport
transpose

Note: For additional prefixes see "Assimilated (Absorbed) Prefixes" and "Number-Related Prefixes and Roots."

NUMBER-RELATED PREFIXES AND ROOTS

bi "two"
bicentennial
biennial
bilateral
bilingual
bimonthly
bipartisan
biped
bipolar
bisect
bivalve
biweekly

cent, centi "hundred"
bicentennial
centenarian
centennial
centigrade
centimeter
centipede
century
percent
percentile

dec, deca "ten"
decade
decagon
decahedron
decameter

mon, mono "one, alone"
monarchy
monastery
monochromatic
monogamy
monograph
monolith
monologue
monomania
monopoly
monorail
monosyllabic
monotheism
monotone
monotonous

multi "many, much"
multicolored
multicultural
multidimensional
multifaceted
multifamily
multilateral
multimedia
multimillionaire
multinational
multiple
multiplex
multiplication
multipurpose
multitude

oct, octa, octo "eight"
octagon
octahedron
octave
October
octogenarian
octopus
octet
octillion

pent, penta "five"
pentadactyl
pentagon
pentameter
pentathlon
pentatonic

poly "many"
polychrome
polydactyl
polygamy
polyglot
polygon
polygraph
polyhedron
polymerization
polymorphous
polynomial
polyp
polyphagia
polyphonic

polyphony
polysyllabic
polytechnic

quad, quadri "four"
quadrangle
quadrant
quadriceps
quadrilateral
quadrille
quadruped
quadruple
quadruplets
squad
square

semi "half, partly"
semiannual
semiautomatic
semicircle
semicolon
semiconscious
semidetached
semidiurnal
semifinal
semiprecious
semiprivate
semisolid
semitropical
semiweekly
semiyearly

tri "three"
triad
triangle
triceps
tricolor
tricuspid
tricycle
trident
triennial
trifocal
trillium
trilobite
trilogy
trimester
trinity

trio
triplet
tripod
triptych

uni "one"
reunion
unicorn
unicycle
uniform
unify
unilateral
union
unique
unison
unit
unite
unity
universal
universe
university

GREEK ROOTS

aer
(aer "air")
aerate
aerator
aerial
aerie
aerobatics
aerobic
aerodynamics
aeronautics
aerosol
aerospace

arch
***(archos "chief,
   ruler")***
anarchy
archangel
archbishop
archduke
archetype
archipelago
architect
hierarchy
matriarch
monarchy
oligarchy
patriarch

aster, astr
(aster "star")
aster
asterisk
asteroid
astrology
astronomy
astronaut
astronomical
astrophysics
disater

bi, bio
(bios "life")
amphibious
antibiotic
autobiography
biochemistry
biodegradable
biography

biopsy
biology
symbiotic

centr
***(kentron
   "center")***
center
centrifugal
centripetal
centrist
concentrate
concentric
eccentric
egocentric
ethnocentric

chron
(chronos "time")
anachronism
chronic
chronicle
chronological
chronology
chronometer
synchronize

cosm
***(kosmos
   "universe,
   world")***
cosmic
cosmogony
cosmography
cosmology
cosmonaut
cosmopolitan
cosmos
macrocosm
microcosm

cris, crit
***(kritikos "to
   judge,
   separate"***
crisis
criterion
critic
criticism

criticize
critique
diacritical
hypocrisy

cycl
(kyklos "circle")
bicycle
cycle
cyclical
cyclist
cyclometer
cyclone
encyclopedia
motorcycle
recycle
tricycle
unicycle

dem
(demos "people")
demagogue
democracy
demographic
endemic
epidemic
epidemiology

derm
(derma "skin")
dermatology
epidermis
hypodermic
pachyderm
taxidermy

geo
(geo "the earth")
geocentric
geode
geographic
geology
geophysics
geothermal

gram
***(graphein "to
   write")***
anagram
cryptogram

diagram
electrocardiogram
epigram
grammar
histogram
hologram
ideogram
monogram
parallelogram
program
telegram

graph
***(graphein "to
   write")***
autobiography
autograph
bibliography
biography
calligraphy
cartographer
choreographer
cinematography
demography
digraph
epigraph
ethnography
geography
graphics
graphite
homograph
lexicographer
lithograph
oceanography
orthography
paragraph
phonograph
photograph
polygraph
seismograph
telegraph
topography

homo
(homos "same")
homogeneous
homogenize
homograph
homophone

(cont.)

GREEK ROOTS (*cont.*)

hydr
(*hydor* "water")
anhydrous
hydra
hydrangea
hydrant
hydrate
hydraulic
hydroelectric
hydrology
hydrophobia
hydroplane
hydroponics

log, ology
(*legein* "to
speak")
analogy
anesthesiology
anthology
anthropology
apologize
archaeology
audiology
biology
cardiology
catalogue
chronology
dermatology
dialogue
ecology
epilogue
entomology
etymologist
eulogy
genealogy
geology
gerontology
hematology
ichthyology
immunology
logical
logo
meteorology
monologue
mythology
ophthalmology
ornithology

pathology
pharmacology
physiology
prologue
psychology
seismology
sociology
technology
terminology
theology
volcanology
zoology

mania
(*mainesthai* "to
rage")
kleptomania
maniac
pyromania
monomania
megalomania

mega
(*megas* "great")
megabyte
megalomania
megalopolis
megaphone
megaton
megawatt

meter
(*metron*
"measure")
altimeter
barometer
centimeter
chronometer
cyclometer
diameter
hydrometer
kilometer
millimeter
micrometer
odometer
parameter
pedometer
pentameter

perimeter
speedometer
tachometer
thermometer

micro
(*mikros* "small")
microbe
microbiology
microchip
microcomputer
microcosm
micrometer
microfiche
micron
microorganism
microphone
microscope
microwave

morph
(*morphe* "having
a form")
amorphous
anthropomorphism
endomorphic
metamorphosis
morpheme
morphology

onym, nym
(*onyma, onoma*
"name")
acronym
anonymous
antonym
eponym
homonym
patronymic
pseudonym
synonymous

ortho
(*orthos* "straight,
correct")
orthodontics
orthography
orthodox
orthopedic

pan
(*pan* "all")
panacea
Pan-American
panchromatic
pandemic
pandemonium
panoply
panorama
pantheon

path(o), *pathy*
(*pathein* "to
suffer")
antipathy
apathetic
empathize
homeopathic
osteopath
pathogen
pathologist
pathetic
pathos
sympathize
telepathy

ped
(*pais/paidos*
"child"*)
encyclopedia
orthopedic
pedagogue
pedagogy
pediatrician

phil, phile
(*philos* "loving")
audiophile
bibliophile
Philadelphia
philanderer
philanthropy
philatelic
philharmonic
philosophy
philter

*See also Latin *ped.*

(*cont.*)

GREEK ROOTS (*cont.*)

phobia
(phobos "fear")
acrophobia
agoraphobia
claustrophobia
hydrophobia
monophobia
phobia
xenophobia

phon, phone
(phone "sound")
antiphony
cacophony
earphone
euphony
headphone
homophone
megaphone
microphone
phoneme
phonetic
phonics
phonograph
polyphonic
saxophone
sousaphone
stereophonic
symphony
telephone
xylophone

photo
(photos "light")
photocell
photocopier
photogenic
photograph
photojournalism
photometry
photosynthesis
telephoto

phys
(physis "nature")
astrophysics
biophysics
geophysics
metaphysics

physics
physical
physician
physiognomy
physiology
physiotherapy
physique

pol, polis
(polis "city")
acropolis
Annapolis
cosmopolitan
Indianapolis
megalopolis
metropolis
Minneapolis
police
policy
politician

proto
(protos "first")
protocol
proton
protoplasm
prototype
protozoan

psych
*(psyche "spirit,
soul")*
psyche
psychedelic
psychiatry
psychic
psychoanalyst
psychology
psychomotor
psychosis
psychosomatic

scope
*(skopein "see,
view")*
gyroscope
horoscope
kaleidoscope
microscope

periscope
scope
stethoscope
stereoscope
telescope

soph
*(sophos "clever,
wise")*
philosophy
sophisticated
sophistry
sophomore

sphere
*(sphaira "ball,
sphere")*
atmosphere
bathysphere
biosphere
chromosphere
hemisphere
ionosphere
sphere
stratosphere
troposphere

tele
(tele "far off")
telecast
telecommunications
teleconference
telecourse
telegraph
telegram
telepathy
telephone
telephoto
telescope
telethon
televise
television

therm
(therme "heat")
geothermal
thermal
thermodynamic
thermometer

thermonuclear
thermos
thermostat
thermotropism

typ, type
*(typtein "to beat,
to strike")*
archetype
daguerreotype
genotype
phenotype
prototype
stereotype
typecast
typesetter
typewriter
typist
typographical

zo
(zoion "animal")
protozoan
zodiac
zoo
zoological
zoologist
zoophobia
zoophyte

LATIN ROOTS

am, amor
(amare "to love")
amateur
amiable
amicable
amity
amorous
enamored

ambl, ambul
(ambulare "to
walk, move")
amble
ambulance
circumambulate
perambulate
preamble
somnambulate

anima
(anima "breath,
air, soul")
animadversion
animal
animate
animosity
magnanimous
pusillanimous
unanimous

aud
(audire "to hear")
audible
audience
audio
audiology
audiometer
audit
audition
auditorium
auditory
audiovisual
inaudible

bell, belli
(bellum "war"
antebellum
bellicose

belligerent
rebellion

bene, beni
(bene "well")
benediction
benefactor
benefactress
beneficence
beneficial
beneficiary
benefit
benevolent
benign
benignant

cand, chand
(candere "to
shine")
candelabra
candid
candidate
candle
candor
chandler
chandelier
incandescent

cap
(caput "the
head")
cape (land)
capillary
capital
capitalize
capitol
capitulate
captain
decapitate
per capita
recapitulate

ce(e)d, ceas, cess
(cedere "to go, to
yield")
accede*
antecedent
cease

cede
concede
decease
exceed*
intercede
precedent
proceed*
recede*
succeed*
secede

cide
(caedere "to kill,
to cut")
circumcise
concise
excise
fungicide
genocide
germicide
herbicide
homicide
incise
insecticide
pesticide
precise
regicide
suicide

clud, clos, clus
(claudere "to
shut")
cl(a)ustrophobia
close
closet
conclude
conclusion
disclose
enclose
exclude
exclusive
foreclose
include
inclusion
occlude
occlusion
preclude

seclude
seclusion
recluse

cogn
(gnoscere "to
know")
cognition
cognizant
incognito
precognition
recognizance
recognize

cor
(cor, cordis
"heart")
accord
concord
cordial
core
discord
record

cor, corp
(corpus "body")
corps
corpse
corpulent
corpus
corpuscle
corporation
corporeal
corset
incorporate

cred
(credere "to trust,
believe")
accredit
credence
credentials
credible
credit
credulous
discredit
incredible

*The noun form which ends in *ess* is not shown (e.g., *success*).

(cont.)

LATIN ROOTS (*cont.*)

cure
(cura "care")
manicure
pedicure
procure
secure
sinecure

dent, dont
(dens, dentis "a
tooth")
dentils
dentine
dentist
dentition
dentures
orthodontist

dic, dict
(dicere "to
speak")
abdicate
benediction
contradict
dedicate
dictate
diction
dictionary
edict
indict
jurisdiction
predicate
predict
valedictorian
verdict
vindicate

doc
(docere "to
teach")
docent
docile
doctor
doctorate
doctrine
document
documentary
indoctrinate

dom
(dominus "lord,
master")
condominium
domain
dominant
dominate
domineer
dominion
predominate

dom
(domus
"building")
dome
domestic
domesticate
domicile
major domo

dorm
(dormire "to
sleep")
dormant
dormer
dormitory
dormouse

duce, duct
(ducere "to
lead")
abduct
adduce
aqueduct
conducive
conduct
conductor
deduce
deduct
duct
educate
educe
induct
introduction
product
reduce
reproduce
semiconductor
viaduct

equa, equi
(aequus "even")
equable
equality
equanimity
equation
equator
equidistant
equilateral
equilibrate
equilibrium
equinox
equity
equivalent
equivocate

fac, fact, fect
(facere "to do")
affect
artifact
benefactor
confection
defect
effect
facile
facilitate
facsimile
fact
faction
factor
factory
faculty
infect
manufacture
perfect
putrefaction
satisfaction

fer
(ferre "to bring,
carry")
aquifer
circumference
conference
conifer
differ
ferry
fertile
inference

prefer
reference
suffer
transfer
vociferous

fid
(fidere "to trust")
affidavit
bona fide
confidant
confident
confidential
diffident
fidelity
infidelity
perfidy

fin
(finis "end")
confinement
definitive
final
finale
fine
finish
finial
infinite
refine

flect, flex
(flectere "to
bend, curve")
circumflex
deflect
flex
flexible
genuflect
inflection
inflexible
reflect
flex

flict
(fligere "to
strike")
afflict
conflict
inflict

(*cont.*)

LATIN ROOTS (*cont.*)

flu
(*fluere* "to flow")
affluence
confluence
fluctuate
fluent
fluid
influence
influx
superfluous

forc, fort
(*fortis* "strong")
comfort
enforcement
force
fortify
fortitude
fortress
perforce
reinforce

form
(*forma* "a shape")
conform
cuneiform
deform
formal
formality
format
formation
formula
formulate
informal
information
malformed
platform
reform
transform
uniform

fract, frag
(*frangere* "to break")
diffraction
fraction
fracture
fragile

fragment
infraction
refraction

fug
(*fugere* "to flee")
centrifuge
fugitive
fugue
refuge
refugee
subterfuge

gest
(*gerere* "to bear, carry")
congestion
decongestant
digest
gestation
gesticulate
gesture
ingest
suggest

grac, grat
(*gratus* "pleasing, thankful")
congratulate
grace
gracious
grateful
gratify
gratitude
gratuitous
gratuity
ingrate
ingratiate
persona non grata

grad, gress
(*gradi* "to step")
aggressive
centigrade
congress
degradable
digress
downgrade

egress
grade
gradient
gradual
graduate
ingress
progress
regress
retrograde
transgress
upgrade

greg
(*grex, gregis* "a flock, herd")
aggregate
congregation
desegregate
gregarious
segregation

hab, hib
(*habere* "to have, hold")
cohabit
exhibit
habit
habitat
habituate
inhabit
inhibit
prohibit

hos
(*hospes* "host, guest")
hospice
hospitable
hospital
hospitality
host(ess)
hostage
hostel

ject
(*jacere* "to throw")
abject
conjecture

dejected
eject
injection
interject
objection
projectile
projector
reject
subjective
trajectory

jud
(*judex* "a judge")
adjudge
adjudicate
injudicious
judge
judgment
judiciary
judicious
prejudice

junct
(*jungere* "to join")
adjunct
conjunction
disjunction
injunction
junction
juncture

langu, lingu
(*lingua* "the tongue")
bilingual
language
lingo
linguine
linguist
linguistics
monolingual
multilingual

lateral
(*latis, lateris* "a side")
bilateral
collateral

(*cont.*)

LATIN ROOTS (*cont.*)

equilateral
multilateral
quadrilateral
unilateral

lect
(*legere* "to
   gather, read")
collect
elect
elective
elector
intellect
lecture
neglect
select

liber
(*liber* "free")
liberal
liberate
libertarian
libertine
liberty

lit
(*litera* "a letter")
alliteration
illiterate
literacy
literal
literary
literati
literature
literate
obliterate

loc, loco
(*locus* "a place")
allocate
collocate
dislocate
local
locate
locomotive
locus

loc, loq
(*loqui* "to speak")
circumlocution
colloquial
colloquy
elocution
eloquent
grandiloquent
interlocutor
loquacious
obloquy
soliloquy
somniloquy
ventriloquist

luc, lum
(*lumen* "a light")
elucidate
illumination
lucid
lumen
luminary
translucent

magn
(*magnus* "great")
Magna Carta
magnanimous
magnate
magnificent
magnify
magnitude

man
(*manus* "hand")
amanuensis
emancipate
manacle
manage
mandate
maneuver
manipulate
manner
manual
manufacture
manuscript
manicure

medi, medio
(*medius*
   "middle")
intermediary
intermediate
medial
median
mediate
medieval
mediocre
Mediterranean
medium

mem
(*memor* "mindful,
   remembering")
commemorate
immemorial
memento
memorabilia
memorable
memorandum
memoir
memorial
memorize
memory
remembrance

mens, ment
(*mens, mentis*
   "the mind")
comment
demented
mental
mention

migra
(*migrare* "to
wander")
emigrate
immigrate
migrate
transmigration

min
(*minuere* "to
   make smaller")
diminish
mince
minimize
minimum
minnow
minor
minuet
minus
minuscule
minute

mir, marv
(*mirari* "to
   wonder at")
admire
admiral
marvel
marvelous
miracle
mirage
mirror

miss, mit
(*mittere* "to
   send")
admission*
commission*
demise
emissary
emission*
intermission
intermittent
missile
mission
missionary
omission*
permission*
promise
promissory
remission*
submission*
transmission*

*The verb forms of these words end in *it* and are not listed (for example, transmit).

(*cont.*)

LATIN ROOTS (*cont.*)

mob, mot
(*movere* "to
     move")
automobile
bookmobile
commotion
demobilize
demote
emotion
immobile
locomotion
mob
mobile
motel
motion
motivate
motor
promote
remote

mod
(*modus*
     "measure,
     manner")
accommodate
commodious
model
moderate
modify
modicum

mon
(*monere* "to
     warn")
admonish
monitor
monster
monstrous
monument
premonition
remonstrance
summon

mort
(*mortis* "death")
immortal
mortal
mortgage

mortician
mortified
mortuary
postmortem
rigor mortis

mot
(*movere* "move")
automotive
commotion
demote
emotion
locomotive
motility
motion
motivation
motive
motor
motel
promote
remote

mur
(*murus* "a wall")
extramural
immure
intramural
mural

nat
(*nasci* "to be
     born")
innate
natal
nation
native
nativity
nature

nov
(*novus* "new")
innovation
nova
novel
novelty
novice
renovation

numer
(*numerus*
     "number")
enumerate
innumerable
number
numeral
numerator
numerical
numerous
supernumerary
omni
(*omnis* "all")
omnibus
omnifarious
omnipotence
omnipresent
omniscient
omnivore

pac
(*pax, pacis*
     "peace")
Pacific Ocean
pacifier
pacifist
pacify

pat(e)r
(*pater* "father")
expatriate
paternal
patriarch
patrimony
patron
patronize
patronymic
repatriated

ped*
(*pes, pedis*
     "foot")
biped
centipede
expedite
impede
millipede
moped

orthopedic
pedal
pedestal
pedestrian
pedicure
pedigree
pedometer
quadruped

pel
(*pellere* "to
     drive")
appellate
appellation
compel
dispel
impel
propel
repellent

pens, pend
(*pendere* "to
     hang")
appendage
appendix
compensate
dependent
dispense
expend
expense
impending
pendant
pending
pendulum
pension
pensive
propensity
stipend
suspend
suspense

pop, pub
(*populus* "the
     people")
populace
popular
population
populous

*See also Greek *ped*.

(*cont.*)

LATIN ROOTS (*cont.*)

public
publicity
publish

port
(**portare** "to carry")
comportment
deport
deportment
disport
export
import
important
portable
portage
porter
portfolio
portmanteau
rapport
report
sport
support
transport

pos, pon(e)
(**ponere** "to put, place")
a propos
apposition
compose
composite
compost
composure
dispose
expose
impose
impostor
opposite
pose
position
positive
postpone
preposition
proponent
proposition
repose
superimpose
suppose
transpose

press
(**premere** "to press")
antidepressant
compress
decompress
depress
express
impress
irrepressible
oppress
pressure
repression
suppress

prim, princ
(**primus** "first")
prima donna
primal
primary
primate
prime
primer
primeval
primitive
primogeniture
primordial
primrose
prince
principal
principality
principle

priv
(**privus** "separate")
deprive
private
privateer
privation
privet
privilege
privy

prop
(**proprius** "one's own")
appropriate
expropriate

proper
property
proprietor
propriety

pug
(**pugnare** "to fight")
impugn
pugilistic
pugnacious
repugnant

punct
(**punctus** "a point")
punctilious
punctual
punctuate
punctuation

qui
(**quies** "rest")
acquiesce
quiet
quit
quite
requiem
requite
tranquil

quer, ques, quir, quis
(**quaerere** "to ask")
acquire
acquisition
conquer
inquire
inquisition
query
quest
question
questionnaire
request
require
requisite
requisition

rect, reg
(**regere** "to lead straight, rule")
correct
direct
erect
regal
regimen
regiment
region

rod
(**rodere** "to gnaw")
corrode
erode
rodent

rupt
(**rumpere** "to break")
abrupt
bankrupt
corrupt
disrupt
erupt
interrupt
irruption
rupture

sacr, sanct
(**sacer** "sacred")
sacrament
sacred
sacrifice
sacrilege
sacristy
sacrosanct
sanctify
sanctimonious
sanction
sanctuary

sal
(**sal** "salt")
salad
salami
salary
saline
salt

(*cont.*)

LATIN ROOTS (*cont.*)

**scend
(*scandere* "to
climb")**
ascend
condescend
descend
transcend

**sci
(*scire* "to know")**
conscience
conscious
conscientious
omniscient
prescience
science
subconscious

**scrib, script
(*scribere* "to
write")**
ascribe
circumscribe
conscription
describe
inscribe
nondescript
postscript
prescription
proscribe
scribble
scribe
script
scripture
subscribe
transcription

**sect, seg
(*secare* "to cut")**
bisect
dissect
insect
intersect
section
sector
segment

**sen
(*senex* "old")**
senate
senator
seneschal
senile
senility
senior

**sent, sens
(*sentire* "to feel,
perceive")**
assent
consent
consensus
dissent
insensate
resent
scent
sensation
sense
sensitive
sensory
sensuous
sentence
sententious
sentient
sentiment
sentinel
sentry

**sequ, sec
(*sequi* "to
follow")**
consecutive
consequence
non sequitur
persecute
prosecute
second
sect
sequel
sequence
subsequent

**sert
(*serere* "to join")**
assert
concert

desert
e(x)ert
insert

**sign
(*signum* "a sign")**
assignment
consign
countersign
design
designate
ensign
insignia
insignificant
resignation
signal
signature
signet
significant

**sist, stat
(*stare* "to stand")**
assist
consistent
desist
insistent
persist
resist
state
station
stationary
statistic
statue
stature
status
subsist

**sol
(*solus* "alone")**
desolate
sole
soliloquy
solitary
solitude
solo

**solv
(*solvere* "to free,
loosen")**
absolve
dissolve
resolve
solve
solvent

**somn
(*somnus* "sleep")**
insomnia
somnambulate
somniloquy
somnolent

**son
(*sonus* "a
sound")**
assonance
consonant
dissonant
resonate
sonata
sonic
sonnet
sonorous
unison
utrasonic

**sort
(*sors, sortis* "a
lot, share")**
assorted
consort
consortium
resort
sort

**spec, spect, spic
(*specere* "to
see")**
aspect
auspicious
circumspect
conspicuous
despicable
inspector
introspection

(*cont.*)

LATIN ROOTS (*cont.*)

perspective
perspicacious
prospect
prospectus
respect
retrospect
specimen
spectacle
spectator
specter
spectrum
speculate
suspect
suspicion

spir
(*spirare* "to
   breathe")
antiperspirant
aspirate
aspire
conspire
dispirit
inspire
perspire
respiration
spirit
transpire

spon
(*spondere* "to
   promise")
correspond
despondent
respond
responsible
sponsor

strict
(*stringere* "to
   draw tight")
boa constrictor
constrict
district
restrict
strict
stricture

stru, struc
(*struere* "to
   build")
construct
construe
destruction
infrastructure
instruct
obstruct
structure

tact, tag, tang
(*tangere* "to
   touch")
contact
contagious
intact
tact
tactile
tangent
tangible

tain
(*tenere* "to hold")
abstain
attain
appertain
contain
detain
entertain
maintain
obtain
pertain
retain
sustain

tempo
(*tempus* "time")
contemporary
extemporaneous
tempo
temporal
temporary

tend, tens
(*tendere* "to
   stretch)
attend
contend

distend
extend
intend
intensify
portend
pretend
superintendent
tendency
tendon
tendril

term
(*terminus* "an end,
   boundary")
determine
exterminate
indeterminate
predetermine
term
terminal
terminate
terminology

terra
(*terra* "earth")
Mediterranean
subterranean
terra cotta
terra firma
terrace
terrain
terrarium
terrestrial
terrier

tort, torq
(*torquere* "to
   twist")
contort
distort
extort
retort
torque
torsion
tortilla
tortuous
torture

tract
(*trahere* "to pull")
abstract
attract
contract
detract
distract
extract
intractable
protract
retract
subtract
tract
traction
tractor

trib
(*tribuere* "to
   assign, allot,
   pay")
attribute
contribute
distribute
retribution
tributary
tribute

vac
(*vacare* "empty")
evacuate
vacant
vacate
vacation
vacuous
vacuum

val
(*valere* "be
   strong, be
   worth")
convalesce
devaluate
equivalent
evaluate
invalid
valediction
valiant
valid
validate

(*cont.*)

LATIN ROOTS (*cont.*)

valor
value

ven, vent
(*venir* "to come")
adventure
avenue
circumvent
convenient
convention
event
eventual
intervene
invent
prevent
revenue
souvenir
venue
venture

ver
(*verus* "true")
aver
veracity
verdict
verify
veritable
verity
very

verb
(*verbum* "a word")
adverb
proverb
verb
verbatim
verbiage
verbose

vers, vert
(*vertere* "to turn")
adverse
advertise
anniversary
avert
controversy
conversation
convert

divert
diverse
extrovert
introvert
inverse
inverted
perverted
reverse
revert
subvert
traverse
transverse
universe
versatile
versus
vertebra
vertex
vertical
vertigo

vid, vis
(*videre* "to see")
advise
audiovisual
envision
evident
improvise
invisible
providence
provision
revision
supervise
televise
video
visa
visage
visible
visit
vista
visual

vinc, vict
(*vincere* "to conquer")
conviction
convince
evict
evince
invincible

victor
victory

viv
(*vivere* "to live")
convivial
revive
survive
vivacious
vivid

voc, vok
(*vocare* "to call")
advocate
avocation
convocation
equivocal
evoke
invocation
provoke
revoke
vocabulary
vocal
vocation
vociferous

vol
(*velle* "to be willing, to will")
benevolent
malevolent
volition
voluntary
volunteer

vol, volv
(*volvere* "to roll")
convoluted
devolve
evolve
involve
revolve
voluble
volume (book)

vor
(*vorare* "to devour")
carnivore
herbivore
insectivore
omnivore
voracious

APPENDIX 2

◆ ◆ ◆

Reproducible Forms

Word Card Template (21 Cards)

Word Card Template (24 Cards)

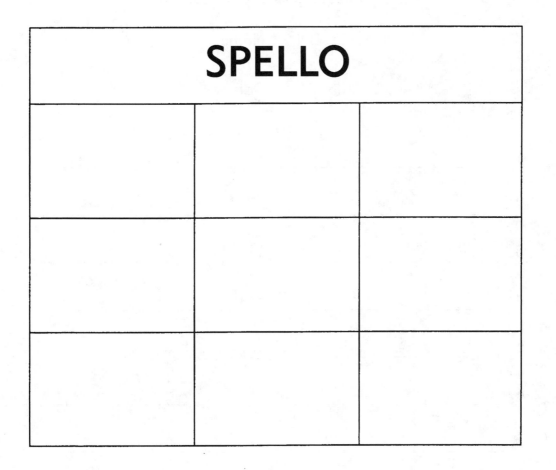

SPELLO

Screening Answer Sheet

Name _____

L   W   S   D   Date _____

1. _____   11. _____

2. _____   12. _____

3. _____   13. _____

4. _____   14. _____

5. _____   15. _____

6. _____   16. _____

7. _____   17. _____

8. _____   18. _____

9. _____   19. _____

10. _____   20. _____

Screening Answer Sheet

Name _____

Date _____

    L   W   S   D

1. _____
2. _____
3. _____
4. _____
5. _____
6. _____
7. _____
8. _____
9. _____
10. _____
11. _____
12. _____
13. _____
14. _____
15. _____
16. _____
17. _____
18. _____
19. _____
20. _____

Screening Answer Sheet

Name _____

Date _____

    L   W   S   D

1. _____
2. _____
3. _____
4. _____
5. _____
6. _____
7. _____
8. _____
9. _____
10. _____
11. _____
12. _____
13. _____
14. _____
15. _____
16. _____
17. _____
18. _____
19. _____
20. _____

From *Word Journeys* by Kathy Ganske. Copyright 2000 by The Guilford Press. See copyright page for photocopying limitations.

Answer Sheet: FORM A

Name _____

Stage _____

Date _____

1. _____

2. _____

3. _____

4. _____

5. _____

6. _____

7. _____

8. _____

9. _____

10. _____

11. _____

12. _____

13. _____

14. _____

15. _____

16. _____

17. _____

18. _____

19. _____

20. _____

21. _____

22. _____

23. _____

24. _____

25. _____

Answer Sheet: FORM B

Name _____

Stage _____

Date _____

1. _____

2. _____

3. _____

4. _____

5. _____

6. _____

7. _____

8. _____

9. _____

10. _____

11. _____

12. _____

13. _____

14. _____

15. _____

16. _____

17. _____

18. _____

19. _____

20. _____

21. _____

22. _____

23. _____

24. _____

25. _____

DSA Class Record

		A	Initial & Final Consonants	LN STAGE
		B	Initial Consonant Blends & Digraphs	
		C	Short Vowels	
		D	Affricate	
		E	Final Consonant Blends & Digraphs	
			STAGE SCORE	
		F	Long Vowels (VCe)	WW STAGE
		G	R-Controlled Vowels	
		H	Other Common Long Vowels	
		I	Complex Consonants	
		J	Abstract Vowels	
			STAGE SCORE	
		K	Doubling & e-Drop with ed & ing	SJ STAGE
		L	Other Syllable Juncture Doubling	
		M	Long Vowel Patterns (Stressed Syllable)	
		N	R-Controlled Vowels (Stressed Syllable)	
		O	Unstressed Syllable Vowel Patterns	
			STAGE SCORE	
		P	Silent & Sounded Consonants	DC STAGE
		Q	Consonant Changes	
		R	Vowel Changes	
		S	Latin-Derived Suffixes	
		T	Assimilated Prefixes	
			STAGE SCORE	
			TOTAL INVENTORY SCORE	

DSA Student Profile

Name: **School:**

Grade										
Teacher										
Date										
Form										
Total Inventory Knowledge										
Total Inventory Score										
Stage Knowledge										
Derivational Constancy										
Syllable Juncture										
Within Word Pattern										
Letter Name										
Feature Knowledge										
T—Assimilated Prefixes										
S—Latin-Derived Suffixes										
R—Vowel Changes										
Q—Consonant Changes										
P—Silent & Sounded Consonants										
O—Unstressed Syllable Vowel Patterns										
N—*R*-Controlled Vowels (Stressed Syllable)										
M—Long Vowels (Stressed Syllable)										
L—Other Syllable Juncture Doubling										
K—Doubling & *e*-Drop with *ed* & *ing*										
J—Abstract Vowels										
I—Complex Consonants										
H—Other Long Vowels										
G—*R*-Controlled Vowels										
F—Long Vowels (VC*e*)										
E—Final Consonant Blends & Digraphs										
D—Affricates										
C—Short Vowels										
B—Initial Consonant Blends & Digraphs										
A—Initial & Final Consonants										

Letter Name Stage Scoring Sample

Answer Sheet: FORM A

Name _____

Stage ___LN___

Date _____

1. Jet
2. SheP
3. BAt
4. got
5. CAP
6. Drm
7. BAp
8. moJ
9. With
10. mAp
11. hop
12. PlAn
13. thAt
14. SeD
15. MAD

16. GAB
17. Cop
18. fAst
19. Dish
20. WAt
21. Win
22. fAD
23. trAP
24. roB
25. fet

Within Word Pattern Stage Scoring Sample

Answer Sheet: FORM A

Name _____

Stage _____WW_____

Date _____

1. _pach_____
2. _cowch_____
3. _steepe_____
4. _cute_____
5. _brigde_____
6. _glar_____
7. _scrap_____
8. _might_____
9. _gril_____
10. _frown_____
11. _smoke_____
12. _flock_____
13. _stod_____
14. _leste_____
15. _short_____

16. _qwight_____
17. _grape_____
18. _yone_____
19. _drive_____
20. _coste_____
21. _hurt_____
22. _point_____
23. _ripe_____
24. _feare_____
25. _pante_____

Syllable Juncture Stage Scoring Sample

Answer Sheet: FORM A

Name _____

Stage _____SJ_____

Date _____

1. *furniss*

2. *making*

3. *sober*

4. *complaint*

5. *pilot*

6. *termite*

7. *polar*

8. *pileing*

9. *claped*

10. *escape*

11. *disturb*

12. *trample*

13. *curcus*

14. *survive*

15. *swimming*

16. *burden*

17. *baggedge*

18. *fountin*

19. *exsplode*

20. *mayor*

21. *solute*

22. *minnow*

23. *trotted*

24. *tenis*

25. *compiet*

Derivational Constancy Stage Scoring Sample

Answer Sheet: FORM A Name _____

Stage DC Date _____

1. electrician
2. impression
3. immature
4. permisive
5. hymn
6. commend
7. grevance
8. moisten
9. assumption
10. explanation
11. dependant
12. acommadate
13. resign
14. sufice
15. incredible
16. hostility
17. erruption
18. vehical
19. condemn
20. provision
21. admiration
22. irresistable
23. compsition
24. majority
25. confident

Error Sort

Emergent	invisable invisible	shad shade	maik make
Letter Name	mod mud	confesion confession	iliterate illiterate
Within Word Pattern	k come	gril girl	lad land
Syllable Juncture	complante complaint	compesition composition	cowch couch
Derivational Constancy	brigde bridge	lt elephant	mottel motel
jrep drip	soler solar	hasen hasten	yat wet
tite tight	t cut	doted dotted	disterb disturb

RESOURCES

Children's Literature

Ahlberg, J., & Ahlberg, A. (1978). *Each peach pear plum*. New York: Scholastic.

Alexander, L. (1964). *The book of three*. New York: Holt, Rinehart, & Winston.

Alexander, L. (1966). *The castle of Llyr*. New York: Holt, Rinehart, & Winston.

Alexander, L. (1968). *The high king*. New York: Holt, Rinehart, & Winston.

Armstrong, J. (1997). *Sunshine, moonshine*. New York: Random House.

Babbitt, N. (1975). *Tuck everlasting*. New York: Farrar, Straus & Giroux.

Bacmeister, R. (1988). "Galoshes." In *Sing a song of popcorn: Every child's book of poems*. New York: Scholastic.

Base, G. (1993). *Animalia*. New York: Harry Abrams.

Blume, J. (1972). *Tales of a fourth grade nothing*. New York: Dutton.

Blume, J. (1978). *Starring Sally J. Freedman as herself*. New York: Dell.

Blume, J. (1980). *Superfudge*. New York: Dutton.

Burnett, F. H. (1967). *A little princess*. New York: Platt & Munk.

Byars, B. (1970). *The summer of the swans*. New York: Viking.

Byars, B. (1987). *The Blossoms meet the vulture lady*. New York: Bantam Doubleday Dell.

Byars, B. (1991). *Wanted . . . Mud Blossom*. New York: Delacorte.

Cameron, A. (1981). *The stories Julian tells*. New York: Alfred A. Knopf.

Cameron, A. (1986). *More stories Julian tells*. New York: Alfred A. Knopf.

Cameron, A. (1994). *The cat sat on the mat*. Boston: Houghton Mifflin.

Carle, E. (1969). *The very hungry caterpillar*. New York: Philomel.

Carter, D. A. (1994). *Alpha bugs*. New York: Simon & Schuster.

Christopher, M. (1976). *Football fugitive*. Boston: Little, Brown.

Christopher, M. (1979). *Dirt bike racer*. Boston: Little, Brown.

Christopher, M. (1995). *Shoot for the hoop*. Boston: Little, Brown.

Cleary, B. (1968). *Ramona the pest*. New York: Morrow Junior.

Cleary, B. (1982). *Ralph S. Mouse*. New York: Morrow Junior.

Cleary, B. (1983). *Dear Mr. Henshaw*. New York: Morrow Junior.

Clements, A. (1997). *Frindle*. New York: Aladdin.

Cobb, A. (1996). *Wheels*. New York: Random House.

Cole, J. (1987). *The magic school bus: Inside the earth*. New York: Scholastic.

Cole, J. (1990). *The magic school bus: Lost in the solar system*. New York: Scholastic.

Cole, J. (1992). *The magic school bus: On the ocean floor*. New York: Scholastic.

Cowley, J. (1998). *The bicycle*. Bothell, WA: Wright.

Cowley, J. (1998). *Dishy-washy.* Bothell, WA: Wright.

Cowley, J. (1998). *The scrubbing machine.* Bothell, WA: Wright.

Coxe, M. (1996). *Cat traps.* New York: Random House.

Cutting, B., & Cutting, J. (1996). *Are you a ladybug?* Bothell, WA: Wright.

Dahl, R. (1961). *James and the giant peach.* New York: Alfred A. Knopf.

Dahl, R. (1982). *The B.F.G.* New York: Trumpet Club.

Dahl, R. (1990). *Matilda.* New York: Puffin.

DeGross, M. (1994). *Donovan's word jar.* New York: HarperCollins.

Fleming, D. (1991). *In the tall, tall grass.* New York: Henry Holt.

Foster, K., & Erickson, G. (1991). *The bug club.* Hauppauge, NY: Barron's.

Foster, K., & Erickson, G. (1991). *The sled surprise.* Hauppauge, NY: Barron's.

Foster, K., & Erickson, G. (1993). *What a day for flying.* Hauppauge, NY: Barron's.

Fox, M. (1993). *Time for bed.* New York: Harcourt, Brace.

Freedman, R. (1993). *Eleanor Roosevelt: A life of discovery.* New York: Clarion.

Fritz, J. (1979). *Stonewall.* New York: Putnam.

Gave, M. (1993). *Monkey see, monkey do.* New York: Scholastic.

Gelman, G. (1977). *More spaghetti, I say!* New York: Scholastic.

Giff, P. R. (1984). *The beast in Ms. Rooney's room.* New York: Dell.

Giff, P. R. (1985). *In the dinosuar's paw.* New York: Dell.

Giff, P. R. (1987). *The secret at the Polk Street School.* New York: Dell.

Gollub, M. (1998). *Cool melons—Turn to frogs! The life and poems of Issa.* New York: Lee & Low.

Gregorich, B. (1996). *Jog, Frog, jog.* Grand Haven, MI: School Zone.

Grossman, B. (1996). *My little sister ate one hare.* New York: Crown.

Guarino, D. (1989). *Is your mama a llama?* New York: Scholastic.

Hass, E. (1986). *Incognito mosquito takes to the air.* New York: Random House.

Hass E. (1987). *Incognito mosquito flies again.* New York: Random House.

Hass E. (1988). *Incognito mosquito makes history.* New York: Random House.

Hesse, K. (1997). *Out of the dust.* New York: Scholastic.

Hoban, L. (1981). *Arthur's funny money.* New York: HarperCollins.

Hoff, S. 1992). *Stanley.* New York: HarperCollins.

Howe, J. (1982). *Howliday Inn.* New York: Atheneum.

Hurwitz, J. (1979). *Aldo Applesauce.* New York: Morrow Junior.

Hurwitz, J. (1983). *Riproaring Russell.* New York: Morrow Junior.

Hurwitz, J. (1987). *Class clown.* New York: Morrow Junior.

Jacques, B. (1986). *Redwall.* New York: Avon.

James, M. (1990). *Shoebag.* New York: Scholastic.

Juster, N. (1961). *The phantom tollbooth.* New York: Random House.

Kalan, R. (1981). *Jump, frog, jump!* New York: Mulberry.

Kellogg, S. (1992). *Aster Aardvaark's alphabet adventure.* New York: Morrow.

Lansky, B. (1993). *The new adventures of Mother Goose: Gentle rhymes for happy times.* New York: Meadowbrook Press.

Le Mieux, A. (1994). *Fruit flies, fish, and fortune cookies.* New York: Morrow.

Lobel, A. (1972). *Frog and toad together.* New York: Harper & Row.

Lobel, A. (1994). *Away from home.* New York: Greenwillow.

Lowry, L. (1979). *Anastasia Krupnik.* Boston: Houghton Mifflin.

Lowry, L. (1982). *Anastasia at your service.* Boston: Houghton Mifflin.

Lowry, L. (1989). *Number the stars.* Boston: Houghton Mifflin.

Marshall, E. (1981). *Three by the sea.* New York: Puffin.

Martin, B., Jr. (1967). *Brown bear, brown bear, what do you see?* New York: Holt.

Martin, B., Jr. (1991). *Polar bear, polar bear, what do you hear?* New York: Holt.

Martin, B., Jr., & Archambault, J. (1988). *Listen to the rain*. New York: Henry Holt.

Milgrim, D. (1994). *Why Benny barks*. New York: Random House.

Most, B. (1992). *There's an ant in Anthony*. New York: Morrow.

Naylor, P. R. (1991). *Shiloh*. New York: Atheneum.

O'Dell. S. (1988). *Black star, bright dawn*. Boston: Houghton Mifflin.

Parish, P. (1963). *Amelia Bedelia*. New York: Harper & Row.

Paterson, K. (1987). *The great Gilly Hopkins*. New York: HarperCollins.

Pilkey, D. (1994). *Dog breath: The horrible trouble with Hally Tosis*. New York: Scholastic.

Polacco, P. (1990). *Thunder cake*. New York: Philomel.

Preller, J. (1994). *Wake me in spring*. New York: Scholastic.

Prelutsky, J. (1984). *The new kid on the block*. New York: Scholastic.

Rowling, J. K. (1997). *Harry Potter and the sorcerer's stone*. New York: Scholastic.

Rowling, J. K. (1999). *Harry Potter and the chamber of secrets*. New York: Scholastic.

Rylant, C. (1987). *Henry and Mudge: The first book*. New York: Aladdin.

Rylant, C. (1992). *Henry and Mudge and the long weekend*. New York: Aladdin.

Rylant, C. (1993). *Henry and Mudge and the wild wind*. New York: Aladdin.

Sachar, L. (1992). *Marvin Redpost: Kidnapped at birth*. New York: Random House.

Sachar, L. (1994). *Marvin Redpost: Alone in his teacher's house*. New York: Random House.

Sachar, L. (1999). *Marvin Redpost: Class president*. New York: Random House.

Scieszka, J. (1991). *Knights of the kitchen table*. New York: Viking.

Scieszka, J. (1992). *The good, the bad, and the goofy*. New York: Viking.

Scieszka, J. (1993). *Your mother was a Neanderthal*. New York: Viking.

Shaw, N. (1991). *Sheep in a shop*. New York: Houghton Mifflin.

Sierra, J. (1998). *Antarctic antics: A book of penguin poems*. New York: Harcourt Brace.

Silverstein, S. (1996). *Falling up* . New York: HarperCollins.

Speare, E. G. (1958). *The witch of blackbird pond*. New York: Dell.

Van Allsburg, C. (1985). *The polar express*. Boston: Houghton Mifflin.

Van Allsburg, C. (1987). *The Z was zapped: A play in 26 acts*. Boston: Houghton Mifflin.

Viorst, J. (1994). *The alphabet from Z to A with much confusion on the way*. New York: Atheneum.

White, E. B. (1952). *Charlotte's web*. New York: Harper.

Wilder, L. I. (1953). *Little house in the big woods*. New York: Harper & Row.

Wilder, L. I. (1953). *Little house on the prairie*. New York: Harper & Row.

Wildsmith, B. (1982). *Cat on the mat*. New York: Oxford University Press.

Yolen, J. (1997). *Nocturne*. Orlando, FL: Harcourt Brace.

Word Play and Word Histories

Agee, J. (1994). *So many dynamos.* East Rutherford, NJ: Farrar, Straus & Giroux.

Agee, J. (1999). *Sit on a potato pan, Otis!* East Rutherford, NJ: Farrar, Straus & Giroux.

Almond, J. (1995). *Dictionary of word origins: A history of the words, expressions and cliches we use.* Secaucus, NJ: Carol.

Ashton, C. (1988). *Words can tell: A book about our language.* Englewood Cliffs, NJ: Julian Messner.

Collins, B. (1993). *Six sick sheep: 101 tongue twisters,* New York: Morrow.

Dickson, P. (1992). *Dickson's word treasury: A connoisseur's collection of old and new, weird and wonderful, useful and outlandish words.* New York: Wiley.

Gwynne, F. (1970). *The king who rained.* New York: Simon & Schuster.

Gwynne, F. (1976). *A chocolate moose for dinner.* New York: Simon & Schuster.

Gwynne, F. (1988). *A little pigeon toad.* New York: Simon & Schuster.

Hanks, P. (1997). *Concise dictionary of first names.* Cary, NC: Oxford University Press.

Heller, R. (1988). *Kites sail high: A book about verbs.* New York: Putnam & Grosset.

Heller, R. (1989). *Many luscious lollipops: A book about adjectives.* New York: Putnam & Grosset.

Heller, R. (1990). *Merry-go-round: A book about nouns.* New York: Grosset & Dunlap.

Heller, R. (1991). *Up, up and away: A book about adverbs.* New York: Grosset & Dunlap.

Hepworth, C. (1992). *Antics,* New York: Putnam.

Levitt, P., Burger, D. A., & Guralnick, E. S. (1990). *The weighty word book.* Boulder: CO: Manuscripts Ltd.

Maestro, B., & Maestro, G. (1992). *All aboard overnight: A book of compound words.* New York: Clarion.

McMillan, B. (1990). *One sun: A book of terse verse.* New York: Holiday House.

Merriam-Webster new book of word histories. (1991). Springfield, MA: Merriam-Webster.

Moore, B., & Moore, M. (1997). *NTC's dictionary of Latin and Greek origins.* Lincolnwood, IL: NTC Publishing Group.

Muschell, D. (1990). *Where in the word? Extraordinary stories behind 801 ordinary words.* Rocklin, CA: Prima Publishing.

Oxford English Dictionary on CD-ROM. (1994). Oxford, England: Oxford University Press.

Presspon, L. (1997). *A dictionary of homophones.* New York: Barron's.

Room, A. (1994). *NTC's dictionary of word origins.* Lincolnwood, IL: National Textbook Co.

Rosenbloom, J. (1999). *The tongue twisters.* New York: Sterling.

Schwartz, A. (1972). *A twister of twists, A tangler of tongues,* New York: Harper & Row.

Schwartz, D. M. (1999). *If you hopped like a frog.* New York: Scholastic.

Soukhanov, A. H., et al. (Eds.). (1996). *The American heritage dictionary of the English language* (3rd ed.). Boston: Houghton Mifflin.

Terban, M. (1985). *Too hot to hoot: Funny palindrome riddles.* New York: Clarion.

Terban, M. (1987). *Mad as a wet hen! And other funny idioms.* New York: Clarion.

Terban, M. (1988). *Guppies in tuxedos: Funny eponyms.* New York: Clarion.

Terban, M. (1989). *Superdupers! Really funny real words.* New York: Clarion.

Terban, M. (1991a). *They hay! A wagonful of funny homonym riddles.* New York: Clarion.

Terban, M. (1991b). *Your foot's on my feet and other tricky nouns.* Boston: Houghton Mifflin.

Terban, M. (1992). *Funny you should ask: How to make up jokes and riddles with word play.* New York: Clarion.

Terban, M. (1993). *Eight ate: A feast of homonym riddles.* New York: Clarion.

Tuleja, T. (1991). *Marvelous monikers: The people behind more than 400 words and expressions.* New York: Crown.

Glossary

abstract vowels   Vowels, other than those influenced by *r*, that are neither long nor short. Most of the abstract vowels discussed in this work are vowel digraphs and diphthongs (for example, *c<u>au</u>ght*, *t<u>oy</u>*, and *h<u>ou</u>se*). See also *digraphs* and *diphthongs*.

acronym   A word formed from the initial letters of a phrase, like NATO (**N**orth **A**tlantic **T**reaty **O**rganization).

anagram   A word or phrase whose letters can be reordered into a new word or phrase—*steal* and *least*.

affixes   Prefixes and suffixes, which are added to base words and word roots—*<u>re</u>view<u>ing</u>* and *<u>sub</u>ject*.

affricate   A speech sound made when the breath stream is first stopped and then slowly forced out at the point of articulation—tongue positioned against the front portion of the roof of the mouth—as when the beginning of *<u>ch</u>op* or *<u>j</u>am* is pronounced. Other letters and letter combinations besides *j* and *ch* that produce the sound of an affricate include *g* (usually before *e*, *i*, and *y*), as in *<u>g</u>em*, *ma<u>g</u>ic*, and *<u>g</u>ym*; *d* and *t* before *r*, as in *<u>dr</u>ip*, and *<u>tr</u>ot*; and the letter name *h* ("aich"). More complex patterns such as *tch* and *dge* also create an affricate sound— *ca<u>tch</u>* and *bri<u>dge</u>*.

alliteration   The repetition of initial consonant sounds in words— *"<u>F</u>ive <u>f</u>owl <u>f</u>lew <u>f</u>ar away."*

alphabetic principle   In alphabetic writing systems, the assumption that letters match to sounds.

alternations   The way derivationally related words change from one form to another. There are consonant alternations (for example, *magi<u>c</u>/magi<u>c</u>ian* and *disrup<u>t</u>/disrup<u>t</u>ion*) and vowel alternations (*comp<u>e</u>te/ comp<u>e</u>tition* and *prep<u>a</u>re/prep<u>a</u>ration*).

anecdotal notes   A recording of observed behaviors.

articulation   The way sounds are formed in the mouth. Novice spellers often base their invented spellings on how sounds are articulated. This can lead to spelling confusions. For example, the beginning of *<u>dr</u>ip* and *<u>tr</u>ip* have similar articulations but different spellings.

assimilated prefixes (also, **absorbed prefixes**)   The sound and spelling of the final consonant in a prefix have been "absorbed" into the initial consonant of the base word or root to

323

which the prefix is joined (for example, *in* + *responsible* = *ir̲responsible* and *in* + *merse* = *im̲merse*).

base word (also, **root word**)   A word to which prefixes and/or suffixes are added. In *return̲-ing* the base word is *turn*. Compare *root*. See also *morpheme*.

blend   The joining of two or more consonants with minimal change in their sounds—*b* + *l* = *bl̲ack*.

blind sorts   A word sort that is completed "blindly"—namely, without looking at the words. Words that exemplify the characteristics of each category are placed in front of the student as key words. As someone calls out the words to be sorted, the student points to the appropriate category. Blind sorts encourage students to use sound clues and their memory for particular spelling patterns.

book talk   A brief discussion lead by a teacher or student that highlights the merits of a particular book in order to prompt students to read it.

brief assessment option   A testing option with the Developmental Spelling Analysis that enables users to assess students' orthographic knowledge by dictating words at their stage of development. Strengths and weaknesses in knowledge of specific spelling features are revealed. Compare *comprehensive assessment option*.

buddy-pairs   Student partners who complete word study activities together. Buddies are usually from the same spelling group but can be from different grade levels (such as, a first grader and a fifth grader).

choral reading   Teachers and student(s) read text aloud together. Choral reading is often used to provide support for beginning readers. Compare *echo reading*.

circle, seat, and center schedule   A rotation cycle for meeting with multiple (usually three) groups of children. During "circle," there is teacher-guided instruction; "seat" is a time when students typically complete assigned tasks independently at their desks; and "center" activities are done in the classroom but usually at a special area. Center activities may be completed independently, with a partner, or as a small group.

class record   A roster that profiles an entire class's performance on the Developmental Spelling Analysis, highlighting specific strengths and weaknesses. Results are used for planning small group word study activities.

closed sorts   Word sorts that rely on predetermined categories for classifying words. Pictures can also be used for closed sorts. Compare *open sorts*.

closed syllable   A syllable that ends in a consonant sound. In polysyllabic words, a closed syllable signals a short vowel sound. The vowel sound is usually "closed" by two consonants, although the consonants may cross syllable boundaries (*mat-ter, cac-tus, tick*-et). Compare *open syllable*.

complex consonants   Consonant units that include three-consonant clusters (*spr̲ain* and *pitc̲h*), two-consonant units that sound like a single letter (*pic̲k* and *k̲nife*), and consonant and vowel units (*bridg̲e* and *squawk̲*).

compound words   Words made up of two or more smaller words. Some compounds are written as a single word (*bookcase*); others are hyphenated (*mother-in-law* and *light-hearted*).

comprehensive assessment option   A testing option with the Developmental Spelling Analysis that begins dictation of words at the stage preceding the student's stage of development and continues with succeeding stages until the child is unable to spell at least 12 of the list words correctly. Strengths and weaknesses in knowledge of specific spelling features are revealed and a total score for the inventory is attained. Compare *brief assessment option*.

concept of word   The ability to match spoken words to printed words. Accurate pointing to words of a memorized text while reading is a common indicator of this. At least one two-syllable word must be included.

concept sort   The categorizing of words or pictures by meaning rather than by spelling feature (such as, *farm animals* and *zoo animals,* or *tornadoes* and *hurricanes*).

content areas   Subject areas like social studies, science, and math. In the elementary grades ,language arts is not considered a content area.

contraction   The shortening of a phrase by omitting one or more letters, as in *didn't* for *did not* and *o'clock* for *of the clock*. An apostrophe indicates where the letters were removed.

cumulative stories   Stories with many details added and a repetition of parts (for example, "The House That Jack Built").

DEAR   An acronym for "**d**rop **e**verything **a**nd **r**ead"— a time when all students in a class (often the teacher as well) read books of their choice. In some classrooms, this time is referred to as *sustained silent reading* (SSR).

derivational constancy spelling stage   The last stage of spelling development. Spellers study relationships between *derived* forms of words—namely, between words that share a common root. They learn that many spelling patterns remain constant across derived forms despite changes in sound. The *g* in *sign* is retained because of its meaning connection with *signal*. See also *alternations*.

developmental spelling   Children progress in their knowledge of the English spelling system from concrete letters and sounds to more abstract pattern and meaning relationships.

Developmental Spelling Analysis (DSA)   A dictated word inventory designed to determine students' stage of spelling development and to highlight strengths and weaknesses in their knowledge of specific spelling features so that appropriate instruction can be planned.

developmentally appropriate spelling instruction   Instruction that is targeted at a child's stage of spelling development, where learning is likely to be maximized.

dialogue journal   A journal in which students and teachers (or students and peers) exchange written conversations about literary works.

dictated experience stories   (also known as the **language experience approach, LEA**) An approach to reading instruction in which students dictate stories to the teacher, an older student, or a parent. The stories are written down using the students' own language. Because the language and experience are familiar to the child, the stories are more easily reread than other stories. Children practice reading the stories with choral or echo reading and independently. Known words are collected from the text for word banks. This type of approach is especially beneficial for students with limited English background and other special needs. See *choral* and *echo reading*.

digraph   Two letters that make one sound. Consonant digraphs (*ship*, *chop*, *that*, *when*) are focused on at the letter name spelling stage; vowel digraphs (*seat*, *boat*, *saw*) receive attention starting at the within word pattern stage.

diphthong   The sound produced by one vowel gliding into another (*boil*, *joy*, *shout*, and *crowd*).

directionality   The left-to-right direction used for reading and writing in English.

doublet   A special type of VCCV across-syllable pattern in which the two consonants (CC) are the same—*butter*. Compare with a normal VCCV pattern like *basket*.

early spellers   Students who correctly spell 0–11 words on a particular stage list of the Developmental Spelling Analysis Feature Inventory but who spell 22–25 words correctly on the previous stage list.

echo reading   An oral reading technique that is used to support readers who have limited sight vocabularies. The teacher (or a peer) reads a section of text, and the student echoes or imitates the reading. Fluent reading is modeled and exercised during echo reading.

emergent   A period of literacy development that precedes conventional reading and writing. Emergent spelling is the first stage of spelling development. It is characterized by writing that shows no letter–sound correspondence until the end of the stage. The emergent spelling stage has also been called the *preliterate stage* (Henderson, 1990). See also *prephonetic writing* and *semiphonetic writing*.

eponyms   Words that are named after people. For example, the word *sandwich* originated with the Earl of Sandwich, whose favorite pastime was gambling. To avoid wasting time, he had his meat wrapped in bread and delivered to the table. In this book, words named after places are also included as eponyms.

etymology   The origin and development of a word. This information is included as a part of dictionary word entries.

expository text   Informational text.

Feature Inventory   A dictated word inventory that is part of the Developmental Spelling Analysis. The inventory is used to assess an individual's (or group's) knowledge of specific spelling features at her stage of spelling development so that instruction can be tailored to meet identified needs.

fluency   The automatic recognition of words—reading that is done smoothly and accurately.

genres   Categories of children's or adolescent literature, such as contemporary realistic fiction, fantasy, historical fiction, biography, poetry, mysteries, and informational text.

homographs   Words that are spelled the same but have different pronunciations and different meanings ("A *desert* is dry" and "The soldier decided to *desert* his regiment," or "What do you *estimate* the answer to be?" and "The insurance company gave an *estimate* for repairing the damaged car").

homonyms   Words with different origins and meanings but with the same spelling or pronunciation. Homographs and homophones are different kinds of homonyms. This word is also sometimes used to refer to words that are spelled *and* pronounced the same but that have different meanings (the *bridge* you cross and the card game of *bridge*).

homophones   Words that sound alike but which have different spellings and meanings (*plain* and *plane*).

inflectional ending   In English, suffixes that indicate verb tense (*ing*, *ed*), adjective and adverb comparisons (*er* and *est*), and noun plurals and possessives (*s*, *es*, *'s*, and *s'*)

intermediate grades   In the United States, usually grades 4–6 in school.

invented spelling   Temporary, incorrect spellings that reflect a writer's current knowledge of the English spelling system. Spelling inventions provide valuable information about children's perceptions of how words work.

key words and key pictures   Words or pictures that are used as category headers during word sorts. They clearly reflect the feature represented by the category. For example, the words *tap*, *bake*, and *car* might be used as key words for a word sort that focuses on the sounds of *short a*, *long a*, and *r-controlled* (or *r-influenced*) *a*.

letter name spelling stage   The second stage of spelling development in which students begin to represent beginning, middle, and ending sounds with letters that are phonetically accurate. Letter choice is often based on the sound of the letter's *name* rather than on the more abstract letter–sound association. Thus, *y* may be used to represent the first sound in *wet*, because the letter's name produces a "wuh" sound. The name of the correct letter, *w* ("double-u"), bears no resemblance to the desired sound.

malapropism   The accidental substitution of incorrect but similar-sounding words, as "Modeling is a good way to *provoke* writing" (*promote*).

meaning-based spelling strategy   The use of meaning units as clues to correct spelling—for example, knowing that *marked* ends in *ed* because of the past tense, rather than *t* as the sound suggests; or that *illegal* is written with two *l*'s, in order to preserve the prefix meaning of "not."

metaphor   A figure of speed in which a word or phrase that normally refers to one thing is used to describe another; an implied comparison. For example, "He had a *mountain* of homework to do." Compare *simile*.

mnemonic   An aid to memory, such as "Never *e*at *s*our *w*heat" for remembering *n*orth, *e*ast, *s*outh, and *w*est on a compass, or associating *ears* with *bears* in order to recall the appropriate *r*-controlled pattern.

morpheme   The smallest unit of meaning, including prefixes, suffixes, and roots. Morphemes can be *free* or *bound*. Free morphemes are actual words and can stand alone, like *talk* or *paper*. Bound morphemes cannot stand alone and must be used with words. Prefixes and suffixes like *pre*, *un*, *re*, *ful*, *ing*, and *es* are bound morphemes, but roots can be either bound or free. *Misspelled* has two bound morphemes (*mis* and *ed*) and one free morpheme (*spell*). By contrast, *baseball* has two free morphemes (*base* and *ball*) but no bound morphemes, and *audible* has two bound morphemes (*aud* and *ible*) but no free morphemes. In this book, the word *root* refers only to bound morphemes, unless otherwise designated. *Base word* is used to indicate a free morpheme. See *base word* and *root*.

onomatopoeia   Words that sound like what they mean (*buzz*, *tinkle*).

onset   The part of a syllable that precedes the vowel, the initial consonant(s). For example, in one-syllable words, the *j* in *jump*, the *ch* in *chop*, the *fl* in *flap*, or the *str* in *string*. Although most syllables have onsets, not all do—*at*, *in*, *air*, *use*. Compare *rime*.

open sorts   A categorizing of words or pictures according to a student's own judgment. Open sorts provide useful diagnostic information by revealing what students are attending to as they work with words—sound, pattern, meaning, word length, and so on. Compare *closed sorts*.

open syllable   A syllable that ends in a vowel sound. When the syllable is stressed, the sound is long (*ba-sic*, *sea-son*, *hi*). Compare *closed syllable*.

orthographic/orthography   Literally, "straight" or "correct" (*ortho*) "writing" (*graphy*). Orthography refers to the writing system of a language. Some writing systems are based on ordered characters or symbols. English orthography relies on correct sequences of letters, standard spelling.

oxymoron   A figure of speech that combines contradictory terms, as "a bitter sweetness."

palindrome   A word, phrase, or number that reads the same forward and backward (*peep*).

pattern sort   A word sort that focuses on spelling patterns rather than sound distinctions. For example, in a pattern sort, the words *thread*, *meat*, and *great* would all be grouped together because they share the *ea* pattern, and *seen* and *been* would be grouped in another category, since they share the *ee* pattern. Compare *sound sort*.

pattern-based spelling strategy   The use of pattern, or sequences of letters that represent a particular sound, in spelling. Students who use patterns when writing words know there is more to spelling than sound. For example, although the single vowel sound in *van* is represented with just one letter, the single vowel sound in *vane* or *vein* is recorded with a pattern that includes silent letters to mark the vowel as long.

patterned text   Books that include rhyme and/or repetition of phrases and sentences. Such books are used to support beginning readers, who are able to use the predictability of the text to anticipate upcoming lines (For example, " 'Is your Mama a llama?' I asked my friend Dave. 'No, she is not,' is the answer Dave gave," Guarino, 1989).

personal voice (also, **author's voice**)   In writing, the unique way in which the author expresses his or her ideas.

phoneme   In speech, the smallest unit of sound that distinguishes one word from another, as /t/ in <u>t</u>ap, /m/ in <u>m</u>ap, and /l/ in <u>l</u>ap. *Map* has three phonemes—/m/ + /ă/ + /p/ and *eight* has two—/ā/ + /t/.

phonemic awareness   An awareness of individual speech sounds. Students who are phonemically aware can produce rhyming words and words that start with the same sound. For example, upon hearing the word <u>s</u>*ack*, a student might respond with *p<u>ack</u>, b<u>ack</u>,* or *wh<u>ack</u>.* Likewise, in response to a word like butter, a student might say <u>b</u>*all,* <u>B</u>*en,* or <u>b</u>*ug.*

phonics   Different people use this term in different ways. Typically, it refers to instructional practices for teaching beginning readers sound–symbol relationships.

phonogram   A sequence of letters (the vowel and what follows it) that is common to many words. Phonograms that occur frequently in single-syllable words include *an, ate, ell, eat, ip, ing, oke, or,* and *ug,* and *ump,* as well as many others. Compare *rime* and *word family.*

phonological awareness   Awareness of word parts. Words can be separated in three ways. The easiest for students is by syllable—*rab-bit, mo-tel, el-e-phant.* A second way involves separating individual syllables into onsets (initial consonant[s]) and rime (the vowel and what follows)—*c-at, br-ing, g-o,* and *b-as / k-et* or *p-a / p-er.* The third and most difficult way is by individual phonemes—/r/-/ea/-/d/, /d/-/ă/-/d/, and /b/-/l/-/ă/-/ck/. See *syllable, onset, rime,* and *phoneme.*

picture sort   The categorizing of pictures according to similarities and differences in their sound or meaning. Picture sorts are usually used with students who have not yet learned to recognize many or any words.

polysyllabic words   Words of more than one syllable. *Lightning* has two syllables, and *hippopotamus* has five.

portmanteau word   A word that is a combination of two other words, like *breakfast + lunch = brunch.*

possessives   Nouns (and pronouns) that show ownership. Possessive nouns are usually formed by adding an apostrophe and *s* (*book → book's cover*) or just an apostrophe (*students → students' work*).

preconsonantal nasal   A nasal sound is one produced through the nose, as the *m* and *n* in *mop* and *not*. *M* and *n* are *preconsonantal* nasals when they appear before another consonant, as in *ju<u>m</u>p* and *la<u>n</u>d*.

predictable text   Books that are written with rhyme, repetition, and rhythm, enabling beginning readers to anticipate words, thereby easing the task of word identification for them.

prefix   A unit of meaning that attaches to the beginning of a base word or word root. Examples of prefixes include *pre, mis, un, in, sub*. Compare *suffix*.

prephonetic writing   Literally, "before sound". Writing that demonstrates no letter–sound correspondence. Scribbles, random marks, wave-like writing, and random letters are all examples of prephonetic writing. This type of writing occurs during the emergent spelling stage. Compare *semiphonetic writing*.

primary grades   In the United States, usually grades 1–3 in school.

***r*-controlled vowels** (also, ***r*-influenced vowels**)   In English, when a vowel is followed by an *r*, the *r* colors the sound of the vowel (compare *burn/bun, hard/had*, and *bird/bid*).

reading to learn   Reading for the purpose of acquiring knowledge.

reading workshop   Usually, a whole-class reading time where students either read independently or with a partner. Teachers often hold conferences with individual students during this time to discuss the story, talk about vocabulary, and listen to oral reading.

reliability   Dependability in test measurement; the extent to which individual differences are measured consistently.

rhyming   Recurring final sounds (the vowel and what follows it) in words (*slate, bait, eight*, and *great* all rhyme, despite their different spellings).

rhythm   A pattern of recurring emphasis in spoken or written words.

rime   The rime of a syllable is the vowel and any consonants that follow it. In the words *tap* and *slap*, the rime is *ap*; in *seat* it is *eat*. Some rimes are common to many words. Compare *phonogram* and *onset*.

root (also, **word root**)   A Greek or Latin meaning unit to which prefixes and suffixes are added, as *chron, derm, spect, fer, mem*. Most word roots are not complete words. Compare *base word*. See also *morpheme*.

scaffolding   Providing necessary support for learners through modeling and practice, then gradually removing the support as the learner moves toward independence.

schwa   In English, the vowel, or vowel pattern, in an unstressed syllable, as in *<u>a</u>bout, foss<u>i</u>l*, and *vill<u>ai</u>n*. Dictionaries represent the schwa sound with the symbol (ə).

Screening Inventory   A component of the Developmental Spelling Analysis. A 20–word dictation list that is composed of words at the letter name, within word pattern, syllable juncture, and derivational constancy stages. It is used to identify an individual's stage of spelling development. Compare *Feature Inventory*. See also *stage of spelling development*.

semiphonetic writing   Literally, "part sound". Writing that shows some awareness of letter sounds. Initial or initial and final consonant sounds are represented (K or KT for *cat* and DD for *daddy*). Vowels are absent. Semiphonetic writing occurs at the end of the emergent stage when children are developing a concept of word. Compare *prephonetic writing*. See *concept of word*.

sight vocabulary   Words that can be automatically recognized.

simile   A comparison of two unlike things, usually with the words *like, than*, or *as*. For example, "Although he was *as skinny as a rail*, he could *run like the wind*." Compare *metaphor*.

sound-based spelling strategy   Using the sounds of individual letters as clues for spelling words. Letter name spellers often rely on the sounds of letter names (*take* = TAK and *sat* = CAT).

sound sort   A word or picture sort that focuses on differences in sound, rather than pattern. For example, in a sound sort, words like *thread* and *deaf* would be grouped with words like *sled, bend*, and even *said* because they all have the short *e* sound. Compare *pattern sort*.

speed sorts   Word or picture sorts intended to help students internalize spelling patterns. Through repeated, timed trials, sorting of the features becomes automatic.

spelling   The correct ordering of letters to represent words, also called *orthography*. See *orthographic*.

spelling inventory   A dictated list of words used to determine a student's spelling competence. The Developmental Spelling Analysis is an example of a spelling inventory.

spoonerism   The accidental mixing up of parts of words, as "The gray mouse ran away" and "The May grouse ran away."

stage of spelling development   Five periods or stages of spelling development are described—emergent, letter name, within word pattern, syllable juncture, and derivational constancy. *Stage of spelling development* refers to the stage at which a student uses spelling features but uses them inconsistently. It is where instruction should be focused, because the learner is ready to acquire new understandings.

stage score   On the Developmental Spelling Analysis, the number of correctly spelled inventory words at a given stage of spelling development.

student profile   A form for recording information about an individual student's spelling performance across time.

suffix   A unit of meaning that attaches to the end of a base word or word root. Examples of suffixes include *ly, er, ing, ness, ible, ity*. Compare *prefix*.

syllable   In spoken language, units of speech that consist minimally of a vowel (*a, I, a-gain, tri-o*). Usually the vowel is preceded and/or followed by several consonants (*string, rab-bit, fe-ver, dic-tion-ar-y*. Dictionaries do not always accurately represent syllable divisions; meaning overrides sound—for example, *grat-ing* not *gra-ting* or *hik-ing* not *hi-king*.

syllable juncture spelling stage   The fourth stage of spelling development. Students work with words of more than one syllable. They learn how syllables join and when to double a final consonant or drop a final *e*; they also learn to extend their vowel pattern knowledge and to correctly represent vowel sounds in unstressed syllables.

syllable stress (also, **accent**)   A syllable that receives the primary emphasis in a spoken word, such as *syl-la-ble* and *to-mor-row*. The symbol (') is used to designate which syllable is accented. In words that have several syllables, a secondary stress (less emphasis) may also be indicated. Syllables that are unstressed usually have a schwa vowel. See *schwa*.

tacit   Tacit understanding is knowledge that one has, but not at a conscious level of awareness.

total inventory score   A score that indicates overall performance on the Developmental Spelling Analysis. Total inventory scores can range from 0 to 100.

tracking   The ability to point to words while reading. Accuracy in tracking is used to determine whether a student has a concept of word. See *concept of word*.

unconventional spelling   Spelling that is not standard or correct.

vowels   *a, e, i, o, u,* and sometimes *y. Long vowel* sounds are those that produce the sound of the letter's name, as in *make, read, bike, boat,* and *tune. Short vowel* sounds are like the *a* in *bat, e* in *pet, i* in *sit, o* in *hot,* and *u* in *cup.* As a vowel, *y* can have different sounds—*baby, cry,* and *myth.*

weekend news writing   A type of journal writing used in primary grades. At the beginning of the week ,students write about their weekend activities.

within word pattern spelling stage   The third stage of spelling development. Students at this stage move beyond strict one-letter–one-sound correspondences and learn to spell by pattern. A primary instructional focus is the marking of long vowels (*gave, wait, tray,* and *vein*), but other vowel and consonant patterns also receive attention (*dart, boil, crouch, caught* and *pitch, fudge,* and *squid*).

word bank   A collection of known words (sight words) used by beginning readers for word study and review. Word bank words are gathered from text children have read and reread. They are kept in a plastic bag, envelope, small box, or elsewhere, so that they are readily accessible. The process of harvesting words for the word bank often works like this: After students are familiar with a story (dictated experience story, rhyme, and so on) the story is cut apart into sentences, which are read, matched to sentences in the story, and sequenced. The sentences are then cut apart and individual words are identified in isolation. Words recognized by sight are added to the bank, reviewed, and used in word study activities. This process may take several days.

word cards   Words that are used in word study are usually written on small (2½" × 1") cards for student manipulation during sorting activities.

word family   Words that share a phonogram (the vowel and letters that follow it). The words *hop, pop, stop, top,* and *flop* share the *op* phonogram and are part of the *op* family. Likewise, *coat, goat, throat,* and *boat* share the *oat* phonogram and belong to the *oat* family. At the derivational constancy stage, word family is used to describe words that share the same base or root, as *receive, deceive, perceive* and *reception, deception, perception* or *dictate, dictator, dictionary, verdict,* and *contradiction.*

word hunt   A word study activity in which students apply their knowledge of spelling features being studied, by hunting through text they have already read for words with the same spelling features.

word play   Activities that arouse students' interest and curiosity in words. Rhyming, word histories, and the use of words for special effect (like similes and metaphors) are a few examples of word play. To introduce a particular type of word play, teachers often share examples from children's or adolescent literature. See *simile, metaphor,* and *rhyming.*

word recognition   The identification of a word—being able to pronounce the word and, usually, understand its meaning to some extent.

word root   See *root.*

word sorts   Compare and contrast activities in which students group like words into categories according to their sound, pattern, or meaning. Each category is usually headed by a key word. See *key words*.

word study   A student-centered approach to phonics, spelling, and vocabulary instruction that actively engages the learner in constructing concepts about the way words work.

word study notebooks   Notebooks that are used by students during word study to record word sorts and discoveries, list word hunt findings, and complete other types of word study activities.

word walk   A teacher-guided introduction to a word feature. Through teacher modeling and guided practice, students are "walked" through words to discover sound, pattern, and meaning principles related to the features under study. Word walks usually include word identification, discussion, sorting, and much student thinking and reflection about words.

word webs   A graphic representation of word relationships. Word webs are often used with the study of word roots. A root is written in a center oval with lines radiating from it. At the end of each line, students record a word that includes the root. For example, *phon* might be written in the oval and words like the following around it: *earphone, homophone, phoneme, symphony, telephone, phonics,* and *microphone.*

writers' workshop   Regularly scheduled writing time during which students use process writing to plan, draft, revise, edit, and publish pieces. Collaboration and feedback from peers are common practices.

writing sorts   A word study activity in which students write their words under category headings. Writing sorts are sometimes used to assess students' ability to spell the week's words.

writing to learn   Writing that is used to gain a deeper understanding of concepts and ideas encountered during reading.

zone of proximal development (ZPD)   A term introduced by Vygotsky, a Russian psychologist. ZPD refers to circumstances that enable a student to maximize learning when given the support of an adult or peer. Instruction targeted at a student's zone of proximal development is neither too easy nor too difficult. For word study, zone of proximal development corresponds to an individual's stage of spelling development. See *stage of spelling development.*

References

Abouzeid, M. P. (1992). Stages of word knowledge in reading disabled children. In S. Templeton & D. R. Bear (Eds.), *Development of orthographic knowledge and the foundations of literacy: A memorial Festschrift for Edmund Henderson* (pp. 279–306). Hillsdale, NJ: Erlbaum.

Adams, M. J. (1990). *Beginning to read.* Cambridge, MA: MIT Press.

Adams, M., Foorman, B., Lundberg, I., & Beeler, T. (1998). *Phonemic awareness in young children.* Baltimore, MD: Brookes.

Atwell, N. (1998). *In the middle: New understandings about writing, reading, and learning.* Portsmouth, NH: Heinemann Boynton/Cook.

Barnes, W. G. (1989). Word sorting: The cultivation of rules for spelling in English. *Reading Psychology, 10,* 293–207.

Bear, D., Invernizzi, M., & Templeton, S. (1996). *Words their way: Word study for phonics, spelling and vocabulary instruction.* Englewood Cliffs, NJ: Prentice-Hall.

Bear, D., & Templeton, S. (1998). Explorations in developmental spelling: Foundations for learning and teaching phonics, spelling, and vocabulary. *The Reading Teacher, 52*(3), 222–242.

Bear, D., Truex, P., & Barone, D. (1989). In search of meaningful diagnoses: Spelling-by-stage assessment of literacy proficiency. *Adult Literacy and Basic Education, 13*(3), 165–185.

Beers, J. (1980). Developmental strategies of spelling competence in primary school children. In E. H. Henderson & J. W. Beers (Eds.), *Cognitive and developmental aspects of learning to spell: A reflection of word knowledge.* Newark, DE: International Reading Association.

Beers, J., & Henderson, E. (1977). A study of developing orthographic concepts among first graders. *Research in the Teaching of English, 2,* 133–148.

Blevins, W. (1997). *Phonemic awareness activities for early reading success.* New York: Scholastic.

Bloodgood, J. (1991). A new approach to spelling instruction in language arts programs. *The Elementary School Journal, 92,* 203–212.

Bruner, J., Goodnow, J., & Austin, G. A. (1956). *A study of thinking.* New York: Wiley.

Cecil, N. L. (1994). The wonder of words. In *Freedom fighters: An affective approach to language arts* (2nd ed., pp. 83–94). Salem, WI: Sheffield.

Cramer, R. L. (1998). *The spelling connection: Integrating reading, writing, and spelling instruction.* New York: Guilford Press.

Cramer, R. L., & Cipielewski, J. (1995). Research in action: A study of spelling errors in 18,599 written compositions of children in grades 1–8. In *Spelling research and information: An overview of current research and practices.* Glenview, IL: Scott, Foresman.

Cunningham, P. M. (1995). *Phonics they use: Words for reading and writing.* New York: HarperCollins.

Cunningham, P. M., & Cunningham, J. W. (1992). Making words: Enhancing the invented spelling–decoding connection. *The Reading Teacher, 46,* 106–115.

Ehri, L. (1980). The development of orthographic images. In U. Frith (Ed.), *Cognitive process in spelling* (pp. 311–338). New York: Academic Press.

Ehri, L. C. (1998). Grapheme-phoneme knowledge is essential for learning to read words in English. In J. L. Metsala & L. C. Ehri (Eds.), *Word recognition in beginning literacy* (pp. 3–40). Hillsdale, NJ: Erlbaum.

Ehri, L. (1997). Learning to read and learning to spell are one and the same, almost. In C. Perfetti, L. Rieben, & M. Fayol (Eds.), *Learning to spell: Research theory and practice across languages* (pp. 237–269). Mahwah, NJ: Erlbaum.

Ericson, L., & Juliebo, M. F. (1998). *The phonological awareness handbook for kindergarten and primary teachers.* Newark, DE: International Reading Association.

Fitzpatrick, J. (1998). *Phonemic awareness: Playing with sounds to strengthen beginning reading skills.* Cypress, CA: Creating Teaching Press.

Fraser, J., & Skolnick, D. (1994). *On their way: Celebrating second graders as they read and write.* Portsmouth, NH: Heinemann.

Ganske, K. (1999). The Developmental Spelling Analysis: A measure of orthographic knowledge. *Educational Assessment, 6*(1), 41–70.

Gentry, J. R. (1980). Three steps to teaching beginning readers to spell. In E. H. Henderson & J. W. Beers (Eds.), *Development of orthographic knowledge and the foundations of literacy* (pp. 79–104). Hillsdale, NJ: Erlbaum.

Gentry, J. R., & Gillet, J. W. (1993). *Teaching kids to spell.* Portsmouth, NH: Heinemann.

Gill, J. T. (1989). The relationship between word recognition and spelling in the primary grades. *Reading Psychology, 10*(2), 117–135.

Gillet, J. W., & Kita, M. J. (1979). Words, kids, and categories. *The Reading Teacher, 32,* 538–542.

Hanna, P., Hanna, J., Hodges, R., & Rudorf, H. (1966). *Phoneme-grapheme correspondences as cues to spelling improvement.* Washington, DC: U.S. Government Printing Office.

Henderson, E. (1990). *Teaching spelling* (rev. ed.). Boston: Houghton Mifflin.

Henderson, E., Estes, T., & Stonecash, S. (1972). An exploratory study of word acquisition among first graders at midyear in a language-experience approach. *Journal of Reading Behavior, 4* (3), 21–31.

Invernizzi, M. A. (1992). The vowel and what follows: A phonological frame of orthographic analysis. In S. Templeton & D. Bear (Eds.), *Development of orthographic knowledge and the foundations of literacy* (pp. 105–136). Hillsdale, NJ: Erlbaum.

Invernizzi, M., Abouzeid, M., & Gill, J. T. (1994). Using students' invented spellings as a guide for spelling instruction that emphasizes word study. *The Elementary School Journal, 95* (2), 155–167.

Johnston, F. R. (1999). The timing and teaching of word families. *The Reading Teacher, 53*(1), 64–75.

Juel, C., Griffith, P., & Gough, P. (1986). Acquisition of literacy: A longitudinal study of children in first and second grade. *Journal of Educational Psychology, 78,* 243–255.

Laminack, L. L., & Wood, K. (1996). *Spelling in use: Looking closely at spelling in whole language classrooms.* Urbana, IL: National Council of Teachers of English.

Lane, B. (1993). *After the end: Teaching and learning creative revision.* Portsmouth, NH: Heinemann.

McCamier, A. (1999). *Interactive writing: How language and literacy come together, K–2.* Portsmouth, NH: Heinmann.

Moats, L. C. (1983). A comparison of spelling errors of older, dyslexic and second-grade normal children. *Annals of Dyslexia, 33,* 121–140.

Moats, L. C. (1995). The missing foundation in teacher education. *American Federation of Teachers, 19,* 43–51.

Morris, D. (1981). Concept of word: A developmental phenomenon in the beginning reading and writing process. *Language Arts, 57,* 659–668.

Morris, D. (1982). "Word sort": A categorization strategy for improving word recognition ability. *Reading Psychology, 3,* 247–257.

Morris, D., Blanton, L., Blanton, W. E., & Perney, J. (1995). Spelling instruction and achievement in six classrooms. *The Elementary School Journal, 96*(2), 145–162.

Padget, R. (1987). *The handbook of poetic forms.* New York: Teachers and Writers Collaborative.

Payne, C. D., & Schulman, M. B. (1998). *Getting the most out of morning message and other shared writing lessons.* New York: Scholastic.

Perfetti, C. (1992). The representation problem in reading acquisition. In P. Gough, L. Ehri, & R. Treiman (Eds.), *Reading acquisition,* (pp. 145–174). Hillsdale, NJ: Erlbaum.

Read, C. (1971). Pre-school children's knowledge of English phonology. *Harvard Educational Review, 41* (1), 150–179.

Read, C. (1975). *Children's categorization of speech sounds in English.* Urbana, IL: National Council of Teachers of English.

Sawyer, D., Lipa-Wade, S., Kim, J., Ritenour, D., & Knight, D. (1997). *Spelling errors as a window on dyslexia.* Paper presented at the Annual Convention of the American Education Research Association, Chicago.

Schlagal, R. (1989). Constancy and change in spelling development. *Reading Psychology, 10* (3), 207–229.

Scragg, D. (1974). *A history of English spelling.* New York: Barnes & Noble.

Snow, C., Burns, S., & Griffin, P. (Eds.). (1998). *Preventing reading difficulties in young children.* Washington, DC: National Academy Press.

Taylor, S. (1996a). *Cardmaker* [Computer software]. Available: staylor@cstone.net.

Taylor, S. (1996b). *Speedsorter* [Computer software]. Available: staylor@cstone.net.

Templeton, S. (1983). Using the spelling/meaning connection to develop word knowledge in older students. *Journal of Reading, 27,* 8–14.

Templeton, S., & Bear, D. (Eds.). (1992). *Development of orthographic knowledge and the foundations of literacy: A memorial Festschrift for Edmund Henderson.* Hillsdale, NJ: Erlbaum.

Templeton, S., & Morris, D. (1999). Questions teachers ask about spelling. *Reading Research Quarterly, 34* (1), 102–112.

Treiman, R. (1992). The role of intrasyllabic units in learning to read and spell. In P. B. Gough, L. C. Ehri, & R. Treiman (Eds.), *Reading acquisition* (pp. 65–106). Hillsdale, NJ: Erlbaum.

Treiman, R. (1998). Why spelling? The benefits of incorporating spelling into beginning reading instruction. In J. L. Metsala & L. C. Ehri (Eds.), *Word recognition in beginning literacy* (pp. 289–313). Hillsdale, NJ: Erlbaum.

Venezky, R. (1970). *The structure of English orthography* . The Hague: Mouton.

Vygotsky, L. (1978). *Mind in society.* Cambridge, MA: Harvard University Press.

Wilde, S. (1990). A proposal for a new spelling curriculum. *The Elementary School Journal, 90,* 275–289.

Worthy, J., & Invernizzi, M. (1990). Spelling errors of normal and disabled students on achievement levels one through four: Instructional implications. *Annals of Dyslexia, 40,* 138–151.

Wylie, R., & Durrell, D. (1970). Teaching vowels through phonograms. *Elementary English, 47,* 787–791.

Yopp, H. (1992). Developing phonemic awareness in young children. *The Reading Teacher, 45*(9), 696–703.

Yopp, H. (1995). Read-aloud books for developing phonemic awareness: An annotated bibliography. *The Reading Teacher, 48*(6), 538–542.

Yopp, H. K., & Yopp, R. H. (1997). *Oo-pples and boo-noo-noos: Songs and activities for phonemic awareness.* Orlando, FL: Harcourt.

Zutell, J. (1998). Word sorting: A developmental spelling approach to word study for delayed readers. *Reading and Writing Quarterly, 14*(2), 219–238.

Zutell, J., & Rasinski, T. (1989). Reading and spelling connections in third and fifth grade students. *Reading Psychology, 10*(2), 137–155.

Index